T0384567

The Age of the Gas Mask

The First World War introduced the widespread use of lethal chemical weapons. In its aftermath, the British government, like that of many states, had to prepare civilians to confront such weapons in a future war. Over the course of the interwar period, it developed individual anti-gas protection as a cornerstone of civil defense. Susan R. Grayzel traces the fascinating history of one object – the civilian gas mask – through the years 1915–45 and, in so doing, reveals the reach of modern, total war and the limits of the state trying to safeguard civilian life in an extensive empire. Drawing on records from Britain's Colonial, Foreign, War, and Home Offices and other archives alongside newspapers, journals, personal accounts, and cultural sources, she connects the histories of the First and Second World Wars, combatants and civilians, men and women, metropole and colony, illuminating how new technologies of warfare shaped culture, politics, and society.

Susan R. Grayzel is Professor of History at Utah State University. Her previous publications include *Women's Identities at War: Gender, Motherhood, and Politics in Britain and France during the First World War* (1999), *At Home and Under Fire: Air Raids and Culture in Britain from the Great War to the Blitz* (2012), and the co-edited volume *Gender and the Great War* (2017).

Studies in the Social and Cultural History of Modern Warfare

General Editor
Robert Gerwarth, *University College Dublin*
Jay Winter, *Yale University*

Advisory Editors
Heather Jones, *University College London*
Rana Mitter, *University of Oxford*
Michelle Moyd, *Indiana University, Bloomington*
Martin Thomas, *University of Exeter*

In recent years the field of modern history has been enriched by the exploration of two parallel histories. These are the social and cultural history of armed conflict, and the impact of military events on social and cultural history.

Studies in the Social and Cultural History of Modern Warfare presents the fruits of this growing area of research, reflecting both the colonization of military history by cultural historians and the reciprocal interest of military historians in social and cultural history, to the benefit of both. The series offers the latest scholarship in European and non-European events from the 1850s to the present day.

A full list of titles in the series can be found at: www.cambridge.org/modernwarfare

The Age of the Gas Mask

How British Civilians Faced the Terrors of Total War

Susan R. Grayzel

Utah State University

CAMBRIDGE
UNIVERSITY PRESS

CAMBRIDGE
UNIVERSITY PRESS

University Printing House, Cambridge CB2 8BS, United Kingdom

One Liberty Plaza, 20th Floor, New York, NY 10006, USA

477 Williamstown Road, Port Melbourne, VIC 3207, Australia

314–321, 3rd Floor, Plot 3, Splendor Forum, Jasola District Centre, New Delhi – 110025, India

103 Penang Road, #05–06/07, Visioncrest Commercial, Singapore 238467

Cambridge University Press is part of the University of Cambridge.

It furthers the University's mission by disseminating knowledge in the pursuit of education, learning, and research at the highest international levels of excellence.

www.cambridge.org
Information on this title: www.cambridge.org/9781108491273
DOI: 10.1017/9781108868068

First published 2022

Printed in the United Kingdom by TJ Books Limited, Padstow Cornwall

A catalogue record for this publication is available from the British Library.

Library of Congress Cataloging-in-Publication Data
Names: Grayzel, Susan R., author.
Title: The age of the gas mask : how British civilians faced the terrors of total war / Susan R. Grayzel, Utah State University.
Description: New York : Cambridge University Press, [2022] | Series: Studies in the social and cultural history of modern warfare | Includes bibliographical references and index.
Identifiers: LCCN 2021056140 (print) | LCCN 2021056141 (ebook) | ISBN 9781108491273 (hardback) | ISBN 9781108811804 (paperback) | ISBN 9781108868068 (epub)
Subjects: LCSH: Gas masks–Great Britain–History–20th century. | Chemical warfare–Great Britain–Safety measures. | Civil defense–Great Britain–History–20th century. | World War, 1939-1945–Social aspects–Great Britain. | World War, 1939-1945–Chemical warfare–Great Britain.
Classification: LCC UA929.G7 G73 2022 (print) | LCC UA929.G7 (ebook) | DDC 363.350941–dc23/eng/20220211
LC record available at https://lccn.loc.gov/2021056140
LC ebook record available at https://lccn.loc.gov/2021056141

ISBN 978-1-108-49127-3 Hardback

For my Transatlantic Support System

Contents

Figures

Acknowledgments

When I started researching the gas mask over a decade ago, I would never have imagined writing these words after taking a walk while wearing a handmade cloth mask, a tangible object that embodies the world of 2020. I anticipated that this journey to think through my research on masks, the state, and the individual, on bodies, emotions, and objects during times of crisis and war would be finished before this year. Yet that this volume came to its final incarnation at this moment has taught me some profound lessons. Witnessing the horrors and challenges of this pandemic has led to a deeper appreciation of the subjects of this book: those living through times of anxiety, fear, and loss, who responded with humor and resistance, anger and hope. It has helped me to understand that this book is about both the many manifestations and meanings of an object and how an object can encapsulate an era.

Initial support came from my former institutional base at the University of Mississippi and sustained help from my new academic home at Utah State University. I am so grateful to the ACLS Collaborative Research Grant that allowed Lucy Noakes and myself to undertake research in Glasgow, Belfast, and London in 2015. That joint project on gender, citizenship, and civil defense is forthcoming, but some of that research deeply benefitted this book. At the final stages, the granting of a visiting fellowship at All Souls College in Oxford and the UK Fulbright Distinguished Chair at the University of Leeds gave me access to incredible resources (both material and human) and, above all, the time to finish this book.

Audiences at conferences and seminars (hosted by the following institutions and facilitated by those noted in the parentheses) all asked sharp questions that improved my work: University of Brighton and University of Essex (Lucy Noakes); University of Edinburgh (Louise Jackson and Wendy Ugolini); University of Huddersfield (Rosie Cresswell and Barry Doyle); University of Leeds (Alison Fell and Erin Pickles); University of Oxford (Yasmin Khan, Senia Paseta, Hew Strachan, and Peter Wilson); University of Sheffield (Julie Gottlieb); University of St Andrews (Gill

Plain); and Trinity College Dublin (John Horne). In the United States, opportunities to speak at the following institutions (each facilitated by the faculty named parenthetically) proved invaluable to the development of my thinking: Amherst College (Ellen Boucher); The Citadel (Kathy Grenier); College of Wooster (Greg Shaya); Columbia University/NYU British Studies Seminar (Susan Pedersen and Guy Ortolano); Duke University (Anna Krylova); MIT (Abigail Jacobson); The Ohio State University (Bruno Cabanes); Southern Methodist University (Erin Hochman); University of California at Irvine (Kai Evers and David Pan); University of Cincinnati (Lily Frierson); University of Kentucky (Karen Petrone); University of Maryland-Baltimore County (Anne Sarah Rubin); University of Northern Iowa (Emily Machen); and the United States Air Force Academy (D'Ann Campbell). Testing out ideas in person at conferences also helped enormously, so my thanks to the organizers and program committees of the 2015 American Historical Association Annual Conference, the 2014 Anglo-American Conference of Historians, the 2014 and 2017 Berkshire Conference on Women, Gender, and Sexualities, the 2016 European Social History Conference, the 2012, 2015, and 2017 North American Conference on British Studies, the 2012 Social History Society Annual Conference, and the 2017 Society for the Space Between, as well as the opportunity to deliver keynote addresses to the 2017 Britain and the World conference, the 2019 Canadian Military History Symposium, the 2014 Southern Conference on British Studies, and the 2016 Western Conference on British Studies.

Over many years, the debt that I owe the staffs at the following archives and libraries has only grown, so my deepest thanks to those at the Bishopsgate Institute; Bodleian Library; British Library; Brotherton Library; Friends Library: Special Collections at the Mitchell Library; the Library at All Souls College; Imperial War Museum; National Archives of Ireland; National Library of Ireland; National Library of Scotland; Labour Party Archives at the People's History Museum; Public Record Office of Northern Ireland; The National Archives; the Wellcome Institute Library; and the Women's Library and special collections at the British Library of Political and Economic Science. Interlibrary loan staff at the Merrill Crozier Library at Utah State University have my utmost thanks as well.

Everyone studying a new topic should be so lucky as to get to co-teach a class with an expert. When Susie Pedigo (professor of biochemistry) and I first conceived of our class on "Science and War," I had no idea how much I would learn from her – I hope our work continues! I likewise wish that everyone writing a book had the benefit of the writing groups that have sustained me throughout this one by allowing me to read their own inspiring work as well as receive critical feedback, including colleagues at the University of Mississippi and at Utah State University but most especially those who constitute the two virtual writing groups that began in 2020: Nadja Durbach, Kate Imy, Michelle Moyd, Tammy Proctor, Melissa Shaw, and Michelle Tusan.

I count myself lucky that so many colleagues over the years have supported my work; those whose assistance made a vital difference include Jessamy Carlson, Judy Coffin, Santanu Das, Laura Doan, Evelyn Funda, Durba Ghosh, Adrian Gregory, Nicky Gullace, John Horne, Kali Israel, Clare Langhamer, Philippa Levine, Laura Mayhall, Susan Pedersen, Jane Potter, the late and deeply missed Sonya Rose, Ingrid Sharp, Kara Dixon Vuic, and Karolina Watroba. I am especially indebted to those who read drafts of chapters: Catherine Coneybeare, Alison Fell, Kathryn Gleadle, Tom Laqueur, Lucy Noakes, Gill Plain, Penny Summerfield, Ian Whittington, and above all Deborah Cohen and Tammy Proctor, who read the entirety at critical moments and made the best suggestions. Finally, I am deeply grateful to William Waters and Sabine Barcetta for their editorial assistance. I apologize in advance for anyone that I may have missed, and of course, for any errors that remain mine alone.

At Cambridge University Press, Michael Watson championed this book and waited patiently for its arrival. I am grateful to him, Emily Sharp, Emily Plater, Lisa Carter, freelance copyeditor Fiona Little, and the other staff whose labor allowed this work to reach to the public. Many thanks as well to David Speicher for his work on the index.

My gratitude to those individuals who made it possible for me to think, research, speak, and finally write is boundless. This volume owes its existence to my transatlantic support system, a community of friends who helped me more than I can ever repay. Stalwarts in that group across the Atlantic include Clare Collins, Alison Fell, Andy Fellows, Jude Higgin, Etta Logan and her family, Ingrid Sharp, and Lucy Noakes – conversations with all have sustained me for decades. On this side, I am so lucky to have the friendship of Julie Anderson, Jessica Beels, Simone Davis, Kirsten Dellinger, Kate Gibson, Branwen Gregory, Lisa Hunter, Vivian Ibrahim, Val Ross, Fara Shook, Jessica Weiss, Marcia Yonemoto, and above all Muriel McClendon (who also invited me to a crucial writers' workshop and has given me and my family so much).

While I dedicate this book to key members of my chosen family, my actual family continues to provide me with reasons for hope and opportunities for joy. Researching and writing this book has made me reflect often on how my grandparents lived through some of these times, especially my beloved immigrant grandmother Sarah Gross Grayzel, who served as a civil defense volunteer in Brooklyn in the Second World War. I am sustained by the memory of my mother, Estherann Grayzel, and ongoing stimulating conversations with my father, Arthur Grayzel, and Claire Lieberwitz, my siblings – Jon and Dave Grayzel – and their incredible families as well as my in-laws. During the entirety of this book project, my children – Sarah, Rebecca, and Max – have grown into young adults who fill me with awe and thankfulness for their critical engagement with the world, their intelligence, humor, and love. As always my gratitude to Joe Ward is the hardest thing to express – every word of this book is better for his critical eye, and every aspect of my life is unimaginable without him.

Abbreviations

ARP	Air Raid Precautions
BL	British Library, London
BLPES	British Library of Political and Economic Science, London School of Economics
CDRD	Chemical Defence Research Department
CDRE	Chemical Defence Research Establishment (India)
GCA	Glasgow City Archives, Mitchell Library, Glasgow
IWM	Imperial War Museum, London
LONA	League of Nations Archives, Geneva
MOA	Mass Observation Archive, University of Sussex
PPU	Peace Pledge Union
SJA	St John Ambulance
TNA	The National Archives, London
UDC	Union of Democratic Control
WILPF	Women's International League for Peace and Freedom
WVS	Women's Voluntary Service

1   Introduction

Introduction

It was a bitterly cold evening, and I had just finished giving a talk that shared the glimmerings of a new research project that looked seriously at how the gas mask, a peculiar object that came into being in 1915, could elucidate what it meant to face total war. At that point, the project had begun by asking why many countries including Britain had decided by 1939 to distribute tens of millions of gas masks as the primary means of protecting their inhabitants against the worst elements of modern war. After I had finished, an older man, buttoning his coat and tying his woolen scarf around his neck, came up to me to report that my remarks had made him recall vividly some of his earliest fears from his childhood in England, when his brother would put on his gas mask and chase him around their house.[1]

This was the first of many anecdotes about gas masks that strangers and acquaintances shared with me in surprising ways. A year or so later, I was discussing this project with a fellow academic in a café in London when a woman interrupted us from the next table. "Were you talking about gas masks?" When I affirmed that we were, she continued: "One of my worst moments in the war was when I left my gas mask on the train. I was in tears coming home. How would we pay to replace it? What would mother say about my not having it about?" Later that year, in South Carolina, an audience member at another lecture came up to me: "I remember getting my gas mask. My sister's was pink and mine was blue. My mum told me, 'Now if you smell a funny smell, put it on.'" Another retired professor told me, "I had a gas mask, but I really wanted the big one, not the one for babies," and a guest at a dinner in London recounted, "I hated that my sister had the pretty one, you know, the one that was red and blue, whilst I had the ugly one." What all of these stories and others like them share is a distinct memory of the gas masks that people received as children. They associated it with a sense or sensation or feeling: "the smell was awful, like rubber"; "it was hot"; "I hated it."[2]

1

Shared memories such as these, largely from those who had been children in England or Scotland, helped me to understand more fully the human dimensions of government decisions to distribute gas masks to civilians as the Second World War approached. Despite having researched and written about air raids, I had not thought through all the implications of imagining and preparing not just for aerial war but for the precise, terrifying spectacle of aero-chemical war, for the massive use of chemical arms, and of what this meant for a far-reaching imperial state. As part of that research, I read many works written during the aftermath of the First World War that sought to use the experience of air power and chemical arms in that conflict as a spur to action. For me, one of the most vivid was a 1922 dystopian novel, *Theodore Savage*, by British feminist Cicely Hamilton, which describes an impending war as the "war of the air and the laboratory," a combination that will utterly destroy civilization.[3] Having served as a volunteer in various capacities in northern France during the First World War, Hamilton was witness to how the civilian experience of modern war had been transformed. Her book, set in a ravaged England where hordes fled clouds of poison and flame, offers a warning about the dangers of not halting such weapons. My primary interest had been in the wars of the air, but Hamilton's account made me realize that I had neglected to consider fully the wars of the laboratory; the wars that gave rise to the civilian gas mask.

The Age of the Gas Mask explores how the emergence of this potent material object that strove to protect all civilians from chemical weapons fostered the creation of the "civil defence state" in the first half of the twentieth century. This development had important implications for the subsequent arrival of the "national security state," which further expanded the role of state power as it claimed to act in order to safeguard individual lives. At its core, this book argues that the invention of the civilian gas mask powerfully reveals the changed landscape of modern war.[4] In the aftermath of the unleashing of chemical weapons in the First World War, and despite the Geneva Gas Protocol of 1925, which restricted the use of chemical agents in warfare, the fundamental issue of whether such weapons should ever be used remained. Interwar antimilitarists, among others, felt that both air power and chemical weapons should be banned. So, when confronted with civil defense measures, including civilian anti-gas measures such as masks, they asked whether this meant that the state acknowledged that such weapons would be deployed. Distributing gas masks meant that using chemical weapons was thinkable. No other artifact or practice of civil defense, from evacuation to shelters to blackouts, so overtly responded to the vivid horrors of deliberately poisoning the air, a step beyond dropping explosive or even incendiary bombs. Moreover, expending public resources in fraught economic times on devices that the government did not envision as being necessary was deemed both illogical and wasteful. Therefore, interwar activists accused their governments of encouraging the illegal and immoral use of such weapons.

Another set of related ethical issues grounded in this historical era motivates this project. When states decided to develop civil defense, questions about which bodies and spaces could be made safe always arose. Governments sought to protect civilian bodies, but they never did so universally. The challenge of determining whom to keep safe – or even how to keep them safe – and who would be given state-sponsored protection for the individual against the devastating consequences of a chemical war preoccupied officials at the time and has long echoes into contemporary policy. For example, on the eve of the Second World War, in June 1939, an imperial offshoot of the British government's facility for chemical warfare, the Chemical Defence Research Establishment (India) (CDRE), issued a report on a recent set of trials for the fitting of general civilian respirators (gas masks) on Indian women. The stated purpose of the trials was to ensure that "families of service personnel" in "vulnerable places" would be prepared for chemical warfare. The fate that might befall the millions of other Indian women and children, not to mention colonial subjects across the empire, in the event of a potential poison gas attack was left unaddressed.[5] The granting of anti-gas protection to imperial subjects – demanded by some in the colonies – remained wrapped up in discussions of whether the gas mask was something to give to those "useful" to (working for) the imperial regime or to try to ensure loyalty to it. The very existence of a facility to test chemical weapons as well as protection against them in an imperial space reveals a government willing to experiment on a population that it might be unwilling or unable to protect. Internal government debates in Britain on all of these issues raise important questions about the relationship between state and citizen, between state and colonial subject, in times of total war.

From a distance of just over 100 years, one striking element emerges about 1915: the air itself was weaponized. New technology, especially aircraft, enabled militaries to strike not only soldiers but also civilians far from the designated battle zone, creating a "home front" that must be defended. The lethal use of chemical weapons also devastated troops as well as the environment. While images of soldiers in gas masks came to symbolize both the modernity and the brutality of the First World War, twenty years later the British government aimed to distribute gas masks to its civilian population in the metropole: in principle, every man, woman, and child, regardless of status or income. The creation and dissemination of the civilian gas mask reflected a pervasive sense of how much war had changed and how little could be done by men in arms to protect the vulnerable – feminized civilians represented by women and children – so this is very much a story with gender at its heart. Among those who campaigned vigorously in the aftermath of the First World War for disarmament rather than gas masks were feminist antimilitarists; the Women's Voluntary Service for Civil Defence (WVS) helped throughout the Second World War to distribute and maintain civilian gas masks. Gender did not predict the response to gas masks, but it inflected it.

From the moment the gas mask arrived during the First World War, it underwent multiple incarnations as a solely military object during that conflict. And one of the factors that made the gas mask unique was its relationship to the body. First placed on soldiers, it took on a much more poignant register when placed on civilian faces, especially those of children.[6] While the civilian gas mask remains powerfully associated with the Second World War, its origins lay in the First World War. It was during this earlier conflict that the gas mask and the emotional responses it elicited entered into the history of modern war. This object was one of the few militarized things shared by combatants and noncombatants, and as such it embodied a complex emotional life that enables us better to understand or even define total war.

That process must begin with the first extensive deployment of lethal chemical gas shells in battle in April 1915, when gas attacks evoked a visceral response of horror. Contemporaries felt there was something insidious about chemical weapons (and one can see echoes of this into the present). No matter that, as their defenders carefully explained, chemical weapons did not kill or maim any more combatants than other forms of munitions utilized during the First World War and that they would never have the devastating impact that opponents predicted. Prominent figures in interwar Britain, such as the scientist J. B. S. Haldane, argued in 1925 that chemical arms were in many ways more "humane" and conventional weaponry "more distressing." Extreme right-wing military strategists such as J. F. C. Fuller continued to advocate for the use of chemical arms through the late 1930s.[7] Yet such opinions did not matter to those who vociferously condemned any use of chemical arms. Both during and after the First World War, chemical weapons provoked acute anxiety about their potential use against civilian. Nation-states across the globe thus began to prepare for a future war that could inflict nearly unimaginable damage upon noncombatants by developing anti-gas protection for their civilian populations. Officials in nearly every government that would later play a decisive role in the Second World War developed some form of individualized anti-gas device to help keep their civilian populations safe from the chemical weapons that they felt certain would be directed against them in the next war.

The invention, production, and eventual distribution of civilian gas masks, therefore, represent a critical break from all previous wars; governments had to acknowledge that they were in the business of protecting individual bodies as well as borders, even if they could not succeed at either endeavor. For the first time, the state recognized the incorporation of civilian lives and domestic spaces into war zones that it could never render immune from wide-scale destruction. Perhaps most significantly for understanding the complicated history of the modern wartime state, the gas mask was an emblem of what it meant to face a war of the imagination.

Unlike air raids, which inflicted visible damage on some domestic spaces, chemical weapons in the First World War remained largely in the purview of the battlefield, even if they loomed large in the imagination. Moreover, the most sustained damage to the body from chemical arms was to the lungs rather than in the form of more visible wounds. Some poison gas was hardly evident until it killed; it thus required new ways to think about modes of warfare. As a result, to prepare for the destruction that a full-scale unleashing of chemical weapons on a densely populated city like London, let alone Singapore, meant engaging in a vast, state-sanctioned cultural project.

In contrast to their totalitarian counterparts, officials in Britain and other states with liberal norms such as a relatively free press and extensive enfranchisement found that such preparations could be (and were) subjected to vociferous public debate and critique. As those planning how to cope with the perceived threat of massive aerially delivered chemical arms slowly explored the best ways to do so, they envisaged engaging in acts of cultural persuasion rather than coercion in order to convince their citizens to accept what amounted to a massive expansion of state power. Lengthy internal government debates, especially in the 1930s, determined that the entire scheme of civilian anti-gas protection had to be voluntary. The British government planned to give a viable gas masks to all of its ciitzens and convince rather than compel them to use them. Planning for chemical warfare at home meant that the state was now actively engaged in the protection of its subjects not merely through supporting the armed forces but also through an almost universal apparatus of civil defense that relied on the willingness of its inhabitants to accept it.

Given the prevalent interwar fears of aero-chemical annihilation, many nations invested heavily in figuring out ways to protect their populations from chemical weapons. The civilian gas mask with its distorting and dehumanizing features embodies this interwar endeavor. Providing such individualized protection also meant extending the apparatus of the state onto not only the domestic sphere but also the very corporeality of its inhabitants. As an empire and an expanding democracy trying to negotiate this process, Britain provides a rich site in which to explore this vital issue. The expansion of the British state through the experiences of modern, total war into one that promised potentially to safeguard the bodies of its subjects by protecting their very breath thus can illuminate how the seemingly limitless borders of modern conflict developed.

The Gas Mask: Some Historical and Theoretical Context

This study builds upon work by historians of war, science, and technology who have traced the immediate impact and consequences of deploying chemical arms and the consequences of doing so for politics and society in the interwar era.[8] The history that unfolds in this book expands the focus of prior studies of chemical arms and of civilians at war by placing the invention and provisioning of gas masks designed to safeguard civil populations at the center of the story. By so doing, it connects the histories of world wars and imperial violence, of combatants and noncombatants, and of state agents and passionate critical activists including antimilitarists, feminists, pacifists, scientists, and socialists.[9] It reveals how the gas mask embodies the notion of total war.

This project also makes use of interdisciplinary studies of material culture that provide ways to rethink the history of modern war.[10] Scholarship since the 1980s has sought to give "things" a place in the understanding of culture beyond the aesthetic and collectible by treating objects not solely as cultural artifacts but also as items that made meaning as they multiplied around modern human populations.[11] While people inherit objects that shape them, over time societies acquire and normalize new objects. But things also emerge suddenly in response to cataclysms and new modes of violence.[12] The potential of these approaches for the study of military and militarized objects as devices that shed light on broader aspects of total war continues to be underutilized by historians of war.[13]

Military and militarized devices personify the violent power that lies at the heart of all war, and the escalation of industrialized warfare in 1914–18 revealed and prompted an array of new things that encapsulated the virulence of modern conflict. The global networks that circulated gunpowder and guns, for example, illustrate the profound political consequences of embracing new military objects.[14] The spread not only of military technology itself but also of ideas and plans for deploying such technology in new ways has fueled and continues to define arms races, the essence of contests over global domination. One important feature of thinking about war's objects and their political lives is the question of how populations accustom themselves to living with the threats they embody.[15] Military devices further take on cultural traits and national trajectories as each state develops its own version of innovations, as can be seen in the history of aerial warfare, tanks, bombs, guns, or bullets. Moreover, the usefulness of new weapons is not always self-evident, and studies of the military contain examples of resistance to the development of new modes of war-making that often shatter prior ideals of how war should be conducted.[16]

Accounts of war-making technology have highlighted their utility for understanding broader social phenomena. As John Ellis's influential study of the machine gun demonstrates, it required a shift in mindset – even emotions – rather than simply in technology to accept and put the machine gun to use to catastrophic effect during the First World War.[17] Fundamentally, wartime objects revolve around activities – most notably killing other humans – that are taboo in ordinary circumstances. The emotions and ideas provoked by and entangled in the objects that enable state-sanctioned violence are thus essential to making war feasible.[18]

Yet, even as military technology developed in the late nineteenth and the early twentieth centuries to make possible the catastrophic injuries experienced during the First World War, so too did ideas that sought to limit their devastating impact. Some of these emerged on the macro level of international law, which sought in the Hague Conventions to limit the use of military technology and tactics, such as efforts to prohibit certain types of bullets or limit the damage that could be inflicted on civilian populations.[19] Some attempts to constrain the use of military technology, such as chemical munitions, proved relatively futile during the First World War. However, the outrage that accompanied reports of the widespread damage sustained by regions invaded and occupied by Germany reflected the popular belief that the German army violated norms for waging war and for the treatment of civilians.[20] These pieces of paper exist as artifacts that also incarnated the efforts of thousands seeking to mitigate the worst possibilities of modern war-making, at least when it came to encounters between European nation-states; the violation of such norms in Europe's colonies failed to provoke similar responses.[21]

Wartime things deserve nuanced study as military violence destroys and otherwise shapes objects in profound ways.[22] As Leora Auslander and Tara Zahra elucidate in their recent work, people need objects during wartime not merely to address their basic needs but also to continue their "humanness," the ability to make and transmit meaning. Such basic needs can be radically altered by sustained acts of violence:

The meaning of things to individuals is often magnified or transformed entirely in the context of war and displacement. War brings with it the destruction of the stuff of identity, of belonging, and of memory: homes, clothing, and landscapes. Wars also destroy the tools needed for productivity and creativity. ... The rescued remnants take on new meanings when they are all that is left of a formerly much larger array of the stuff of everyday life. ...[23]

Such insights offer new ways of seeing how investigating war's materiality leads to a deeper appreciation of the violence and trauma of conflict, and of efforts to recover from them. Perhaps most importantly for this study, Auslander and Zahra reflect on the objects of war as things that "are not fully subject to human intent. They do not have agency or will, but they can be recalcitrant."[24] The gas mask represents just such a recalcitrant object, one that continually defied some of the purposes for which it was designed.

Unlike the technology that led to chemical gas shells and the artillery that delivered them, the gas mask was designed to be *life-preserving* rather than life-taking, although its role as a defensive weapon meant that it enabled its wearers to continue to act violently. Its improvised arrival in 1915 in the face of deliberately poisoned air drew upon models created to sustain life under particular, *nonviolent* circumstances, such as working in a mine or responding to fire.[25] As it evolved from its most primitive designs – a piece of cloth, moistened with some liquid, tied over the nose and mouth – into the more sophisticated helmets with separate filters and eye holes for protection and visibility, the gas mask became emblematic of the emerging barbarism of modern, industrialized warfare over the course of the First World War.

In addition to gas masks being used to trace the development of shifting emotional regimes over time, such masks' emotive resonances deserve to be considered in all their contexts from local to imperial, from social to political.[26] Recent work on the emotions and material culture, in addition to the pioneering work in *Objects of War* mentioned above, has begun to trace "how a history of feeling which is engaged with the material world unlocks new ways of conceiving how emotions are manifest, and the sources in which they are found," even as our feelings about objects as well as the things themselves change over time.[27] All of this is critical for understanding circumstances such as modern war, in which maintaining constraints on emotions has become linked with national survival. As a widespread, devastating series of events with violence at their core, the twentieth century's total wars produced new emotional states not only in those directly engaged in military action but also in everyone caught up in their expanding maw.

Fear would seem a cornerstone for this type of emotional regime: the thing necessary to control in those engaged in fighting, but perhaps in the citizen-soldier above all.[28] For the First World War, in particular, studies have focussed on how the new diagnosis of shell shock came to describe what happens when traumatic stress and modern weaponry meet the mass mobilization of men who are not professional soldiers.[29] The very recognition of fear in combatants coincided with the rise of military psychology as a distinct field of expertise and practice.[30] The issue of fear is an essential factor in modern war.[31] Among soldiers, training and the provision of rest, food, and various forms of "comfort" could mitigate fear. When it came to civilians, survival techniques to address fear included appeals to the supernatural, such as seeking assurance from superstitions and astrology as well as more traditional religion.[32]

The provision of *objects* to manage fear or to convey a sense of safety, however elusive, was also part of the experience of increasingly militarized life for both combatants and noncombatants under the conditions of total war. These came to include many concrete things designed for their association with security and safety. There is a striking shift between the First and Second World Wars. Having initially provided objects such as the gas mask overwhelmingly to combatants only, governments offered them extensively to noncombatants as well by the 1940s. And the gas mask, with its associations with technology and science, its intimacy with the body, and its mimicking of bodily forms, made these objects both reassuring and terrifying.[33]

Masks are a particular kind of object in terms of their capacity to elicit as well as conceal emotions. The role of masks in the First World War offers two salient examples of their uncanniness. New forms of masks made of tin or painted fabric, for example, were used to cover facial disfigurement and hide the shattered visages of the First World War wounded, and scholars have pointed to the uncanny effect of such facial coverings.[34] However, the gas mask that had developed by the end of the war embodies even more powerfully Freud's concept of the uncanny. When Freud investigates the term itself, he goes back to the concept of "das Unheimliche" or the un-homelike, the "class of the terrifying which leads us back to something long known to us, once very familiar."[35] The gas mask may well exemplify the uncanny in this early twentieth-century moment. The "something" known is the face, now obscured and altered yet bearing a semblance of the original. In part because everyone at the front possessed and wore such devices, the face hidden by the gas mask became familiar and also tacitly served as a reminder of the hidden horror of mass industrialized warfare that was literally carried on the body. When it was transferred to civilian bodies en masse, the uncanniness of the gas mask only intensified.

Created as a device designed to enable civilians to withstand mass industrialized aero-chemical warfare, the civilian gas mask personified the state's recognition of the new stakes of modern war. The emergence of such protection for civilians reveals the necessity that the state now had to think about its role in protecting *all* bodies. But first the state had to engage in acts of imagination, to visualize and then realize via this object what kind of war to come *would* come.

Wartime objects can be both imagined and material, and the civilian gas mask was emblematic of "imagined" and "materialized" modern war, of potential and actual modes of warfare that killed populations at home by poisoning their air. Carrying a gas mask, as the Second World War went on, was increasingly seen by the government as a sign of positive morale and high confidence in the state's ability to safeguard its people. But this was always illusory. Waging and winning modern conflict relied on a fantasy that the state could protect civilian bodies, or at least most of them. The figure in the gas mask who haunted the interwar imaginary was the incarnation of a welfare state expanded to protect the individual body and to secure its most basic function: breathing. The gas mask proclaimed the state's insistence that the only way to protect life was to militarize it. It is in this way that the gas mask allows us to see the new relationship between bodies, objects, emotions, and modern war.

The Age of the Gas Mask

One does not need to read critical studies about bodies, objects, and emotions to recognize that the history of war is filled with objects. Soldiers have kits, the basic materials that they need in order to survive, which are strapped onto their bodies so that they can transport what enables them to wage war. During the First World War, the things they carried remained consistent across national borders, including those solely for military and death-dealing purposes like grenades and those adapted from civilian life like canteens. Tucked away in rucksacks and pockets were relatively new objects like photographs of loved ones that offered critical emotional support, alongside letters from home in an increasingly literate European society.[36] By the end of 1915, like those in other mass armies, soldiers in the British military also transported powerful innovative objects: gas masks. Critically, and unlike the other military devices of this war, the gas mask would come to play a central role in the complicated management of entire populations during wartime, both combatants and noncombatants. In part this occurred because the gas mask has an uneasy intimacy with the body that is unique among the objects associated with modern conflict.

There have long been objects used by armies to protect the bodies of soldiers, such as body armor, which sheltered men performing military service – traditionally the most elite kinds of warriors. The gas mask was different, for between the First and Second World Wars, a gas mask became an object that could be attached to *every* body in order to allow humans to perform functions vital to basic survival, not merely to the waging of war.[37] Gas masks allowed individuals to breathe in an empoisoned world. They extended life by filtering the air everyone inhaled. And the masks did so by hiding human features – eyes, noses, mouths – behind distorting sacks, bits of metal, celluloid, mica, cloth, and rubber.

Gas masks thus transformed humans into mechanical inhuman forms. On the one hand, figures in gas masks feature in images that were indelibly artificial with robot-like uncanny masks replacing the face. On the other hand, humans in gas masks are also reduced to the level of any organism struggling to breathe, to their essential relationship to nonhuman animals, with the protruding hose or filter of masks being compared to (and depicted as) the snouts of pigs and anteaters, the trunks of elephants, or the protruding jaws of simians. The gas mask made humans both less and more than ordinary, natural, or even human.

Such reactions and representations date to the emergence of these objects at a precise historical moment. They allow us to see a span of time, the era of the two world wars, as being truly the "age of the gas mask."[38] This marks an acceleration of both the warfare and the welfare state; weapons became more lethal, but the efforts to save civilian lives became more extensive as well. One sign of this was that as the threat of modern industrial warfare represented by aerial and chemical arms spread, the state embarked on an odyssey to try to protect people from such attacks by developing the gas mask. In order to understand this era and why this object encapsulates it, it is essential to return to the origins of both chemical arms and the gas mask in the middle of April 1915.

The story of the gas mask begins on the Western Front after lethal poison gas was introduced by the German army at the Second Battle of Ypres in April 1915. Britain and its allies quickly responded by coming up with a respirator to help counter the effects of this new weapon. Despite widespread condemnation at the time, both sides in the conflict escalated the use of chemical arms in part because they developed relatively effective defensive measures against them. But gas masks did not remain the purview of the military, and the next chapter demonstrates how information about chemical warfare and the production of gas masks at home, including devices marketed for civilians in Britain, changed the understanding of what warfare had come to entail.

At the war's conclusion, as Chapter 2 explores, debates about the legacy of the chemical war ensued. Many advocated curtailing chemical weapons; others argued that Britain must be prepared to use them in the future and that this would require extensive anti-gas protection. In the war's immediate aftermath, scientists and engineers continued to test gas masks in Britain and in India. By the mid-1920s, the public could read works about future aero-chemical warfare in strategic treatises such as *The Riddle of the Rhine* and *Callinius* as well as in cautionary fiction such as *Theodore Savage* or *Poison Gas*. Despite the arrival of a major contribution to disarmament, the 1925 Geneva Gas Protocol, with its seeming prohibition on chemical weapons, a decade after the first use of gas masks, Britain and many other states had come to believe that what war would now entail would require them to protect the individual body as well as national, let alone imperial, borders.

Chapter 3 then focusses on the official (and largely secret) accelerated development of civilian anti-gas protection as part of civil defense in the 1930s. This involves analyzing the cultural impact of the gas mask in the interwar period and its growing effect on the popular imagination by examining representations and discussions of gas masks in scientific, medical, and military treatises, disarmament campaigns, and personal reflections. Given the increasingly bellicose international situation of that decade, the chapter traces how the development of civilian anti-gas protection escalated as a direct result of the use of poison gas in the Italo-Ethiopian War of 1935–36, which gave rise to the gas mask as the harbinger of civil defense in the war to come. This reflected a new incorporation of domestic bodies and spaces within the United Kingdom into the waging of war and raised questions about the extent to which this could be replicated in the empire.

With the outbreak of another world war looming by the decade's end, the gas mask entered into the public sphere and popular imagination more fully between 1937 and 1938. Chapter 4 examines government policies and popular reactions to the potential (and actual) distribution of gas masks in the British metropole and empire until "Gas Mask Sunday" in September 1938. The aftermath of these efforts through the outbreak of the long dreaded next war in September 1939 appears in Chapter 5, which then analyzes the ambivalent official, cultural, and personal perspectives on the gas mask during the so-called phony war between the declaration of war in 1939 through the devastating air raids that arrived in Britain in the early autumn of 1940. Throughout this time, criticism and even overt rejection of the provision of gas masks met every effort from the state to reassure its civilian population that it had the means to offer protection from a chemical war. When war threatened in 1938, moreover, there were as yet no devices to protect babies, a glaring oversight that required intensive work to overcome. The limits of the gas mask's capacity and questions about who was left out of the calculations of government planning – colonial subjects, British nationals abroad, criminals – remained to be addressed when the war's violence came home to the United Kingdom. At the war's start, the government commissioned surveys to determine who among the population was following the dictate to "always carry your gas mask," believing that this would be an important gauge of civilian morale. As the last of the Battle of Britain faded away in spring 1941, the government redoubled its efforts to urge citizens always to carry their gas masks and show their commitment to war preparedness. In this way, the gas mask became a mechanism for the state to curate identity, to see who really was the kind of reliable, civic-minded individual who would help save the now acutely vulnerable nation as well as the empire.

Chapter 6 traces how, over the remaining course of the Second World War, gas masks took on various emblematic meanings. Gas masks increasingly became the punch lines to jokes; objects that embodied the calculated poisoning of the air in order to kill civilians turned into fodder for music hall songs. When shortages of rubber and the continued absence of chemical attacks on British soil continued, the government shifted some of its gas mask policy in the middle of the war. It went from saying it was vital to take the gas mask everywhere to stating it was no longer necessary to "always have it with you," but rather to know where it was. Nonetheless, at no point during this war did the British government withdraw gas masks or admit their futility. It continued to calculate how many masks were available, to produce, inspect, and repair them, and to orchestrate a policy for its empire, even if it never delivered masks to its colonial subjects. At the war's end, gas masks remained in the homes in the metropole to which they had been delivered: the property of the state with reminders to keep them ready, just in case. In a way, there was no need to retrieve the gas mask, for the militarization of civilian bodies would never end.

The study concludes in Chapter 7 by addressing what the gas mask's story tells us about modern, total war and about how states faced new threats to their civilian populations in this era. The Epilogue briefly illuminates the long afterlife of the gas mask as a material object and vector of popular memory for the British home front in the Second World War, as it has been incorporated into British popular culture, and as it has played a critical role in popular political protests against other twentieth-century and, indeed, twenty-first-century wars and emergencies, including our current, overwhelming climate crisis.

This study is fundamentally about people and objects in a militarized state. I wrote this book in part for those people whose stories I briefly recounted at the beginning of this introduction.[39] Above all, my aim is never to tell the history of military developments – the evolution of anti-gas protection – divorced from their human wreckage, potential and real. I hope to capture how ordinary people came to understand the harrowing world they inhabited after the First World War. For this was a world where the enemy might deliberately poison the air around you to kill without discrimination, a world where you carried the tangible reminder that, at any moment and without warning, you could cease to breathe. How did such a world become normal? For it is some version of this world in the post-atomic age of accelerated climate change and the age of mass terror that we inhabit, and understanding how we got here may help us to survive, resist, and, perhaps most elusively, undo it.

2 Inventing an Object for Modern Conflict
The Gas Mask in War and Peace, 1915–1929

Introduction

"GAS! Gas! Quick, boys! An ecstasy of fumbling,
Fitting the clumsy helmets just in time;
But someone still was yelling out and stumbling
And floundering like a man in fire or lime.
Dim, through the misty panes and thick green light
As under a green sea, I saw him drowning.
…
If in some smothering dreams you too could pace
Behind the wagon that we flung him in,
…
If you could hear, at every jolt, the blood
Come gargling from the froth-corrupted lungs,
…
My friend, you would not tell with such high zest
To children ardent for some desperate glory,
The old Lie: *Dulce et Decorum est*
Pro patria mori.[1]

These lines from the iconic British text of the First World War written by
an active combatant, Wilfred Owen's poem "Dulce et decorum est," take
us to the heart of an extraordinary transformation. In this often-quoted
verse, suffering combatants, whose blood pours from "froth-corrupted
lungs," haunt the disillusioned and heartsick soldier. When the body of
yet another gas-poisoned soldier is thrown into the wagon with the rest of
the dead, the poet acutely realizes the "old Lie," which is the entire
notion that it is "sweet and honorable to die for one's country." A far
less famous line is the one about "fitting the clumsy helmets just in time."
If the image of toxic plumes crossing the muddy fields of Flanders and
leaving helpless men choking to death remains deeply embedded in every
narrative of this war, then why have we lost sight of the fact that this
innovative weapon yielded an immediate counterpart designed to render
it less effective? What about "the clumsy helmet," perhaps one of the

most enduring material legacies of this war: the gas mask? What would a history of this war and its legacy that put this material object at its center do to our understanding of what it bequeathed to the modern world?[2]

One of the truisms about the First World War is that its history is in part a history of new ways to die. It is not that what came to be called "chemical warfare" was itself new. However, on an unprecedented scale dying in this war could be the result of asphyxiation.[3] In addition to the suffocating qualities of the chemical weapons of phosgene and chlorine, the agent mustard gas, once deployed later in the war, blinded troops, burned their exposed skin, and degraded their lungs. Official statistics on gas-related casualties, according to the leading scholars on the subject, tended to exaggerate their numbers, but these numbers suggest that chemical arms account for between 2.4 and 3.3 percent of wartime casualties for the United Kingdom.[4] What such quantitative data from the war years themselves fail to reveal is the extent to which chemical weapons contributed to lowered life expectancies and quality even if they did not kill their victims outright, nor do they account for the ongoing psychological trauma of poison gas.

Immediate and harsh condemnation followed the first lethal deployment of chemical arms at the Second Battle of Ypres on April 22, 1915, but both sides eventually made use of them. While not the only novel means of waging war that inspired critiques as being "uncivilized" or even an "atrocity," poison gas evoked a particular and visceral horror. Gas weapons and the material responses to them had a long and potent afterlife, which this chapter traces from their origins in 1915 through the end of the 1920s, when Britain in 1929 ratified the Geneva Gas Protocol of 1925. Although it promised to prohibit use of chemical arms, the protocol did not stop the government from experimenting with both chemical weapons and defenses against them.[5]

The modern prohibition of the use of such weapons dated back to the nineteenth century. In 1868, the nations that signed the Declaration of St. Petersburg agreed to limit the types of projectiles that could be used by both armies and navies. Several decades later, Declaration II of the first Hague Conventions of 1899, claiming to find inspiration in this initial agreement, further bound signatory powers to "abstain from the use of projectiles the object of which is the diffusion of asphyxiating or deleterious gases." This provision was further explicitly incorporated into the Hague Convention of 1907, Article 23, which simply prohibited the deployment of "poison or poisoned weapons" as well as "arms, projectiles, or material calculated to cause unnecessary suffering."[6] Such international standards may help explain, in part, the lack of widespread readiness to combat poison gas in 1915. As one of the definitive histories of chemical weapons points out, the belligerents of August 1914 "had no conception of the practicalities of chemical warfare."[7] Participant states on the receiving end of poisoned air had to improvise quickly the first anti-gas devices for troops. Thus did the respirator and what would eventually become the gas mask enter the war and the modern world.

The Invention of the Gas Mask during the First World War

Chemical weapons took the Allied side by surprise. On April 22, 1915, Germany unleashed chlorine gas against colonial troops in the Ypres salient. This change in tactics was initiated at the behest of Germany's chemical industry rather than the military. This meant that the appearance of some form of German anti-gas protection also accompanied the first use of chemical arms and seemingly confirmed the premeditation behind using weapons that had been thought beyond the pale. Yet even here, the decision to deploy chlorine did not lead immediately to the production of anti-gas protection in sufficient quantities to protect all troops. Adopting devices modeled on those used in mines and by workers in the chemical industry, Germany issued a basic respirator only to select military personnel. According to the postwar memoir of Fritz Haber, the 1918 Nobel Prize-winning civilian chemist involved in the development of the chlorine weapon, "it was impossible to convince the military authorities beforehand of the necessity for providing special equipment." Initially, German troops were required to hold pads to their faces; only after April 15 did some of the offensive troops receive respirators that had tapes to hold them up, and such "hasty, final improvisations" on the German side "showed a remarkable lack of foresight and, incidentally, served to alert Belgian intelligence."[8]

Evidence was available to both French and British authorities in the Ypres sector that the Germans were planning to use chemical arms. Yet the Allies chose not to make effective preparations. Rather than acknowledging their lack of readiness, the official British postwar history of its responses to chemical arms claimed that immediately after the battle, "energetic efforts were made at once to devise means to protect our men in as complete a manner as possible." These included "respirators ... made locally, the first one adopted consisted of two layers of flannel (with tapes attached to tie over the mouth) which were meant to be soaked in soda solution before use. One bottle of solution was to be kept in each bay of the trenches." Lacking this, "a cloth or handkerchief soaked in hyposulfite solution, water or even urine was to be used."[9] This was a strikingly improvised response to mass industrial warfare, composed as it was of such basic materials, even of bodily fluids.

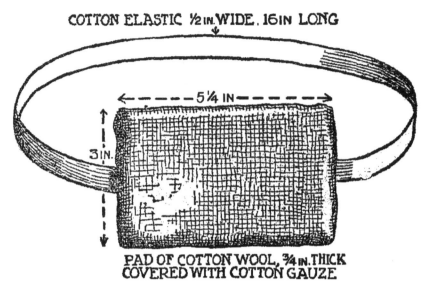

Figure 2.1 A week after the Second Battle of Ypres, the War Office issued an appeal for respirators. Here is the pattern for that basic respirator, as circulated in the *Daily Mail*, April 29, 1915. Public Domain.

The desperate search for anti-gas protection soon led to a rather startling intermingling of the military and domestic spheres of the war. On April 29, about a week after Germany unleashed its chlorine weapon at Ypres, the British government sought help from its civilian population. The War Office launched an appeal in the national press with a simple pattern and instructions for how civilians could transform ordinary *household* materials – bleached cotton wool and three layers of bleached cotton gauze along with elastic – into a respirator. It urged volunteers to send them in packages of no fewer than 100 to the Chief Ordinance Officer of the Royal Army Clothing Depot (Fig. 2.1).[10]

The wording of the official call for respirators did not specify who was to make these devices. While the *Daily Mirror* announced the government initiative with the simple headline "Respirators Wanted by Troops at the Front," the *Evening Despatch* posed it as a query to everyone: "Will You Make a Respirator?" However, some members of the media (especially the *Daily Mail*) instantly framed the call as singling out the women of the nation as the ones to produce these objects, using the headline "Rush Job for Women." Others followed suit; the *Birmingham Daily Post* described the initiative as "An Opportunity for Women," and the *Daily Express* called attention to this with the subheading "Women's Response to War Office Appeal" following the lead "Rush to Make Respirators."[11] Accompanying the appeal, in several papers, including the *Express*, came accounts of women who eagerly and enthusiastically took on this new civic task. The manager of the Royal Army Clothing Depot in Pimlico (the destination for finished respirators listed in the War Office appeal) described himself as having "done nothing all day except willingly answer questions ... the first lady called as soon as the offices were open, and promised to send 5,000 respirators a day." All offer examples of women eager to help the war effort. By early evening, the basic supplies – cotton wool, cotton gauze, and elastic – were running low, and the *Daily Express* took it upon itself to assure readers that "black elastic" would work as well as the white elastic listed in descriptions (although brightly colored material would not).[12]

Commercial establishments seized the opportunity to show women the way. The *Daily Express* further took credit for suggesting that the proprietors of Selfridge's, one of the larger London department stores, "give a practical demonstration at their Oxford Street premises throughout the day" for the benefit of "those who would like to see the process in detail." It also advertised that a female demonstrator would be "in attendance in the surgical instrument department on the ground floor from 10 a.m. onwards" and that a basket in which completed respirators might be placed would be available from that day. In the meantime, in the store's workrooms, "rows of expert women were making respirator pads."[13] Not to be outdone, another West End department store, Harrods, which was already planning a patriotic fashion display, responded to the appeal by stocking the basic components in its store while featuring several samples of homemade gas masks placed in its display windows. Harrods further called attention to this fact by advertising in newspapers that its drug department could supply cotton wool, gauze, and elastic while its wool department could provide "scoured wool for knitting respirators" (although there was certainly no such official demand for woolen respirators).[14]

British women responded enthusiastically to such calls to action as reported in newspapers across the United Kingdom. Among many press accounts was one in the *Manchester Evening News* noting that "ladies at the War Hospital Supply Depot Hove, yesterday, devoted themselves entirely to make respirators for the troops, and 1,000 had been completed."[15] The *Daily Express* noted that Mrs. Winston Churchill used the occasion of opening a sale of work in aid of the West Ealing Tipperary Club (one of the many charitable organizations raising funds to support the troops) to ask the members if they were willing to make respirators at once, as she had brought along a quantity of material for this purpose. The paper recorded this challenge as being met with a resounding "yes."[16] The public nature of this appeal to women in the aftermath of poison gas at Ypres caught private attention. London wife and mother Georgina Lee wrote in her diary that "an appeal is launched to all the women of England to make respirators, thousands and millions of them," revealing the engagement with and recognition by those at home of this new turn in the war, and the resulting new opportunity for women to contribute to the national effort.[17]

The campaign succeeded in engaging civilian time and energy. Stores soon ran out of cotton wool and gauze, and on April 30, barely eight days after the battle, newspapers across Britain posted headlines like "Deluge of Respirators" and notifications that the War Office had "withdrawn" its appeal twenty-four hours after issuing it.[18] An article in the *Irish Times* that day lamented that "Irishwomen had no real chance to help, so short was the time which it took to produce the requisite number of respirators."[19] The triumphant headline in the *Daily Mail* proclaimed "Women Foil the Poisoners," suggesting that the "magnificent" response of women throughout the nation had directly affected the war.[20] The appeal had been interpreted as calling upon the women of Britain to redirect their domestic skills toward the service of military, into making out of ordinary household materials a military object to protect a soldier from modern industrial warfare. The emotional work of this effort gave women a chance to relieve their anxiety by doing something for their menfolk under threat. Such directed labor went far beyond the knitting of socks, balaclavas, and mufflers: it was the creation of a personal, handcrafted emblem of protection against modern military technology.

Tens of thousands of such basic masks were sent to the Western Front in the late spring of 1915. The official postwar account recorded: "A cotton wool respirator in a gauze envelope on the pattern of the naval smoke respirator was also issued. 1,000,000 of these respirators were made in a single day by the women of ENGLAND at the instance of the 'Daily Mail' and of the Red Cross Society." This sentence formed the basis for how the story of these early respirators appeared in most historical accounts of chemical warfare on the Western Front. However, most of these histories also emphasized this effort as showing the futility and waste of the war. The thick cotton pads in this rudimentary design proved a danger: when dry they could not block out chlorine, and when they were wet, the wearer could not breathe.[21] In the official War Office chronology, this failure is obscured: the entry for April 22–30 simply reads, "the women of England were asked to make 1,000,000 respirators in one day." This is followed by an entry for May 5 that states, without further explanation, that a telegram went out ordering that "small cotton wool respirators were not to be used."[22] There is no notation as to why this became the case. So the official record contributed to setting up a myth of heroic women contributing at home to the war generally, and particularly to the struggle against chemical arms, without acknowledging that it proved a useless effort, except perhaps in managing morale at home.[23]

In response to this initial setback in creating anti-gas protection, leading physiologist John Scott Haldane devised a respirator constructed from the black cotton netting commonly used for widows' veils. The netting held in place cotton waste (unfinished cotton) suffused with thiosulphate. Haldane decided on these components after seeking advice from those working in the coal industry and using data showing that woven fabrics worked better than unrefined cotton to absorb poisonous gas. The use of the veil material came as a practical measure since there were ample supplies even as female mourning practices began to change.[24] However, the transformation of a female emblem for mourning in wartime, when it was most clearly associated with signifying a relationship to a dead combatant, into a device to protect the combatant body remains noteworthy. This is especially so when read alongside the public call to women to produce masks to protect men, potentially their loved ones, in the battle zones. This incorporation of feminized materials (widows' veils) and women themselves into the making of an object fully associated with modern war anticipated later developments in puncturing, if not erasing, the borders between combat and the home.

If there remained some trial and error in creating effective respirators, then Britain alongside its allies and enemies fairly rapidly developed mechanisms to enable those facing the clouds of poison gas to breathe. After experimenting with helmets and hoods, by May 1915, Major Cluny McPherson, a Canadian medical officer, had built an anti-gas helmet made of flannel with a celluloid window treated with glycerin, hyposulphite, and bicarbonate of soda as neutralizing agents against chlorine. McPherson's model worked so well that it was the main form of British anti-gas protection until 1916 – although efforts were made both within the military and by others to keep improving designs in response to new types of chemical arms.[25]

Another example of initiatives taken by women to aid in defeating gas attacks can be seen in the effort by Herta Ayrton to have the War Office adopt her "anti-gas fan," designed to help clear trenches of accumulations of gas. A graduate of Girton College, one of the University of Cambridge's rare women's colleges, and a pioneering female electrical engineer, Ayrton designed in 1915 a hand-operated canvas and wooden fan that used air vortices to propel gas away from troops. The utility of the fans, which had to be used in a particular way, was twofold: to help keep gas out of a trench during an attack and to clear gas out of a trench or dugout more swiftly than other methods after an attack. Despite her offering proof that her simple design worked well and could save lives, Ayrton's efforts were met with skepticism by military officials and regular troops both during the war and afterward. She then argued, "however perfect the respirators (and they were finally very perfect) the need for getting rid of poison gases as quickly as possible remained imperative." [26] In the end, the gas mask with its ability to protect the individual body would remain the focal point of anti-chemical warfare provisions.

From roughly the middle of 1915, then, the invention, production, and distribution of gas masks stymied in a substantive way the initial effectiveness of chemical arms.[27] The gas mask became part and parcel of a soldier's kit, be he French, German, Austro-Hungarian, Italian, or British. This did not mean the end of chemical warfare, which was seen in the use of poison gas in battles in Italy and on the Western and Eastern Fronts as well as in Palestine.[28] In Britain, the manufacturing shifted from a simple respirator to increasingly sophisticated devices, resulting in the small box respirator that became the standard in the summer of 1916.

The small box respirator was the invention of chemist Edward Harrison, hailed as the "inventor of the gas mask" when he died from pneumonia on the eve of the war's end in November 1918. Although he joined the army at age forty-five, he shifted roles after the first use of poison gas in the spring of 1915 prompted calls for chemists to join the Royal Engineers in what would become in 1917 a new feature of the military, the Chemical Warfare Department. After conducting tests on a number of devices, often by wearing them in the presence of the poison gases being deployed, Harrison helped design a respirator that fulfilled a variety of needs. It offered adequate protection, so as to give troops confidence in their anti-gas device, while also being readily mass-produced. In addition, it was compact enough that when worn, it would interfere as little as possible with the other tasks required of soldiers. Harrison's design became the basis for anti-gas protection for British, American, and Italian troops.

The many news articles at the time of Harrison's death melded the personal and the historical in listing his notable accomplishments. First, this was a scientific genius plucked from the ranks who, despite joining up as a private, successfully "robbed German gas of its terrors."[29] Further, he did so while mourning the death of one son in the Battle of the Somme and supporting his other son as a soldier. In addition, his design of the soldier's box respirator became "as useful to the soldier as was his rifle."[30] Finally, by testing gas masks on himself and working tirelessly to ensure the design, production, and distribution of adequate protection, "he gave his life in the service of his country as truly as if he had met his death in the fighting line."[31] As a sign of the significance of Harrison's achievement, he received a funeral with full military honors and a postwar memorial plaque that proclaimed, "to save our armies from poison gas he gave the last full measure of devotion." Unlike the inventors of chemical weapons such as Haber, who would be condemned ever after for their role, the inventors of the gas mask received approbation as heroes.[32]

Gas Masks and Civilians

In the months after the Second Battle of Ypres, British civilians began to wonder whether they also would need gas masks. While not directly exposed to chemical weapons as British troops in France had been, civilians learned about their harrowing consequences from both public and private sources – and from rumors amid a climate in the late spring of 1915 filled with a renewed sense of the alleged ruthlessness of Germany. In addition to the arrival of aerial attacks on Britain's coast and reports of chemical warfare in France, by late April 1915 British civilians could read in their newspapers excerpts from the release of the Bryce Report on alleged German atrocities in occupied Belgium. Soon after, they were horrified by accounts of the German sinking of the passenger-laden ocean liner *Lusitania* on May 7. In all of these cases, the emphasis on German attacks on innocent victims, on women and children, dominated the press coverage. In the language of the time, these were "outrages," offering evidence that Germany was capable of anything. After all, Prussia (Germany's antecedent) had signed the treaty guaranteeing the Belgian neutrality it subsequently violated, just as it had signed prewar documents that prohibited the use of poison gas. Like the use of chemical weapons, the sinking of the *Lusitania* by German U-boats seemingly revealed a German willingness to use the triumphs of modern science to inflict death and destruction in novel and thus shocking ways.

Civilians living in Britain could soon imagine other frightening developments on the horizon. In mid-May 1915, London housewife Georgina Lee recorded in her diary that her dentist had advised her "to have in the house respirators against the German gas-bombs as they are said to be about to throw those down at us from Zeppelins shortly."[33] Lady Annette Matthews, who was keeping a diary for her children, recorded it all: air raids, the sinking of the *Lusitania*, the Bryce Report, and the use of poison gas at Ypres. Her reaction to air raids in late May: "People are quite calm. Some have brought respirators, as a precaution against poisonous gas. Some have got a solution of bicarbonate & hypo-sulphate of soda ready to dip their masks in."[34] Enterprising companies further tried to take advantage of such rumors and the emotions they may have provoked. By late May, the Surgical Manufacturing Company was advertising in the mainstream press "the life-saving Cavendish inhaler" designed "for use at home or to send to your friends in the trenches" and promising efficient protection against "the danger of Gas Bombs."[35]

By the last week of May 1915, the *Daily Mail* engaged popular anxiety when it ran a short article entitled "Gas Bombs on London." It noted that in response to a police warning advising people to keep windows closed in the event of an air raid, there had been "a rush to buy respirators" and "stores were sold out within an hour or two."[36] London had not yet experienced an air raid when the "Gas Bombs" article appeared, but the first such attack, a Zeppelin raid on May 31, provided the British public with compelling accounts of how war had changed. On the night of the raid, Elsie Legett and her sister Elizabeth were asleep in bed with three other siblings when a bomb fell directly on their house. The girls' father tried to rescue all the children, but he failed to do so, receiving severe burns in the process. Elsie was three years old when she died that night; Elizabeth was eleven when she subsequently died from injuries sustained in the raid. As a headline in one of the large daily newspapers put it, this was the "tragedy of the Zeppelins" and a vivid reminder that no one was safe from German aggression and ruthlessness.[37]

Partially in response, the Hospitals and General Contracts Company was marketing a new respirator to civilians by early June 1915. Under the heading "Be Prepared for Zeppelin Bombs," it claimed that its device offered protection against "asphyxiating gases."[38] Significantly, this company mailed a circular targeting women (the cover letter was addressed "Dear Madam") that begins as follows:

Having long since disregarded the common Laws of Humanity, will the Germans hesitate to use asphyxiating gases in their premeditated raids on London? ... If they abuse the teachings of science, why, let us show them that we are prepared to meet their dastardly attacks in an *Organized and Scientific* way by using a simple but efficient appliance, in effect, a mask that will protect the respiratory organs and eyes against chlorine.[39]

The covering letter for the announcement reminded the women of the home: "an effective mask will save a life, and prevent intense agony." This marked a profound and disturbing shift in the borders of the war, as it underscored the risk that British families might now face directly.

"WELL, MADAM, WE SELL A GOOD MANY OF BOTH. THE SOLID RUBBER IS PERHAPS THE MORE SERVICEABLE ARTICLE, BUT THE OTHER IS GENERALLY CONSIDERED THE MORE BECOMING."

Figure 2.2 Among the popular reactions to the need for gas masks for civilians was this Lewis Baumier cartoon, "Well, Madam ..." appearing in *Punch*, August 18, 1915. Punch Cartoon Library/TopFoto.

Inside every British home, the family had to prepare itself for "dastardly" weapons attacking its most intimate spaces, even if these weapons had not yet appeared.

By the summer of 1915, Lewis Baumier in famed British humor magazine *Punch* was able to make fun of efforts to sell gas masks to civilians in a cartoon that showed a mother from the leisure class being helped by a sales clerk to choose between two types of such masks. While both gas masks depicted in the cartoon were potentially ridiculous in appearance, and the idea of asking a mother to choose a device to protect herself and/or her children against chemical warfare on the basis of its attractiveness was nonsensical, the cowering daughter reminded the viewer of the less comical aspects of what was under consideration. The choice was seemingly about the type of protection, but the prospect of women and children needing to safeguard themselves from a weapon of such horror was also apparent (Fig. 2.2).[40]

Moreover, although chemical attacks specifically directed at civilian populations did not occur, fears that poison gas might be launched from the air against noncombatants persisted, especially as air raids intensified. One of the problems with using poison gas was that it was weather-dependent; wind could cause it to drift away from intended targets. By 1916, this factor had caused the French army to distribute gas masks to civilians living near the Western Front, including those in such cities as Reims, and French civilians, like their British counterparts, had become victims of air raids.[41] Then, with the development of new planes, heavy bombers known as Gothas, German attacks on British civilian lives and spaces in the metropole intensified in 1917. Several things made the air raids of 1917 more traumatic than earlier attacks: they took place in daylight, they had a broad geographic range, and they struck a variety of targets. On June 13, 1917, Londoners experienced the most deadly raid of the war, which was upsetting both because it occurred during the middle of the day and because it included a direct hit on an infants' school. Press accounts of the increasingly deadly raids emphasized the changing nature of war and the redrawing of borders between battle front and home.[42]

Uncertainty about the potential for Germany to use poison gas against British civilians continued. In the autumn of 1917, the jury at the inquest following the death of ten-week-old Lillian Alice Trower declared that the baby girl's death was "caused by irritant gases caused by bombs dropped from enemy aircraft at Shoreditch during the night of 1 October 1917."[43] Given the possibility that this could involve chemical weapons as well as evidence that inhabitants might believe such weapons now to be in place, New Scotland Yard undertook an investigation into the death. Investigators found that the infant most likely suffocated from breathing air contaminated by leaks from gas mains ruptured during a conventional air raid. That the raid caused this gas leak made Trower an indirect victim of air power but not of chemical arms as such. The imagined fear prompted investigative action, regardless of the lack of chemical attacks on the British Isles.[44]

Despite the apparent German reluctance (or inability) to deploy chemical weapons against British civilians by the air, the gas mask as a visible emblem of the war itself found its way into the homeland throughout the war, carried there by soldiers and prominently featured in the illustrated press. On August 1, 1917, the *Daily Mirror* showed a "novel" sporting event for military men, a race where "the competitors had to wear a gas mask, run a certain distance and then change into another mask before making the return journey." A month later, a photograph of men in uniform and masks demonstrated that the "gas mask drill now forms

Figure 2.3 Undated photograph of a mother and child in gas masks. Agence Rol/Public Domain

an important item in the military curriculum."[45] Well into the last year of the war, images of soldiers doing "ordinary" activities while wearing gas masks featured in the press, as in a March 23, 1918 image of "Football Frightfulness" that depicted gas-masked soldiers on a soccer pitch.[46] Such coverage served to highlight the oddity of this new normal: it was "frightful" after all, but still had become just part of a uniform that did not stop British troops from waging war or being good sports.

One of the more startling images of a gas mask worn by civilians appeared in the *Daily Mirror* in 1918. In a clearly staged photograph, a mother and child sit before an open hearth wearing their anti-gas protection.[47] When the image is examined more closely, two countervailing types of objects take precedence. The first are the sacks with eyeholes – improvised gas masks – that hide the faces of the woman and the small child on her lap. The second is the large iron pot hanging in the fireplace. One object signals modernity; one object signals tradition. Somewhere, this image implies, inside a home, in a country stricken by war, a very ordinary domestic scene has become an uncanny realm of horror (Fig. 2.3).[48]

Figure 2.4 The undated photograph of the mother and child in gas masks (centre) appearing in the British media in January 1918 as the central image in an array of illustrations about the war. *Daily Mirror*, January 15, 1918. Mirrorpix/Reach Publishing Licensing

This image and what it represents reveal an overlooked way in which the First World War stands as a watershed moment. If the aftermath of the war allowed us to see what modern war did to the combatant epitomized in the Tomb of the Unknown Soldier (mass death, the destruction of bodies so that they could not be identified), then this photograph is its counterpart: the Hearth of the Unknown Mother.[49] This is what modern war does to the home, to domesticity, to the sacral figure of mother and child: in the heart of the household, it subjects them to mass industrial warfare. When the *Daily Mirror* published this photograph for a British audience, it provided no comment other than noting that in this "pathetic scene in the poor cottage of a Flanders peasant a little behind the front … [e]verybody, women and children included wears the gas mask" (Fig. 2.4).

A month later the same paper published an image of "Alsatian children" wearing or carrying primitive anti-gas helmets.[50] The captions for these photographs claimed that they were official French photographs. Their being reprinted in an English newspaper continued to highlight the shocking and disturbing sight of the most innocent of civilians forced to protect themselves against this most frightening weapon of modern war.

As the war's end approached, British newspapers still reported on horrifying scenes in French territory as the German army retreated: "the shopkeeper told me how he had managed to secure a gas mask for his mother, and how they remained, silent and masked in the darkness of their underground retreat."[51] If everybody near this front had to wear a mask, and if the front had expanded to include the British Isles in aerial attacks, then the pictures from France that appeared in the British press served to reinforce the ongoing specter of what might occur in poor British cottages in a future war. At this stage in the war, such images might serve the function of cultural remobilization, a reminder that the war was still worth fighting and winning despite the sacrifices that this had entailed, given the actions of the enemy.[52]

As the making of combatants' gas masks became industrialized in British factories, more civilians became aware of the realities of chemical warfare. Firms such as the Boots the Chemists took on this task, as the official report on its war activities notes: "practically all the granules required for the gas masks used in the Great War were made in Nottingham and the majority of the gas masks filled and assembled there." Women were among the workers in such factories. 1918 images from the Imperial War Museum's "home front" Women's Work Collection, which contains photographs that the government's Ministry of Information staged to show women's contributions to the war effort, reveals young women creating gas masks in an assembly line in a British factory.[53]

In a commemorative volume celebrating the wartime role of its firm, which made gas masks in Oxford, John Bell, Hills & Lucas Ltd claimed that theirs was a story illustrating "a true romance of War and Industry." Although the book speaks of the "men who beat the Germans," the volume is filled with photographs that depict almost entirely women workers, from those in the helmet shop to those testing valves to those preparing eye filters. These women workers are praised for their zeal: "they were the women behind the men who served the guns. ... Their zest in their work ran sometimes very near the border-line of tears." Two posters from the factory also appear, one reminding women that soldiers owe their lives to their gas masks, and thus the workers must be silent and focused: "bear in mind the life of the man dearest to you may depend on your work." The other cautions the women to stick to their work despite the air raids. By so doing, they are showing their concern for "your country and your Men. They will admire your pluck and thank you for it. Carry On." The text extolling the female gas mask makers explains that these were signs for the minority of workers as most showed their dedication. And the mainly young women surrounded by gas masks or gas mask components do look focussed, even among these surreal objects (Figs. 2.5–2.7).[54]

Figure 2.5 Women factory workers fitting gas mask helmets with eye pieces, photograph from *Lest We Forget* (London: John Bell, Hills & Lucas Ltd, 1918). With kind permission of Nick Hills

Figure 2.6 Women factory workers assembling the small box respirator, the main military gas mask, photograph from *Lest We Forget* (London: John Bell, Hills & Lucas Ltd, 1918). With kind permission of Nick Hills

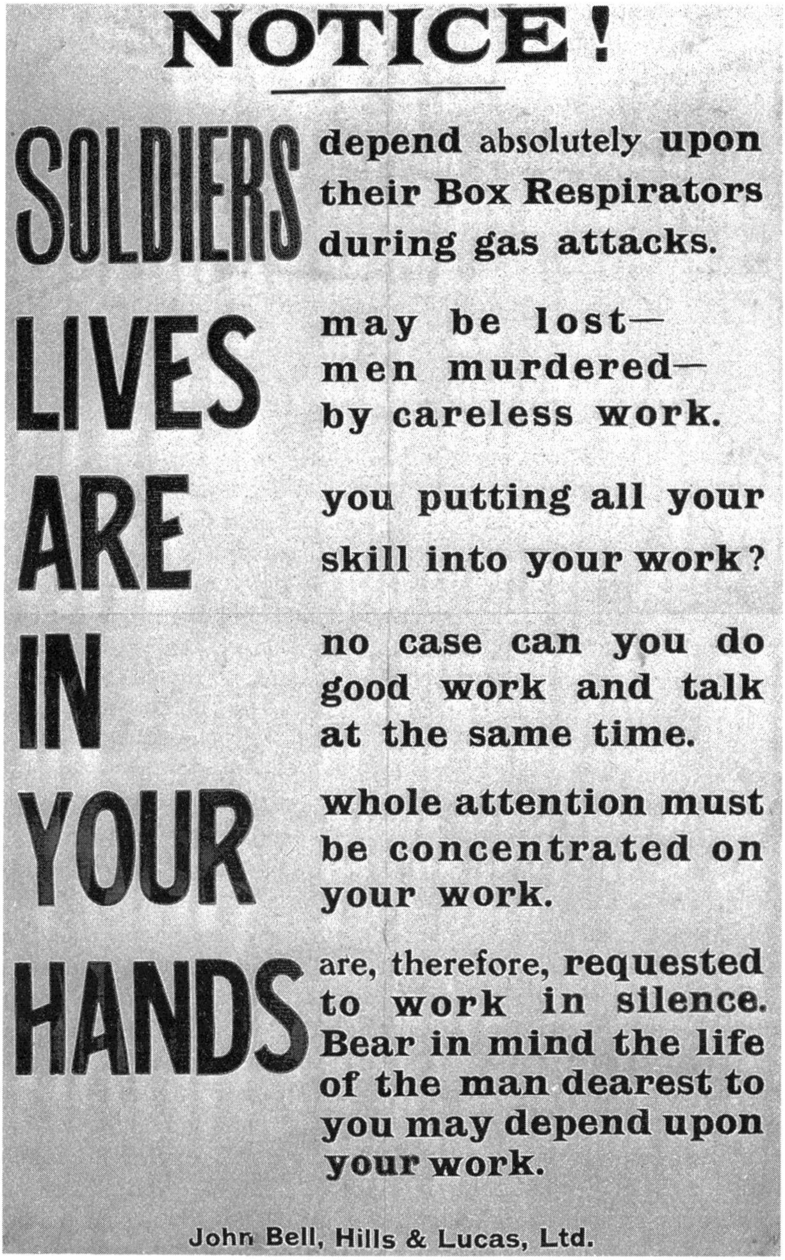

Figure 2.7 "Soldiers Lives Are in Your Hands" poster at a wartime gas mask factory, photograph from *Lest We Forget* (London: John Bell, Hills & Lucas, Ltd, 1918). With kind permission of Nick Hills

After the war ended, some British soldiers carried their gas masks home along with other superfluous items. As the many tributes to the "father of the gas mask" noted on the eve of this occasion, a single object – the gas mask – had saved lives by making the use of poison gas less effective and therefore presumably less tempting to use.[55] Yet the legacy of the unleashing of chemical arms led to an urgent imperative: What was the postwar world to make of the new weapons that could violate the borders between home and war zones and promise new means of death en masse? What would be needed to curtail their power? The long afterlife of the Great War's gas mask was only beginning.

The Immediate Afterlife of the Gas Mask

Gas masks entered into postwar life in two ways: as material devices carried home by men returning from battle and as symbols of a variety of conflicting lessons from the war just past that would shape responses to a future war. Many of those who had experienced air raids and poison gas attacks were forever altered by having encountered these new modes of waging war. They were concerned about their impact in another war, particularly if their lethality could be combined in a rain of toxic chemicals unleashed on unsuspecting civilians in densely crowded cities. One vivid example of this can be found in the preface to British feminist Cicely Hamilton's 1922 dystopian novel *Theodore Savage*, which describes future war as the "war of the air and the laboratory," a combination that would utterly destroy civilization. Witnessing air raids while working in northern France, Hamilton attempted to show others how the First World War had transformed the civilian experience of modern war. And she was not alone.

Media portrayals of the gas mask in postwar civilian spaces echoed the wartime mixture of dark humor and visceral horror. The combatants' gas mask could be practically (and comically) put to use in peacetime Britain, as in a photograph taken almost a year after the armistice, captioned "Demobbed Gas Mask." It shows a painter, "engaged in spraying turpentine, [who] protects himself from the fumes by using a mask that often saved his life in the trenches."[56] This turned the wartime object into a workaday one. However, in 1923, the *Daily Express* sought to sell papers by heralding the story of the "Fatal Gas Mask." Beneath this headline came the cautionary and tragic tale of a three-year-old boy who managed to place the gas mask his father had carried back from his military service over his face and connect its hose to the home's gas bracket. He was found dead, wearing the mask, with the gas turned on.

The instrument that saved a life now caused a death, a reminder of the gas mask's sinister associations.[57]

More significantly, debates about the strategic lessons of the conflict normalized the gas mask as a new part of preparing for war. In one of the earliest book-length attempts to defend chemical arms, Victor Lefebure's 1921 *The Riddle of the Rhine: Chemical Strategy in Peace and War*, the author explains his decision not to focus on protective devices because the gas mask was "a part of the equipment of every soldier" and thus familiar to everyone. Lefebure, who, among other wartime roles, had served as liaison between Britain and France on chemical warfare, asserts that both sides advanced the design of their gas masks in response to a development in their opponent's offensive weapons. Keeping up with anti-gas technology became a vital part of the war effort because Britain had been "absolutely unprepared" for the first use of these weapons, so much so that "nearly every household contributed to our first inefficient and improvised mask." Lefebure thus sums up the basic history of chemical weapons during the war as a "struggle between gas protection and aggression."[58]

This leads Lefebure to a set of conclusions that emphasizes the importance of gas masks in any future war. He insists that "to be within reach of enemy gas without a mask is true nakedness. A modern army without a gas mask is much more helpless and beaten than one without boots." Lefebure adds that "gas discipline thus became one of the most important features of general training, a feature which can never be abandoned by the armies of civilised nations in the future without disastrous results."[59] Despite the intense criticism and discomfort with chemical arms during the war, no nation expected them *not* to be used in a future conflict, and so nations would need to plan accordingly. Such preparations would need to be not only practical but also imaginative in order to produce the necessary actions (the gas discipline) to use objects like gas masks correctly and avoid panic.

Just as armies required gas masks and the training to use them, so, too, would civilians. An essay in the *British Medical Journal* at the end of 1921 asserts that Lefebure's work, other similar American-based studies, and the British daily press had collectively lifted the veil of secrecy that had surrounded chemical warfare. The author notes that this had been "a wise precaution when our defence against gas was inadequate" and also when retaliatory measures benefitted from the element of surprise. The article further highlights that despite the success of masks in safeguarding ocular and respiratory functions, there remained no adequate means to defend against the burns caused by mustard gas. Moreover, this perspective takes seriously Lefebure's point about the undercurrent of danger presented by the very existence of a robust chemical industry and the ease with which factories could be turned from producing chemicals for industry to producing poison gas for war. Despite the terms of the Treaty of Versailles that specifically prohibited Germany (and Germany alone) from using chemical warfare, as long as industrial chemistry flourished there, the danger persisted. The *British Medical Journal* article concludes that although the abolition of gas warfare would be ideal, "no convention, guarantee, or disarmament safeguard will prevent an unscrupulous enemy from employing poison gas if he has the whip-hand in its production – other methods must be looked for." These methods might include providing devices to enable targeted populations to survive this type of weaponry.[60]

Other postwar writers and activists grasped Lefebure's point about the inevitability of chemical weapons, and thus also of gas masks, becoming part of preparing for war. One can further complicate the story of postwar pacifism and antimilitarism by looking at the ways in which the specific dangers posed by *new* modes of warfare captured the attention not only of interwar strategists like Lefebure but also, and more importantly, of the interwar imagination. The danger of not following a path toward disarmament and control of scientifically enhanced warfare resonated in fiction published early in the interwar period, such as Hamilton's *Theodore Savage* (1922).[61]

Theodore Savage serves as one important example of a range of cultural and political responses to the First World War's legacy as a conflict that used modern technology in innovative ways. Hamilton took the powerful images of civilians flocking to the countryside to seek shelter from aerial bombardment and transfigured them into something horrifying. It is not flame and destruction that the characters in her novel try to escape but the profound devastation, through the use of poisoned weapons, of cities, lives, and the very earth upon which humans depend for survival.

In Hamilton's novel, we find not an acceptance of chemical arms, but instead a clear warning that scientific knowledge applied to warfare could lead to the utter destruction of the civilized world. The plot of *Theodore Savage* is relatively simple. It begins in a recognizable post-1919 European world, and its titular character is a protagonist who epitomizes civilization, a middle-aged and middle-class male bureaucrat. It quickly becomes apparent that all is not well in this world despite the existence of a "League" devoted to ensuring peace and prosperity. Soon enough, international tensions spiral out of control, and Savage finds himself stationed in the north of England to ensure the equitable distribution of resources in the conflagration to come.

When war breaks out, a scientifically enhanced fall from grace brings with it clouds of poison and flame. This causes "a wave of vagrant destitution [rushing] suddenly and blindly northward – anywhere away from the ruin of explosive, the flames and death by suffocation while authority strove vainly to control and direct the torrent of overpowering misery" (75–76). Nameless crowds flee the devastation of chemical war against which they have no recourse and, even more tellingly, against which the state has no remedy. Despite his position as a government agent, Savage can only look helplessly at "a man with bandaged eyes and puffed face whom his wife had led blindfold. ... The man himself sat dumb and suffering, breathing heavily through blistered lips." Even more significantly, "the woman raged vulgarly against the Government which had neglected to supply them with gas masks, to have the place properly defended to warn people!" (76).

Hamilton's message to the reader delivered in this cry expands upon the failure of the government to prepare soldiers for poison gas in 1915 and Lefebure's call for gas masks to become as essential as boots. If the nation-state cannot cope materially with the prospect of chemical warfare, then the only solution is for humanity, acting internationally, to disavow militarism and the use of such weapons. In the catastrophic world of the novel after the ruin, any rational system for coping with the collapse of civil society has failed. This ultimately reduces the few survivors of both the weapons of war and the panic and starvation that follow to a condition of small bands ruled by physical force and violence in a world of chronic depravation: "the daily, personal and barbaric form of war, wherein every man's hand was raised against his neighbour and enemy. That warfare ceased not and could not cease – until the human herd had reduced itself to the point at which the bare earth could support it" (128). There can be no more dire consequences of aero-chemical war to come. The same government that failed to provide gas masks or warnings to its civilian population was unable to prevent the collapse of civilization.

Theodore Savage received a mixed critical reaction. Some praised Hamilton's "conception of this wrecked world ... [as] a really great creation of the imagination ... worked out with a mastery of history and the human mind that is startling."[62] Others criticized that "it hardly makes inspiriting reading for survivors of the latest earthquake, still struggling hopefully among the ruins of their house." Yet, given the circumstances of its creation and appearance, one might concur with another critic who found in it "a moral for the times."[63]

It was a moral that the state was willing to acknowledge. It was the sort of catastrophe outlined in *Theodore Savage*, both in the physical devastation caused by chemical arms and in the criticism against an impotent authority unable to protect its citizens, that the government sought to avoid when it launched its first foray into planning for the aero-chemical war to come.[64] The prospect of total and potentially devastating attacks on civilian life compelled state action in order to prepare to face the very prospect of this new way of waging war. Through its establishment in 1924 of a Committee of Imperial Defence Sub-Committee on Air Raid Precautions, the British government took its first steps toward creating civil defense that took seriously the threat of a chemical attack. It pledged to create "a defensive organisation designed to protect the civilian population against the effects of gas," largely because of the "serious effect that the employment of gas may have on the *morale* of a population ignorant of the subject."[65] From the start, it was something cultural – "morale" and its corollary "character" – and not merely strategy or economics that motivated planners. To ensure civilian morale, some concrete form of protection would be necessary.

Britain was not unique in terms of preparing theoretical and practical means to defend civilians from chemical weapons, nor was it the first to do so. Perhaps the experiences of chemical weapons on French soil inspired the French government to enact its version of civil defense, or "défense passive," as early as 1922, one of the first states to initiate policies for civilians to prepare for a war that would involve scientific, modern tactics and weapons. France, too, had its theorists about the next war against civilians, such as André Michelin and Captain Brifaut, both of whom published articles on this topic that appeared in the mid-1920s in the *English Review*.[66] As structured in the 1920s, anti-gas protection in peacetime fell to various levels of the French bureaucracy, at least in terms of determining its practicalities – such as the allocation of gas masks – but it crucially relied on municipalities to fund civil defense measures. This meant (practically) that planning proceeded without actually developing the mechanisms with which to carry it out.[67]

In the meantime, in Britain (as elsewhere), alongside fictional visions of the dangers of gas weaponry and faint hopes of amelioration came political treatises and organized protests. A 1924 League of Nations Union pamphlet, *Chemical Warfare*, explained:

It is much to be hoped that some means of protecting the civil population from such an attack may be found. But it is right to point out that the problem is a difficult one. To furnish a whole population with gas masks would seem almost impracticable, and methods for collective protection have yet to be proved efficient; yet, short of that, and especially in the absence of any knowledge as to where the attack was to be delivered, no complete protection could be secured.[68]

As would be the case throughout the interwar period, the strongest voices warning of the impossibility of preventing the devastation that a future use of chemical weapons would produce arose from advocates of disarmament and antimilitarism, often from a feminist perspective. Despite the potential for gas masks to mitigate some of the effects of chemical munitions, such voices consistently emphasized that the best recourse remained prohibition, disarmament, and international cooperation. One can, therefore, complicate the story of postwar pacifism and antimilitarism by looking at the ways in which the specific dangers posed by new modes of warfare captured the attention of interwar feminist activists.

Key figures embracing the internationalist and antimilitarist strands of the postwar women's movement, especially Dr. Gertrud Woker (of Switzerland) and Dr. Naima Sahlbom (of Sweden), chose to focus on responding to "scientific warfare." Their campaign emerged from initial efforts specifically targeting chemical weapons that arose at the 1924 Fourth International Congress of Women in Washington, DC, and led to them, founding an "International Committee Against Chemical Warfare." Later that year, in October, this group met for the first time – in Berlin. As a Women's International League for Peace and Freedom (WILPF) newsletter reported, these leaders determined "not to restrict the work of the Committee to the fight against Chemical Warfare, but to direct it against all scientific methods of destruction." The group thus adopted the new name of the Committee Against Scientific Warfare, and its members set as their overarching goal to ask technical experts to help forge a popular appeal and then to publicize the dangers of such methods of warfare to "working people." Along with others, this group was determined to prevent not only war, but particularly the devastation caused by this type of warfare.[69]

The work of the Committee Against Scientific Warfare continued under the auspices of WILPF when that group met in May in Geneva to discuss how to work in tandem with the League of Nations' disarmament efforts. It had some success in obtaining support for a "Declaration against Chemical Weapons," penned by eminent French scientist Paul Langevin. It then adopted a strategy to solicit statements from other international scientific figures – including the American Dr. Alice Hamilton – as well as trying to have such individuals sign Langevin's declaration – all to publicize efforts to stop this form of war.

In order to enlist further aid for these efforts, Woker herself published work emphasizing the dangers that chemical weapons particularly posed to women and children. She was able to distribute a hundred thousand copies of her pamphlet *A Hell of Poison and Fire*, which appeared in 1924 with illustrations by renowned German artist Käthe Kollwitz, by the middle of the decade. In 1925, the German section of WILPF published Woker's *The Next War: A War of Poison Gas* – a volume that went into nine editions by 1932 (and would later be banned and burned by the Nazi Party).[70] The 1927 English translation of this text eloquently lays out the stakes for women (especially as mothers) in such a conflict:

There can scarcely be a greater contradiction than that between the far-reaching protection which the state guarantees its citizens in their civil rights and the brutality with which the same state exposes the same citizens to absolute annihilation. … Moreover, the modern so-called civilized state has many advantages over a savage tribe in methods of killing. It kills in a wholesale manner … the whole people, whose only crime lies in the fact that they were born beyond the boundaries of the attacking country.[71]

Thus every citizen must ask: "Will this terrible possibility become a fact? … Shall humanity … destroy itself by the most cruel death imaginable? … Why should we thus sacrifice ourselves, we who are bound to this wonderful earth by the thousand ties of happiness and joy?" This passage offers a powerful example of the mingling of the warfare and welfare state concerns of postwar feminists.[72]

Against this type of rhetoric, governments had seemingly stark choices: commitment to the abolition of chemical arms or to protection against them. Despite the vocal protests of pacifists and antimilitarists, Britain spent the interwar era preparing to develop simultaneously offensive uses for chemical weapons and anti-gas protection.[73] The ongoing work of what started as the Chemical Warfare Department and eventually became the Chemical Defence Research Department (CDRD) at Porton Down, Wiltshire, and the development of devices and mechanisms to safeguard individuals from chemical attacks continued to the end of the decade.[74] In Britain, ongoing secret testing occurred against a backdrop of substantial public discussion about the stakes of preparing (or not preparing) for an aero-chemical war.[75]

In contrast to advocates of disarmament and prohibition, defenders of chemical arms made clear that they felt there was no option but to prepare to face poison gas. One of the most well-known defenses of such weapons came from J. B. S. Haldane, the son of John Scott Haldane, the scientist who had developed one of the first respirators and who also worked on anti-gas protection during the First World War. John Burton Sanderson Haldane served in the military in the war on both the Western and Mesopotamian fronts, and he would go on to be one of the founders of modern genetics, a popular writer on science, and eventually a member of the British Communist Party.[76] His 1925 *Callinicus* points out that when people object to chemical warfare, they are merely expressing their discomfort with an unfamiliar method of killing. Haldane also notes, almost as an aside, that "apart, however, from the extreme terror and agitation produced by the gassing of uneducated people," the wounds produced by standard artillery shells are far "more distressing" than the results of phosgene or chlorine attacks. Haldane argues that those opposed to the horrors of chemical arms are mistaken: chemical weapons are more "humane" than others because the death toll they produce is lower than that from other forms of artillery. Such an argument discounts the "extreme terror" and the psychological effects of using chemical arms, something that continued to concern military and civilian authorities after the war. Given that the emotional response occurs, in this analysis, in "uneducated people," the solution would seem to be educating the public, training them to understand and thus control their fears.[77]

Moreover, Haldane also points out the obvious technological solution to such weapons, concluding that gas attacks "became more and more ineffective as the efficiency of the respirators used on both sides increased." He urges any postwar government to "seriously consider the provision of gas-masks for the population of London and other large towns and the instruction of school-children in their use." If such protection and training were not made available, he cautions, "a disaster of the very first magnitude" was a distinct possibility in the early phases of the next war. Interestingly enough, he also defends this idea by stating that it is "one of the few military measures which could hardly be regarded as provocative" by either militarists or pacifists. The more serious danger lies in not continuously working on anti-gas measures so as to be prepared not only for the gases previously used but also for new chemical arms that might emerge.[78] Thus a major point of contention between the interwar advocates for using all available weapons and opponents of specific means of waging war (especially chemical and air power) became the issue of protection. In essence, as a practical matter in terms of facing poison gas, the question remained: Could the government give everyone a gas mask that offered effective protection?

As far as Haldane was concerned, the challenge of preparing civilians for chemical attacks in a future war was not new. "[W]e were threatened with gas bombs during the war," he notes, "and certain London pharmacists made very large sums by the sale of alleged anti-gas masks." While acknowledging that these masks may have served a useful purpose, for "the carrying of these curious objects seemed to calm the civilian population in a moment of national emergency," Haldane likens them to "amulets and other pious frauds." For Haldane, the fact that the masks worked in psychological instead of practical terms is reason to dismiss them. He scathingly condemns those who sold such masks which "inspired such faith (for they ... looked like one's idea of what a gas-mask ought to be) that some thousands were sent out by fond relatives to soldiers at the front, a number of whom in consequence perished miserably."[79] Yet implicitly one can read in *Callinicus* an argument for the provision of masks precisely to ensure another vital component of modern war: civilian morale.[80]

Ideally, of course, masks should protect both civilian morale and lives. Above all, Haldane concludes, "the objection to scientific weapons such as the gases of the late war ... is essentially an objection to the unknown." The problem for Haldane is the moral or psychological effect of poison gas that is based on its newness, an effect that could be countered with education and gas masks.[81] As a favorable review of the book in the *Times Literary Supplement* noted, as a scientist and a soldier Haldane had a unique perspective and a reasoned argument in favor of chemical arms: "the most general lesson he draws is the need of education" on this issue, and "it would not be a bad beginning to read his book."[82]

Haldane's *Callinicus* unequivocally and influentially defended chemical warfare at the start of 1925, yet those opposed to such weapons and tactics achieved an important goal that year. In June, postwar international disarmament and antimilitarist campaigns accomplished their aim of starting to limit chemical arms with the issuing of the Geneva Gas Protocol. This document began by acknowledging that "the use in war of asphyxiating, poisonous or other gases, and of all analogous liquids, materials or devices, has been justly condemned by the general opinion of the civilised world."[83] It confirmed for the signatory powers an agreement to prohibit the use of chemical and biological weapons in warfare. As an article in the *Times* explained that month, despite some debate, the General Committee of the Conference on the Control of the International Arms Trade agreed to "a protocol on the prohibition of chemical warfare by the representatives of the Powers assembled at the Conference."[84]

From the start, the all-encompassing language of the Geneva Gas Protocol hid its limitations. These included the fact that it was binding only on signatories who ratified the agreement; it did not discuss retaliatory use of these weapons; it provided no means to enforce the agreement; and it made no mention of the specific dangers faced by civilians. It also did not apply to the use of agents such as tear gas as an allegedly non-lethal gas, especially when used against internal or colonial uprisings.[85] An especially glaring lapse was that the protocol forbade the use but not the development or storage of chemical weapons or devices to defend against them.[86] Moreover, while France, Germany, India, Italy,

Japan, Poland, Portugal, Spain, Turkey, the United Kingdom, and the United States all signed the agreement in 1925, ratification was a different matter. France was the first country to ratify in May 1926, but Italy waited until 1928, Germany until 1929, and Britain until 1930. (The United States did not do so for fifty years – until 1975.)[87]

This lack of precision within the protocol, coupled with the fact that Britain did not ratify it until the start of the next decade, meant that anxiety about chemical weapons and their consequences for civilians as well as governments continued to engage the interwar imagination. In addition to *Theodore Savage*, other fictional works published in the mid-1920s sought to depict the newly altered postwar and thus prewar future. One of these took inspiration directly from Haldane and appeared in 1926, a year after the publication of *Callinicus*: the novel *1944*, whose author Lord Halsbury (Hardinge Giffard) was a First World War veteran. The book's subtitle, "A Novel of Gas War Annihilation," effectively encapsulates the aim of the exercise. The preface explicitly reminds skeptical readers to turn to Haldane's *Callinicus* as a counterweight to believing that "the whole idea is purely fantastical and that such an attack upon the centres of civilisation as I have ventured to suggest is and always will be an impossibility."[88]

The novel's plot is set in motion by a prologue that details the meeting of three friends – English, Scottish, and French veterans of the Great War – in 1925. Their wartime service and the emergence of new weaponry have convinced them that the next war will yield the "total obliteration of civilization." So they make a pact that they will do whatever they can to save themselves and their loved ones when that calamity occurs. The leading figure is the English veteran Sir John Blundell MP, who comes across in these initial conversations as the rational advocate for taking matters into their own hands. His French friend, Pierre De Marnac, proposes that the gas mask is a solution to this potential danger, echoing the ideas expressed in *Callinicus*. Blundell reacts to the idea instantly: "What! For the whole civilian population of London! And against an unknown gas!" (26), dismissing the proposition as nonsensical. This framing chapter ends with all three deciding there are only two options: maintaining boats and planes, so that they can escape the coming destruction and start civilization anew, or trying to stop the looming aero-chemical war from taking place.

The book's main action begins in the year 1944, with the children of the original three protagonists meeting at a June garden party. The text then switches to explaining why a planned disarmament conference is failing – a combination of power-mad dictators in Russia and China – and the prospect of war breaking out. Since our three heroes have spent years closely monitoring all international events, John Blundell receives advance word that Germany and Russia collectively are launching a poison gas attack on London. He rushes to Parliament to try to have a general warning issued but is too late. Once it becomes clear that the attack is already en route, the government can do little but promise reprisals and urge the population to prepare. At this precise moment in London, Dick Blundell and Sylvie De Marnac (respectively the son and daughter of the two friends) witness hundreds of bombs falling: "and from each a mass of poison gas was spreading. Women screamed, and a few men also" (95). There are no gas masks, no devices to protect them.

Much of the rest of the novel traces the harrowing journey of Dick and Sylvie as they try to escape London and reach a place of greater safety, encountering more poison gas, roving bands of cannibals, enemy troops trying to corral the local population, and lack of food and water. In the penultimate chapter, the bruised and battered couple are finally able to join their parents and a few others on a boat setting off for somewhere unaffected by the devastation just unleashed.

However, in something of a twist, as the survivors gather in the chart room to plot where to go, John Blundell rejects the spot on the middle of the map, which is nowhere special but not in danger. Instead, he persuades them all to return to London, for China and Russia have effectively destroyed one another as the war has spread: "it is up to us to go back and save what remains" of an England "stricken as no civilized country has ever been in the whole history of the world" (290–92). The last scenes have them moving slowly up the Thames, beginning the process of rebuilding and burying the dead as the morning sun rises.

Read as part of the ongoing cultural conversation about the state, protection from poison gas, and the war to come, *1944* comes across as both fantastical and sobering. Halsbury presents his protagonists as devising possible strategies for coping with the threat of war in 1925. One is working to inform the populace of exactly what might await them in a chemical attack so as to encourage their advocacy for the abolition or prohibition of such weapons. As the novel vividly demonstrates, this plan of action fails; descriptions of horrific destruction with no prospect of countermeasures occupy much of the text. Yet *1944* itself provides an example of this option. Advertisements for the book noted that it was in its second printing and quoted the critic in the *Morning Post*, who explained that while there had been "several stories of aerial warfare on a grand scale ... '1944' is surely the most powerful and provocative of them all."[89] There are enough scenes of political, moral, and scientific failure to illustrate the path that should not be taken and certainly to increase the fear of chemical arms. That the forethought and ultimately the courage of these veterans are alleged to derive from their war experience suggests something of the immediate legacy of the innovations of the First World War. The lesson of the war and the greater danger lies in not taking action – in not having gas masks.

Gas masks as the solution to a world facing chemical Armageddon permeate another work of fiction that appeared two years later. Norman Anglin, a sometime journalist and author, published his play *Poison Gas* in 1928. Anglin used as his epigraph two quotes: The relevant one is from an undated speech by then Conservative Prime Minister Stanley Baldwin claiming that the government is studying "the problem of the protection of the civil population against gas attack ... both in its technical and non-technical aspects."[90] The play sets out to explore the latter.

The play begins in August 1950; the setting is a boat off the coast of Port Said, with one scene set in a café in that city. The main character, Harber Mansleeve, has devoted his life to atoning for the death of his eldest son during what is referred to as the Great European War. Before meeting the great man, others talk about him as someone who in 1917 "had a great belief in the humanity of asphyxiation. But his own son was killed humanely, and it took the egg out of his enthusiasm" (27). One result was that Mansleeve has seemingly devoted himself to "anti-chemical warfare propaganda" and the designing and manufacturing of gas masks that he has sold around the world (27). He has made a fortune out of so doing, and while those awaiting his appearance, including his third wife, Roma, and his secretary, Garcarth, debate his motives, Roma makes it clear that Mansleeve has profited immensely from advertising "his old pattern of respirators as obsolete and offering the public a better article." She points to the contradiction of his being hallowed for leading "the world revolt against the menace of extermination," all the while living on a boat equipped with every anti-gas precaution (27–28).

When seventy-nine-year-old Mansleeve finally appears, he is obsessed with "the sudden release of gas, the secret gasses, the gasses we all fear but whose composition we cannot foresee" (33). It becomes apparent by the end of Act I that Mansleeve has no mission to save humanity because its fate is sealed: "there is no end to science, when once it has been devoted to the cause of death." For every new device of protection created, a gas or a weapon will render it obsolete (36). The remainder of the play traces the legitimacy of this notion in two ways.

First, it illustrates the widespread necessity of the gas mask in a world on alert for the unleashing of chemical arms. In the opening of Act II, Roma and Enyd (Mansleeve's great-niece) listen to dance music, explaining that dancing is the one activity for which no one wears their respirator: "That's the charm of dancing ... two people can't possibly dance together, if the chest of each is plastered over by a huge, ugly metal box, having an incongruously comic, rubber nozzle, waggling at the top of it" (42). The absence of the gas mask is an emblem of freedom in an otherwise constrained society where "everywhere clergymen carry them, so do doctors … and solicitors" (43). When the scene shifts to a café in Port Said in Act III, the first figure who appears is an enterprising door-to-door salesman, Mohamed, "laden with a large bundle of respirators (in cases) slung from his shoulder. He is wearing one himself. … Secured to his head by elastic bands is a mask with large glass eyepieces and a metal-ringed mouth-opening" (69). His first words are: "Gas Mask! Gas Mask! Very good, very safe, very clean," and most importantly, he claims, endorsed by the great Mansleeve. He makes one sale to a customer, but the Greek proprietor of the café informs him that he keeps many gas masks on hand for his customers "in case some day – poof!" (71).

Conversations among the locals at the café reveal that gas masks are available in automatic machines in the great hotels, the railway, and the post office, and that everyone has something for protection from gas. Those with faith in religion rather than science have constructed their own version of a respirator, described as having "tapes over head, holes for eyes, and over the mouth something is stitched within material." The student in the café who has devised this homemade mask explains that he has stitched the first chapter of the Qur'an inside the green silk to protect himself from poison gas. All of this suggests that the gas mask is ubiquitous because the threat of chemical annihilation is as well. Moreover, everyone in this future is prepared on some level for a war of poison gas at any moment, even if not all are willing to put their trust in scientific methods of protection against a scientific menace.

Second, the play shows the futility of believing that anything can protect people from science bent on destruction and governments bent on survival through maintaining their own power, expressed in this future by competing poison gas arsenals. When a young couple, consisting of Maisie (Mansleeve's daughter) and a crusading journalist, Lewis Farrant, rendezvous at the café, the journalist denounces all anti-gas efforts as only having "robbed the people of hope." As he further explains, all the anti-gas efforts have created a belief that everything is doomed and they have "frightened the ordinary people into living recklessly" (78–79). Farrant later elaborates that "everyone's equally helpless" and that this has led to a society embarked on living a kind of danse macabre (94). Predictably, the last scenes of the play illustrate the gas menace with cries of "gas" and the putting on of gas masks. The final scene in the allegedly secure quarters of Mansleeve's ship ends with the sound of a ringing bell (signaling that the gas indicator has gone off) as the characters collapse to the floor. Unleashing chemical weapons may kill people, the play suggests, but the constant threat of obliteration in a world where poison gas weapons are widely available already destroys lives, because it destroys hope. No device can defend against that.

Placing this play within the larger frame of discussions about chemical warfare and anti-gas protection in the 1920s, like that in the novel *1944*, reveals that it similarly uses science fiction to show the dangers of a present course of action. In the year in which *Poison Gas* was published, after all, fifteen nations, including the United Kingdom, signed the Kellogg-Briand Pact of August 27, 1928. Signatories to this treaty agreed to "condemn recourse to war for the solution of international controversies, and renounce it, as an instrument of national policy in their relations with one another." This was a measure that attacked "aggressive" wars but preserved the idea of wars for defensive reasons.[91] By showing imaginatively the worse consequences of an unbridled commitment to developing not just chemical weapons but also the individual means of combating them via the gas mask, *Poison Gas* reads as an antimilitarist cautionary tale. Yet it also shows how easily populations might accustom themselves to living with an existential threat, and by so doing, it highlights the potential for new weapons to destroy what makes us human as much as life itself.

Gas Masks and Plans for the Next War

Cultural anxiety and international arrangements did not stop the British government from funding and developing an apparatus to prepare for a potential chemical war. Debates could appear in public about whether gas weapons were "humane" (as Haldane put it) or capable of destroying humanity (as imaginative literature suggested). Nonetheless, the testing of both gas masks and chemical weapons at Porton Down continued well beyond the armistice. Planning to defend civilians against potential aero-chemical annihilation coexisted with efforts to develop chemical arms for future conflicts.

In 1919, what had been the Chemical Warfare Department under the Ministry of Munitions came under the purview of the War Office. Work continued on prototype chemical arms as well as on respirators through the 1920s as the Chemical Warfare Research Department became the CDRD. One major preoccupation of the immediate postwar years was the evaluation of the condition of wartime gas masks and the development of improved designs for military anti-gas protection. By 1926, the search for a suitable civilian respirator also became part of the research agenda at Porton.[92]

While the work of the CDRD was hidden from public view, even more obscure were efforts to have imperial spaces serve as a laboratory for devices and practices. By March 1920, Major W. A. Salt, a "chemical advisor" working in India, was reporting back to the CDRD on tests conducted in Mussoorie on the persistence of mustard and chlorine on soil and subsoil. He followed this report by proposing additional experiments in India, noting for example that while respirators should be designed in England, modifications for their use in India would be necessary. As he elaborated:

[the] beard and knob of hair of the Sikh must affect the fit and speed of adjustment of the mask; the great variety in length of hair, from the close cropped hair of many regiments to the long locks of the Baluchi calls for plenty of room for adjustment of the head bands; the present nose clip will not suit everybody, particularly men of the Mongolian type, Gurkhas, Nepalese and Burmese.[93]

The incorporation of colonial subjects serving in the military into such plans may not be surprising, but the detailed list of racially charged "variations" (presumably not found among white British troops) suggests something deeper at work. The extent to which standard anti-gas protections (chiefly the gas mask) could be effective for all of Britain's subjects – military and civilian – was being worked out during the entire interwar era.[94] At this early moment, Major Salt proposed ordering about 50,000 respirators to be sent to India from England, with 20,000 to be kept in storage "and the remainder issued for training on a scale of 10% for the establishment of units."[95] While Salt's plan received a skeptical response, less than a year after Versailles, plans to test the fitness of anti-gas protection displayed an acceptance of this form of warfare and its potential use in imperial settings as well as the metropole.

Other experiments conducted at Porton Down reflected ongoing efforts and concern about protecting civilians, especially within the United Kingdom, as the basic form of civil defense took shape. This emerges vividly in a test conducted in 1928, one which illustrated another aspect of the postwar legacy of the gas mask. In addition to ongoing attempts to prepare civilians to face the war to come, a September report from Porton Down about an experiment that had failed revealed a crucial way in which the quest for civilian anti-gas protection was developing.

A month after the signing of the Kellogg-Briand Pact, the top secret "Investigation on Possibilities of Producing a Simple Civilian

Respirator" by Porton Down scientists A. E. Childs and W. A. Salt (now back from India) reached the War Office in September 1928. It reported on a series of experiments to determine the feasibility of producing a defense against both phosgene and mustard gas in the form of "a respirator which could easily and cheaply be made from substances usually available in an *ordinary household*."[96] Systematically, the scientists had tested pads impregnated with various household substances that "could be quickly and cheaply obtained in quantity" first against phosgene and then against mustard gas.

Using what were presumably readily available household goods including liquids more commonly associated with cleaning or cooking (oils and fats, soap flakes), scientists had found that most substances offered little or no protection. Defense of a "much higher order" was made possible only by using activated charcoal. The next-best result (a towel soaked in washing soda and then treated with melted butter, lard, or olive oil) did not offer much in the way of "adequate" protection. Only a device that more closely mimicked the gas masks of the First World War and used activated charcoal as a kind of filter had any chance of relatively cheaply offering "very good protection for the air passages against even considerable concentrations of gas."[97] Among other things, the experiment implied that any truly useful respirator could not rely on something that the civilian population had readily to hand; it would need to be manufactured elsewhere and distributed widely.

Moreover, much like the call for gas masks to be created by British women in April 1915, this experiment once again explored turning the manufacturing of a military object to safeguard life against a formidable modern weapon into a domestic task. The idea of making a gas mask not only in the home but also from the materials of daily home life illustrated succinctly the militarization of the domestic sphere after the First World War. And not just militarization as such: It demonstrated an acceptance that civilians would now confront a war of potential annihilation. Within a decade of the armistice, new efforts arose to cope with the unprecedented suffering that might come home, and the gas mask lay at the center of that struggle.

Conclusion

From the moment at which chlorine plumes drifted across the battlefield at Ypres in 1915, those on the receiving end of lethal chemical warfare responded both imaginatively and practically. The unprecedented use of chemical arms in 1915 changed the conduct of war, and, facing an unanticipated threat, the British government developed individual anti-gas protection. It started with the most basic form of a covering for nose and mouth and ended by providing each soldier with a small box respirator, protecting eyes as well as airways. Gas warfare seeped into culture, not only in the famous poetry of Wilfred Owen but also in the visual iconography of this war and the ways in which this war came home. When the conflict ended, the future of chemical arms was still open to question.

As the First World War concluded, debates broke out about the extent to which states should assume that chemical weapons would be part of a future conflict. Given the advent of air power, those planning and imagining future war had to contend with the possibility of the widespread deployment of poison gas against entire populations. Given this potential, states had to ask whether civilians should have gas masks. While the British government slowly began measures to accept the new stakes of modern warfare, publicly expressed anxiety about wars yet to come focussed on the state's ability to keep its civilian population safe. The stakes were high, because the government had been so unprepared for poison gas in 1915 that it first had to ask women at home to make basic respirators out of cotton gauze and wool. Might Britain be haunted by the prospect of women, like the wife in *Theodore Savage*, railing against a government that had not provided masks? Throughout the 1920s and despite its decision to ratify the Geneva Gas Protocol at the decade's close, the British government and individual scientists, strategists, and writers prepared to face the gas menace at home. The solution that was developed over the decade and half after the war's end was to provide individual anti-gas protection – a civilian gas mask – for all.

3   Defending Civilians
Developing the Gas Mask in Britain and Its Empire, c. 1930–1936

Introduction

In July 1935, the British government offered its first sustained public statement on civil defense when it released a circular on ARP. As we saw in the last chapter, a core group of officials had been preparing for this moment for at least a decade. As if acknowledging the ways in which ideas about a future war had begun to reach the public, the state offered the following matter-of-fact rationale for these new measures:

> The necessity for such measures must be apparent, and the Government would be neglecting their duty to the civil population – men, women, and children – if they failed to take these precautions. Developments in the air have made it possible for air attacks on a large scale to be delivered. ... It is impossible to guarantee immunity from attack.[1]

It was a vivid reminder that everyone was now at risk, noncombatants and combatants of all ages and in all spaces. While emphasizing that the primary danger in the next war would come from the air, it clearly indicated that such air raids could include chemical as well as conventional weapons. However, even though gas masks had become an increasingly important part of public discussions about future wars and the British Empire's readiness for them, all the statements about anti-gas protection in this document appeared in the future tense.

In the early years of the decade, the government had begun to enlist the British Red Cross and the St John Ambulance (SJA) as the primary national organizations that promoted first aid to train their members in basic health care for a chemical war. It is then not surprising that leading figures in the first aid work of the SJA had opinions about the 1935 ARP Circular and the work of first aiders in preparing for the implementation of civil defense. In the August 1935 issue of *First Aid: The Independent Journal for the Ambulance and Nursing Services*, Captain Norman Hammer offers his perspective on the war to come and the SJA's readiness to care for those who might be wounded by air raids deploying chemical and explosive weapons. Hammer's extended essay "An Ambulance Man

Looks at Gas" appears serially for several issues and begins by acknowledging that "the subject of the protection of the civil population against the effects of poisonous gases has occupied the public mind very much of late." He was proud that the SJA, "ever in the forefront of activity in all that concerns the relief of suffering and the saving of life," had already undertaken extensive work to instruct its members about addressing the wounds inflicted by such weapons.

Hammer then tries to reassure those worried about gas attacks "as inevitably terrorising and casualty producing." This did not have to be the case so long as a population prepared and gained "proper gas discipline," something that could be achieved by individuals as well as by the community as a whole. He continues:

We can say without exaggeration that an attack by poisonous gas is another form of the effect of the environment to secure the survival of the fittest and the elimination of decadent and untrustworthy persons and races; for it is only those persons and races that are too slack and too unintelligent to face up to facts before the event, and so prepare themselves for it, and too lacking in self-control and self-discipline to submit to a little discomfort during the short time of the actual exposure, who will suffer.

Clearly, some inhabitants of Britain – presumably those who were white, middle-class, educated, responsible, full of self-control – constituted the "fittest," who could confront and survive these weapons, and Hammer seemed confident that those willing to volunteer for the SJA would be among them.

A familiar theme of those who claimed that gas was nothing to fear emerges as Hammer develops his ambulance man's take on gas. The greatest danger to the population is not the poison gas itself but the panic that might ensue were such a weapon to be used: panic that would cause laborers to stop vital work, shutting down production, distribution, and communication across the nation. Luckily, "all of these damaging effects can be rendered slight, if not prevented, if the elementary outlines of individual and collective protection are understood." If one trained, one could recognize war gases and know how to treat them. Finally, if one learned how to wear a gas mask properly, then the nation could make "a gas-attack little more disturbing than a local fog." Hammer developed his ideas across the next five issues of *First Aid*, with each installment of "An Ambulance Man Looks at Gas" offering details about gas masks and protective clothing, decontamination, hygiene, and gas-proof shelters. When he wrote his concluding piece in January 1936, he felt that "enough has been said to demonstrate than an attack by gas need not cause casualties and need not cause fear."[2] The key to securing this outcome was disciplined preparation, which became the clarion call as ARP unfolded across Britain.

The 1930s were the crucial decade for efforts to figure out the most effective methods for preparing civilians for future war as imaginary wars turned into actual ones. And it was during this decade that the gas mask emerged as a cornerstone of these plans, for its capacity as much to manage emotions as to protect bodies. It was a challenging time, as alongside disastrous economic conditions, the looming "next war" focussed the attention of governments in many parts of the world. Many studies state matter-of-factly that the Second World War began on September 1, 1939, when Hitler invaded Poland and Britain and France declared war, but large-scale armed conflict took place much earlier in Asia, Ethiopia, and Spain, in addition to the violence within many other countries.[3] European governments also faced ongoing, often violent, resistance to their colonial control, which for Britain included the Indian subcontinent and parts of Africa.[4] Although lethal chemical weapons were deployed in Ethiopia to great condemnation, all of the major zones of conflict in the 1930s witnessed the types of industrial warfare introduced during the First World War now being utilized against civilians.[5] In different ways, these external crises encouraged the rise of civil defense in Britain, which increasingly focussed on the government's commitment to individualized anti-gas protection. It was during this decade that the gas mask fully entered into public life as a key feature of civil defense, a process for which the first half of the decade proved decisive.

Gas masks also became the focal point of debates about the likelihood of any measure of civil defense succeeding. Opponents of air power pinned their hopes on a long-awaited disarmament conference that convened in Geneva in 1932. In the months leading up to its opening, antimilitarists and other activists urged politicians to take a stand against new weaponry, especially air power, in hopes of securing a lasting commitment to eradicate the most terrifying weapons that could target civilians indiscriminately. As part of such efforts, images of babies in gas masks became a shorthand to illustrate the new, horrific stakes of modern war. Such evocations indicated a lack of faith in previous agreements to limit chemical weapons, and they reflected the broadly accepted idea that aircraft would inevitably be used to deploy poison gas against civilians in the wars to come.

Even as advocates of disarmament considered the mere idea of gas masks for all to be emblematic of what was wrong with the current direction of international politics, the British government readied itself to defend civilians against both aerial and chemical warfare. The testing of gas masks continued in both the metropole and colonies, and there was fervent interest in the anti-gas protection being designed abroad. At the same time, with the announcement of ARP in July 1935, public discussions intensified about how the state should address the dangers civilians could face in a future conflict.

This was especially the case after word of the Italians' use of gas weapons in their war with Ethiopia first appeared in the *Times* in October 1935.[6] By March 1936, debates in Parliament focussed on the recurring accounts of poison gases deployed against unarmed civilians, with MPs demanding action from the British government and the League of Nations. The efforts made at the start of the decade to try to balance the need to prepare civilians for war and eradicate the most pernicious of new weapons had reached a critical stage.

Protesting Gas and Gas Masks: The Disarmament Conference and Its Aftermath

In the early years of the decade, efforts to stop the military deployment of new technologies culminated in the Conference for the Reduction and Limitation of Armaments. This was the formal name for what was more often referred to as the World Disarmament Conference, or Geneva Disarmament Conference, which opened in February 1932. Interwar calls for disarmament reflected both the desire to mitigate the cost of continuous arms production and the related belief that the pre-1914 competition over armaments had precipitated the outbreak of the First World War. The British delegation assumed that its role at Geneva was to mediate the competing aims of France and Germany.[7] Yet the specific kind of war that loomed – an industrial and "scientific" one – also motivated advocates outside governments to call for specific limitations on the trauma that could be inflicted on civilians by modern war. Many antimilitarist activists had been asking for the conference for at least a decade, and as the economic circumstances of the Great Depression made governments seemingly more sympathetic to reductions in arms spending, they began preparations in 1929 for what they assumed would be such a conference in earnest. One principal aim became reducing the threat of aero-chemical war in the future.

A key organization working for both the conference and for educating the public to urge a reduction in air power and chemical arms was WILPF. When WILPF organized an international conference on "Modern Methods of Warfare and the Protection of the Civil Population" in January 1929 in Frankfurt, Gertrud Woker, the chemical warfare expert and antiwar activist who helped found the Committee

Against Scientific Warfare, was one of the featured speakers. She here continued her campaign against chemical arms by insisting that "the worst of the past gives little idea of what would be the horrible reality of a future war ... [where] the civil population ... will be massacred by gas bombs from thousands of aeroplanes, and peace will only be concluded over the dead bodies of the enemy nation. In comparison even Dante's hell pales into insignificance."[8] Far from being immune or shielded, civilians would become the main target of such a war. Protecting the civilian mattered in a new way, and the choice was deemed to lie between securing the collective civil population (through communal shelters, including gas-proof ones) and securing individual bodies (through such measures as gas masks).

The prospect of a civilian gas mask providing a respite from this threat, as defenders of chemical weapons such as J. B. S. Haldane had proposed earlier in the decade, was dismissed at the meeting in Frankfurt by another expert, Dr. Nestler, who had assisted the German army in its chemical weapons defense. Nestler explained that it would be especially dangerous if anti-gas protection were thought of as an "individual" problem to be solved with a mask. For Nestler, in addition to the costs of preparing such gas masks, there were psychological barriers to their effectiveness:

To wear a gas-mask requires extraordinary discipline; people put them on with teeth clenched. If discipline is difficult for trained soldiers, how much more so with civilians. A mother could not endure to hear her child crying under its mask. Women and children will certainly not be able to make full use of protective apparatus; every gas attack would cause a panic.[9]

This dire warning signaled how gender might influence the use of gas masks and reveal the limits of the protection then available. If "women and children" could not utilize gas masks because they could not be trained to do so given their "inherent" tendency to panic, there seemed no way for them to survive. By concluding damningly that "all protective measures against modern scientific methods of war were useless," conference speakers on behalf of WILPF at Frankfurt urged instead a renewed commitment to disarmament as the way to ensure survival.[10]

That further restrictions on specific types of arms, especially chemical ones, might also be a crucial element of the upcoming conference at Geneva became clear as the date for convening that meeting approached. As part of the official Preparatory Commission for the Disarmament Conference, the British government announced on April 30, 1929 that it had now decided to ratify immediately the Geneva Gas Protocol of 1925. It did so, however, with the following provisos. First, it considered itself bound not to use chemical or bacteriological weapons only against other countries that had ratified the protocol. Second, it would not be constrained when confronting an enemy state that did not respect these restrictions. In other words, Britain and its dominions who joined in ratifying the protocol at this moment reserved the right to use chemical arms against states that were willing to deploy them. This permitted Britain to make a public statement in support of limitations on one of the most dreaded modes of new warfare while preserving its right to engage (certainly clandestinely) in developing both the weapons and the means to defend against them.[11]

Two years later, Victor Lefebure joined these new conversations about limiting arms by publishing *Scientific Disarmament*, calling for a rational approach to chemical weapons. This book, which appeared nearly a decade after his influential treatise *The Riddle of the Rhine*, includes prefaces by leading advocates for peace and disarmament such as Jane Addams, Gilbert Murray, and H. G. Wells. Perhaps counterintuitively, Lefebure argues for the development and production of gas masks as an aid to disarmament:

The gas mask is a good illustration of the fact that disarmament is real if it leaves the nations with this kind of work not yet completed and mainly to be done at the outbreak of war. ... In another sense, however, it is a bad example, because the gas mask is probably the one feature of armament which should be developed to the utmost in the interests of disarmament.

He elaborates as to why this is so: "Chemical disarmament must be more effective if means of defence are developed to such an extent that the chemical weapons at that time are ineffective. The bigger the gap between defence and aggression in favour of the former, then the less will be the incentive to make chemical war."[12] This was another variation on the argument that had circulated since chemical weapons were first employed in 1915: No rational state would deploy a weapon against which there was an effective remedy.

Lefebure's solution to the threat of chemical arms and scientific warfare relies on the universal availability of gas masks. He asserts that any proposed limit to chemical arms must ensure that an equilibrium be reached between the main powers not only about their weapons but also about the defense against them: "the interesting question arises as to what policy regarding the gas mask is most consistent with a stable peace ... based on essential defence as against unlimited offence" (256). Lefebure then concludes "in plain language" that "all the great nations, if they adopted a rational disarmament policy as regards chemical warfare would standardize on the same gas mask." For if they were to do so, even allowing for "national peculiarities" that would impose design differences in terms of shape, each state could make a decision on the best type of device based on "strictly technical grounds" in order that "the essential protective features of national masks would be the same" (257). Given the possible creation of new types of poison gas, there would need to be ongoing research into the development of gas masks. Nonetheless, this could be limited to perfecting devices against known gases, not the unknown ones (while also discouraging research into them). Lefebure thus proposes a simple solution to chemical weapons, namely an international effort to create a standard prototype for the gas mask.

Lefebure also cautions that while "it might be possible to equip a whole nation with gas-masks," there would remain the uncertainty of knowing that all were in working order and that everyone knew how to use them. There might be "masses of children, invalids, women and careless individuals who would be virtually unprotected, and we have to take the view that the use of gas on civilian populations from the air is substantially and technically the use on an unprotected objective" (281). On the one hand, an internationally recognized, standard gas mask would make the offensive use of poison gas unappealing. On the other, the only effective limits involved curtailing the planes that would ultimately deploy poison gas. The key: "whether we wish war to retain some of its former less repugnant characteristics or to become a chaotic slaughter-house for women and children" (282). This hearkens back to conversations unleashed during the Great War about the barbarism of those willing to use such weapons.

That a future war might involve the slaughter of innocents emerges vividly in the essays that constitute *What Would Be the Character of a New War?*, a volume sponsored by the Inter-Parliamentary Union that also appeared in 1931.[13] Like Lefebure's text, this collection of essays aimed to inform the public of the stakes of future wars so they could take action in light of the looming disarmament conference at Geneva. As its introduction explains, in order for negotiators to do their job properly, they needed the support of "enlightened public opinion" based on scientific expertise. This 400-page tome begins with the general military characteristics of future wars and then considers protection and defense against new means of waging war, including the impact on morale, demography, and economics. Its contributors range from Lefebure, discussing "the decisive aggressive value of the new agencies of war," to left-wing British MP Norman Angell on the effect of a new war on the world financial system.

Gertrud Woker, the sole female contributor, once again weighs in on both chemical and bacteriological warfare in her essay, especially on poison gas as being "an essential, if not the most important, factor in the preparation for a fresh war."[14] Woker calls out the "very lukewarm attitude" of the League of Nations to the disarmament of "scientific warfare" and "the terrible fact that nothing is being done to avoid the danger" (357). This was especially worrying given the number of American, French, German, Russian, and British experts who insisted on the utter destruction that an attack using poison gas would inflict on their nations. As part of her evidence, Woker presents the findings of an International Committee of the Red Cross report that condemned possible defensive measures against gas. Woker calls attention to the fact that collective defense and gas-proof shelters would not work and that gas masks alone would not protect against substances that attacked the skin. Her worst-case scenario ends in a rhetorical question:

> We will suppose then that men, women and children, even the smallest, clothed in a protective suit, gas masks, shoes and gloves of some impervious material, attempt to flee through the streets which are infected by mustard gas and reduced to a burning heap of ruins by incendiary and high-explosive bombs. Where can they go? (382)

For Woker and others helping to define the "character" of a new war, there was no safe place to go. There would be no device that could counter the horrors of modern, industrialized, and inevitably chemical warfare.

More concrete actions also preceded the opening of the Geneva conference in February 1932 both in Britain and elsewhere. In late October 1931, the *Daily Telegraph* showed a group of "hundreds of people" from across the nation who converged in Warsaw, Poland, all wearing some form of gas mask to protest the use of poison gas in war.[15] Antimilitarist organizations such as WILPF worked internationally, and its British section was joined by the National Committee for the Prevention of War to help gather and then deliver at least two million signatures calling for disarmament to the opening meeting in Geneva.[16] Critics of chemical weapons called upon the British government to take action. A pamphlet published by the Chemical Worker's Union issued in the spring of 1932 entitled *The Menace of Chemical Warfare to Civilian Populations* proclaimed that only "enlightened Public Opinion" could "prevent THE NEXT WAR and the mass murder of defenceless men, women and children."[17] Gas masks were not enough to keep women and children safe; only disarming such weapons would work.

As the conference got underway in 1932, the media continued to discuss the arrival of gas masks for everyone – if not in Britain, then elsewhere on the continent. Britain was not the only nation also preparing civil defense at the same time, for a newspaper commented that it seemed "very cynical" in light of the upcoming disarmament conference to have the French government showing off its designs for shelters and gas masks, while another took note that Germany was developing "gas masks for all – even animals."[18]

Reports from the conference kept British readers informed about its workings and about the issues surrounding disarmament more generally. In November 1932, for instance, newspapers reported on debates that included expressions of concern that the manufacture of gas masks might then lead to "inventions counter-acting their efficacy."[19] In Parliament, Lord Marley asked why the government was opposing measures like the suppression of the private manufacturing of arms. Displaying a gas mask that, he claimed, French children were practicing wearing, he argued that the "very unpleasant" object was being used to train a new generation to accept "the worst side of warfare." In turn, Marley was accused of being a communist and asked whether the gas masks being given to every man, woman, and child in Russia were a larger threat, insinuating that the Soviet Union and communism more generally posed the greater menace to world peace.[20] And other papers reported on advertisements in Berlin for gas masks as sensible Christmas presents that December.[21]

If the prospect of gas masks for Christmas did not alarm the population, word of further scientific developments that could fuel the use of poison gas emerged that might do so. In January 1933, the *Times*, under the heading "Terrors of Modern War," publicized recent statements by Lord Halsbury on the development of new war gases. It quoted Halsbury extensively:

War on a large scale to-day would mean a conflict in which masses of civilians would be blotted out in scarcely conceivable conditions of horror. It would be war in which civilisation, as we know it might be utterly destroyed. If large towns such as London were bombed with gas it would be impossible for their inhabitants to use effective measures against poisoning and asphyxiation. Even if respirators could be issued to our urban millions, thorough gas-drill would be necessary, and frequent inspections to ensure that the masks were kept in a state of repair.[22]

The gas mask in this account reflects a familiar refrain: it promises safety, but as an object *alone*, it will fail to work.

Beverley Nichols's bestselling 1933 book *Cry Havoc* crystallized calls for disarmament, highlighting the dangers of modern forms of war. Nichols was, as one reviewer of this book put it, someone "always in the news; opportunist and versatile."[23] After dedicating his book "to those mothers whose sons are still alive," Nichols begins with a letter to H. G. Wells in which he explores his position toward the next war as a pacifist, starting with an examination of the preparations for both offense and defense in this conflict to come.[24] Nichols acknowledges straight-away that under present conditions "the margin between 'defense' and 'offense' is vague and indeterminate." However, he was also prepared to "guess that for every man who was engaged in manufacturing gas masks there would be at least a hundred men engaged in manufacturing poi-sonous gases, directly or indirectly" (12). Given these circumstances, Nichols concludes his introduction by asserting that the very word "war" had become obsolete as soon "as the first shot in the air was fired." It thus required a new word not to describe a conflict of men in arms against other men in arms, but one "which could be applied to the latest possibilities of blowing up babies in Baghdad by pressing a button in Birmingham." Yet still, he claims, most English people, "even in the middle of an air-raid, still carried a subconscious mental image of 'war' as a fight of one group of men against another group of men, whereas the image they *should* have carried was the universal struggle of all mankind against a common enemy ... whose arms were steel and whose breath was a sickly, yellow death" (16).

In asserting that modern warfare had created entirely new circum-stances, Nichols was hardly unique, certainly not in 1933. However, his assertion that the word "war" should be replaced in every instance by the phrase "mass murder of civilians" summed up his argument. Subsequent chapters set out to describe how this would be accomplished unless humanity came to its senses. By describing visits to armaments factories, including those manufacturing poison gas, he aims to show the preparations for offensive war, a section that he cut short "because all the world knows that its neighbours are arming" (57). Addressing the com-placent "average citizen" – especially "the middle-aged man living in a quiet suburb" for whom the prospect of war seemed remote and "the actual prospect of personal pain, of tearing and gasping agony ... unthinkable" – Nichols has a one-word response: "gas" (58).

To begin his exploration of gas, "a word which, not unnaturally, makes people hysterical when they discuss it," Nichols references Haldane and those who had defended gas warfare. He calls special attention to Haldane's assumptions about the survivability of gas warfare being based on the idea *"that the whole population is wearing gas-masks"* (61, emphasis in original). This struck Nichols as the height of absurdity because daily life cannot be carried out in a gas mask: "you cannot eat or drink or speak when you are wearing a gas-mask. You can do nothing but sit tight, or lumber clumsily about" (61). And, he continues, the insidious danger of chemical arms is that "you can no more 'outlaw' gas than you can 'outlaw' the wind or the waves," insisting that no agreement to curtail its usage would last beyond the outbreak of war (63). As evidence of the inevitability of gas warfare, Nichols quotes American, French, and German as well as British experts – all of whom had testified to the efficiency with which the population of a major city could be wiped out by poison gas.

Having established the capacity of various states to wage a chemical war, Nichols turns his attention to the "apathy" and "inefficiency" of the measures for defense, starting with the gas mask. In a chapter entitled "Behind the Mask," Nichols recounts his visit to what he claims was the only English gas mask firm in the last days of 1932, in order to show the feeble and problematic defensive measures against modern war. Once he steps inside, the first thing he encounters is "a glass case, filled with little dolls, all wearing gas-masks" (75). In deeply sarcastic tones, Nichols then praises this idea "as far the most sensible Christmas present which any mother could possibly give to her child" (76). Even when he realizes that these are models, he feels sure that "any mother with sense" would happily provide them as toys for children, for it will accustom them to think of wearing the gas mask as normal. Yet a sense that such a sight could and should never be ordinary emerges when Nichols confronts a wall of "the face coverings, which are at once so hideously human and yet so far removed from life. There they hung ... row upon row of them, grim and grey, still and sightless. Their blank faces were turned dead towards me, and their canvas features seemed to droop in dejection and despair" (78, ellipsis in original). Even more troubling, many of the devices being produced were destined for export – to be used to prepare potential enemies to withstand British chemical arms. Underlying Nichols's entire encounter is horror not only about the object but also about the willingness of the manufacturer to commercialize and profit from the prospect of chemical warfare.

Nichols then asks his guide whether it were possible to provide every man, woman, and child with gas masks, to which he responds, "we could manufacture forty million gas-masks and retail them at five shilling apiece" (79). However, when asked what he would do for his own family, the guide speaks of creating a gas-proof room. Nichols denounces this idea as not worth the paper on which the plans are written, for it would require the entire population to sit still while sheltering from something like the fog.

Finally, Nichols obtains a chance to test a gas mask himself, since he has been told that the "psychological effect" of practicing with a mask is "terribly important" (82). Going into a chamber filled with gas while wearing a borrowed mask, Nichols reports on these effects. The tenor of one's breathing changes; "the world, now, was only a whirling of grey veils, a choking and a gasping, a foul nightmare" (83). Even knowing that the mask was working, that the gas in the room was not fatal, "one felt so helpless, like a trussed animal in a burning building" (84). He quickly decides he has had enough, despite being told that someone could wear such a mask for twenty-four hours and even sleep in it. This cannot be, he concludes, and he deploys a powerful anecdote to illustrate this point:

> Now will you please stop reading for a moment, and do a little mental exercise. It is a very simple exercise. You know what a gas-mask looks like. Well, just picture, for a moment, a mask on the face of some woman you love. Imagine it, for example, shoved over your mother's head. ... When she has it on she won't be able to talk to you nor you to her, for you will be wearing a mask too. You will have to sit, silently, gasping. If she has a weak heart – as my mother has – I fear she will not gasp for long. She will suddenly crumple up, and the face you have always loved, that one day you had thought to kiss, in its last stillness, will be kissed and crumpled by the mask. And if you tear it off, it will be stained and pock-marked by the encroaching acid, as she lies on the floor. (83–84)

This represents the unbearable: that gas will attack at home the most domesticated and idealized figure, the mother. By calling upon his readers to picture their mothers in gas masks, Nichols asks them to do the impossible and so to join him in fully resisting all efforts to prepare to face such a future, such a war. The greatest danger, according to Nichols, lies in acting as if any such conflict would resemble the wars of history: science has turned war into something that will target beloved domestic figures in their homes, with no hope of escape, and so it must be resisted.[25] His views led military figures to write letters to the editor of the *Daily Mail* that suggested Nichols knew nothing about modern gas masks, and critics such as Malcolm Elwin in the *Saturday Review* to claim that he allowed "sentimental idealism" to muddle his arguments, to express horror "at the unmoral realism of commerce" instead of accepting that profits were to be made in armaments and gas masks.[26]

Despite Britain's ratifying the Geneva Gas Protocol and the related issues raised by proponents of international disarmament, by the early 1930s a variety of voices in the media had begun to provide a common vernacular with which to think about protection from chemical weapons. The gas-proof room was deemed either a fallacy or prohibitively expensive; so collective protection was out. And even if the government forged ahead (as it would) with its plans to develop gas masks, this might still not be enough. Critics insisted that individual protection – the gas mask – could not work; yet it would soon become a crucial object upon which the edifice of civil defense would be built.

Preparing to Mask the World

Under the auspices of the Cabinet's Committee on Imperial Defence Sub-Committee on Air Raid Precautions, which had met regularly since its creation in 1924, British war planners took up the issue of defending the civilian population against both aerial and chemical attacks. Britain's imminent ratifying of the Geneva Protocol led to a heated consideration at an ARP Sub-Committee meeting that May as to how plans should now proceed. The longtime committee chair, Sir John Anderson, began the meeting by pointing out "that up till now the question of protection against gas attack has been regarded as one of the foremost necessities" and that, in his opinion, this might not need to change until the committee decided "how much importance could be attached to pledges" not to use gas warfare. Sir Maurice Hankey, another leading figure on the committee, concurred that "he did not attach very great weight to the keeping of pledges by nations in time of war." He therefore urged the committee to adopt the perspective it had expressed in the first ARP Sub-Committee report in 1925 that "it is unlikely that gas will be employed against us at the very commencement of hostilities," so that there would be time to determine what would need to be done and thus who might require protection.[27] Nonetheless, Hankey also insisted that although defense against gas attacks might assume a lower priority, efforts along these lines absolutely should not be abandoned.

Further discussion at the May 1929 meeting highlighted the significant vulnerability of London to aerial gas attack and the ease with which chemicals produced for peacetime measures could be adapted to warlike ones. The production of offensive means of waging gas war could be easily hidden, but defensive preparations had to be public. Anderson commented, "the fact that we have ratified the Geneva Gas Protocol might be used as a stick to beat us with if too much publicity was accorded to any preparations at present." The committee concluded that it would continue to work on measures to safeguard domestic spaces against high-explosive aerial bombs but defer, for a limited time, the next stage in developing anti-gas protection. As Hankey elaborated, even if "international law eventually went overboard" in the last war, the process took time, and the moral indignation that the use of poison gas would raise made it unlikely that it would be a weapon of first resort.[28]

Nonetheless, the government began efforts to train volunteers in first aid in case of chemical attacks, and such training was done discreetly but not secretly. When the Gloucester City Detachment of the British Red Cross Society underwent such training in November 1932, the local paper emphasized that this had involved drills in the latest gas masks

Figure 3.1 Gas mask exercises for medical personnel nurses in London, c. 1933. Imagno/Hulton Archive/Getty Images

and that although it "was an optional experiment, there were no shirkers." By using "shirker" – a common term for "coward" during the First World War – the paper suggested a link between the willingness to accept gas masks in a future war and military courage.[29] That December, the head of the SJA announced that its members would all be instructed and equipped to deal with the effects of gas warfare, and he commented, "make no mistake that with methods of gas and chemical attack now known any future war would be a horror for the civilian population." Members of the SJA were preparing to use gas masks so that they could give first aid to anyone affected by such an attack (Figs. 3.1 and 3.2).[30]

The ARP Sub-Committee always paid attention to how developments were proceeding in other countries. It noted that civil defense drills had begun in France and Germany, and Anderson wondered whether Britain could "gradually be worked up to a realisation of the whole situation" emulating actions undertaken in these nations.[31] He insisted in later meetings that "so much was being done in other countries who did not in the least mind publicity, that we should ourselves have to come out into the open."[32] In the meantime, Britain was waiting for the CDRD of the War Office to complete a civilian gas manual and refine the design for a civilian gas mask, and this group had started to carry out tests only in

Figure 3.2 Plymouth St John Ambulance Service practicing anti-gas
protection. Cover of the *St. John Ambulance Gazette*, September 1933.
With kind permission of Order of St John Archive, London

the middle of 1931.[33] In contrast, by the end of 1932, the committee
noted the development of gas masks for use by civil populations in
France, Germany, and Italy.[34]

Concern emerged during a meeting of the ARP Sub-Committee in
July 1932 about publicizing the development and testing of a civilian gas
mask while the government was also committed to the work of the
Geneva Disarmament Conference. The subcommittee at this time was
wrestling with deciding upon a number of measures to keep the population safe, including evacuation plans, shelters, gas-proof buildings or
rooms, and individual anti-gas protection. It spent time debating whether
it would it make more sense to gas-proof telephone exchanges or to
develop gas masks for the largely female workforce that operated them.
The Chemical Defence Research League wrote to the subcommittee
asking for tests on female workers, as the representative of Porton
Down researchers at the subcommittee noted: "if provisions would have
to be made for respirators for a considerable number of females then it
might be necessary to produce a smaller mask." Maurice Hankey then
responded that the researchers would need to determine the number of
vital female workers who might require a gas mask, including "telephone

operators, nurses, and people of this kind." That being the case, it would be far simpler to provide gas masks than to try to seal up rooms to render them gas-proof. In the view of Porton's representative, "individual protection was the only solution" and might require a gas mask "with special speaking facilities" for such workers.[35] Hankey may have summed up the prevailing attitude to international agreements in this meeting when he stated that the idea that gas warfare had been abolished "did not seem ... to have made any difference to countries in their defensive gas preparations." The only valuable development that might come from the Geneva conference would be an increase in the space between the declaration of war and the first aerial raids; this would be regardless of whether the attacks employed chemical or other weapons.[36]

As Germany fell under Nazi control in the early months of 1933, the hopes for any concrete results from the disarmament conference diminished, even though the conference limped along until its end in 1934. The darkening mood in Geneva gave a heightened sense of urgency to the ARP Sub-Committee's interest in anti-gas protection. The subcommittee noted in October 1932 that there had been "satisfactory trials" of a model civilian gas mask and, a month later, that the SJA had reached out for advice about updating its pamphlet on first aid requirements for gas warfare.[37] The ARP Sub-Committee also recommended in its annual report for 1932 that the government set up a new subcommittee to address civilian anti-gas protection. Although the recommendation was approved in March 1933, the committee would not get to work until 1934.

In the meantime, the ARP (Organisation) Sub-Committee met in early January 1934 to determine its own policy regarding respirators. It included a vigorous discussion of whether or not the government should pursue the formation of a private company that would then be authorized to create official gas masks for the general public rather than having the government alone take charge. Clipped into the committee's minutes are cuttings from the press noting that gas masks were already being offered for sale as well as separate queries from firms that had begun to sell gas masks a major concern was that without regulation, masks might be offered to the public that would not provide protection. Without reaching a definitive conclusion, this subcommittee confirmed that the government had to ensure that gas masks offered to civilians worked and that sufficient quantity be ready before the outbreak of war.[38]

All of these efforts coincided with the ongoing development during 1935 of the first ARP handbook, which included a section on anti-gas measures for individual protection. After meeting regularly in various subcommittees, those refining civil defense measures concluded in the middle of that year that urging the civilian population to purchase a device of absolutely no use during peacetime would fail. Thus there was "no alternative" to the government taking responsibility for providing (and financing) gas masks adequate to meet "overwhelming public demand."[39]

The ARP Sub-Committee had a number of concerns to balance. If gas masks were to be provided, how would they be paid for? Would they be constructed in government factories or in private factories fulfilling government contracts and using the government's approved design? In January 1935, the subcommittee considered a draft report on gas masks and concurred with its findings – for example, that the government must ensure that "the design of any gas respirators on sale to public is suitable" and "the construction and materials of any such respirators do not fall below a certain minimum standard." It needed a separate committee to look directly at this as well as other questions. How long would respirators last before needing replacement? How could costs be controlled and yet minimum effectiveness maintained? And, finally, how would the public be informed, not only about their availability but, even more importantly, about how to use them – would radio, recorded instructions that could be played in homes on a gramophone, or short instructional films shown at the cinema be more helpful in instructing the public how to use a gas mask?[40]

At an April meeting, after it had been determined to have a separate subcommittee, a key related issue emerged: If the government created an awareness that it would supply gas masks, "the public would expect this." The government thus had to decide whether it was going to take on the expense of doing so, as no manufacturer would be willing to produce these for a presumably small demand in peacetime.[41] Within the larger ARP planning committee, as the members went over the policy on gas masks in July that the smaller specialized committee would consider, some grew concerned. If they urged the population to buy government-produced gas masks in peacetime, not only could the government be accused of being "alarmist," but it was also opening itself up "to the charge of creating a market for respirators for private profit." Yet, as one of the main committee members offering expertise on air power, Wing Commander E. J. Hodsoll, explained, if war came, there would be "an overwhelming demand," and failure to meet such a demand would have disastrous consequences for the government. Moreover, unless the nation could distribute gas masks quickly in an emergency, they would be of no use.

The committee concluded, "it was necessary that immediately on an outbreak of war there should be available in the country enough respirators for every person who was within an area of probably hostile air attack." The quality needed to be such that a person could reach a place beyond the contaminated area and remain there. The working-out of these details would be the task of the respirator subcommittee, but the response of the public – emotional as much as political – to these measures remained a vital piece of civil defense planning.[42]

A sense of this potential demand and the raised expectations about gas masks as well as signs of public confidence in the gas mask as a way to be safe in a future war had also emerged in the mid-1930s. In contrast to those voices dismissing the gas mask as being useless, Boyd Cable, who had been a First World War correspondent and was now writing in the *Saturday Review* in February 1934, criticized the government for not having already acted. He pointed out that in the First World War, it took months to get even the most primitive of gas masks to soldiers in war zones.

Perhaps it is idle to ask how long it would take to equip the civilian population with even the crudest masks, because experts have already declared it impossible to attempt. If we leave ourselves vulnerable to poison-gas attack, we must just accept that we shall be massacred helplessly by the scores of thousands.

Given the expansion of air power, "*every city in the kingdom is ... liable to gas attack.*"[43] A few months later, in an essay in the same journal contemplating an air attack on London, Cable urged readers to imagine the suffering and the sheer numbers of men, women, and children who would die without some form of protection. He asked for the public to demand of its government adequate protection, to ask for gas masks.[44]

Don't Be Afraid of Poison Gas, a pamphlet by mechanical engineer F. N. Pickett, weighed in on this debate. In a foreword dated March 1934, Pickett claims that now it was akin to the "honourable attainment" of training men for war "to instruct the innocent non-combatant in an elementary knowledge of the art of self-defence against that invention of the devil – poison gas."[45] He begins by tracing the origins of chemical warfare to 1915 and demonstrates what had acted as a certain counterweight to it, asserting that "by superhuman efforts on the part of France and Great Britain, our armies had been provided with gas masks that were defensively little short of marvels" (5). According to Pickett, the British were able to match each innovation in chemical weapons by developing a superior gas mask and possessing greater "gas discipline." He concludes his discussion of the Great War's chemical arms by asserting, "what would have happened to the German soldier with his inadequate gas mask had the armistice not come when it did, may be imagined" (8). For Pickett, the implication was clear: The gas mask was key to victory for Britain and its allies.

The rest of Pickett's pamphlet devotes itself to providing the promised "hints for civilians in the event of a poison gas attack." The most significant point, presented in boldface, is that "poison gas is not the menace it is popularly supposed to be" (11). What makes it potent is not its physiological effects, but its psychological ones: "a dread of poison gas … is entirely psychological, and a *recognition* of this dread which almost amounts to hysteria is the first step in defeating gas" (12). Hysteria was a particularly gendered concept, usually applied to women. Moreover, as a term it had been displaced during the war by the notion of shell shock, war-induced and therefore understandable mental ailments experienced by men and presumably caused by exposure to the modern weapons of war.[46] In Pickett's analysis, the fear of chemical weapons was "hysterical" and yet nothing to be ashamed of; so long as everyone acquired a gas mask and practiced using it, anxiety would dissipate. The main thing to fear was panic rather than chemical weapons (13).

Fortunately for Britons, according to Pickett, superior gas mask technology was at hand. Over the course of the First World War, the small box respirator ("a marvel of design and construction") had saved countless lives, but even the most rudimentary form of anti-gas protection – the simple respirator or the "hydro helmet" (a porous hood covering the entire head with a celluloid eyepiece, and impregnated with a special hypo solution) – offered basic protection against many poisons (11–16). Furthermore, "it should not be beyond the capacity of any housewife to construct any number of these helmets, and if it is found that a modern box respirator is more expensive than one can afford, then this mask, properly impregnated is a reasonably satisfactory article" (15). As with the respirators made by thousands of British women in 1915 or the experiments at Porton Down in 1928 to create anti-gas protection from household ingredients, this assertion that individual anti-gas protection could be made easily – at home and by women – demonstrated a recalculation of the parameters of modern war.

In his final analysis, Pickett further asserts that gas masks are the key defensive weapon. Persons who valued their lives and the lives of family members needed to "take steps to acquire some form of gas mask" as a top priority, for its lifesaving qualities extended beyond its ability to protect one individual. In his view, "maybe, you will never need it to protect your life, because a hostile nation is hardly likely to see any purpose in attacking a civilian population that has protection and knows how to use it" (18). If the most dangerous aspect of chemical weapons was their capacity to create panic, fear, or hysteria, then the solution was the gas mask: "a great comfort and standby in time of crisis, although it may not and probably will not ever be used" (25). The scale upon which anti-gas protection would need to be provided meant that it either required a vast voluntary organization capable of collecting fees to produce masks and equipment at cost or required that the state itself orchestrate this (39). While claiming to "have no politics," Pickett asserts that "citizens of Soviet Russia, France, Germany and Japan are being furnished with Gas Masks and are being schooled in their use" (40).[47] He thus implies that the British government should have an acute interest in providing gas masks to its citizens and training them in gas discipline. Pickett's pamphlet contributed to a broader call for state action to protect the civilian, the innocent bystander, in a future war involving chemical arms.

Developing the best form of protection from gas weapons had been an ongoing focus of the CDRD at Porton Down. Alternating between preparing military personnel and civilians for gas warfare, scientists were actively investigating how to equip the population both efficiently and inexpensively. A Porton report on respirators for civilians in May 1930 had not abandoned the idea that collective measures were preferable – i.e., it was still best to tell the population to stay in their homes – but it suggested that a model gas mask for civilians could be created. Provisions of gas masks might be especially vital in "poorer quarters," where gas-proof shelters would need to be external to homes and where "some form of individual protection" would be required to get people from their homes to the shelters. The concern throughout the experiments conducted at Porton in the first half of the 1930s was cost and feasibility, evolving into a growing consensus on a design for the general civilian respirator by the middle of the decade.[48]

Such efforts were not restricted to the metropole. By 1929, the CDRE (India) based in Rawalpindi had four scientific officers, although it was in a precarious position by the early 1930s, when the government weighed shutting it down to save money. In March 1932, a report from the Army Council to the Undersecretary of State for India argued for the continuance of the facility: "It will be seen that in certain cases a stage has been reached where the work remaining to be done is chiefly of a routine nature, for example, work on respirators, both from the design and physiological points of view. ..." It had been determined in 1931, for example, that gas masks designed for regular troops would be "suitable for all classes of Indian troops," with no mention of the concerns raised a decade earlier about hair length and beards. Moreover, the letter concluded that "there is no tropical country which is more likely to be subjected to gas attack than India." Although this implies that India was facing an external threat, the facility could be used to develop offensive chemical weapons as well as protection against them, much as was the case at Porton Down. For these, and perhaps other, reasons, the CDRE station was sustained, and its work, which included testing human reactions to chemical weapons, continued.

It was under the auspices of the CDRE, for instance, that larger-scale experiments on both gas masks and chemical weapons occurred a few years later. By the mid-1930s, comparative studies of the effects of mustard gas involving both British and Indian personnel had taken place. In a 1933 memorandum, "On Preliminary Experiments Carried Out to Obtain Data for a Large Scale Test of the Sensitivity to Mustard Gas of British Troops in India and of Indian Troops," investigators at the CDRE observed that "while there was considerable variation between individuals in each group of observers there was a very striking difference between the two groups as a whole, and that the reactions on British skins developed much more rapidly than on Indian skins." Moreover, the explicit racialization of Indian troops – "subdivided into 3 groups in accordance with their colouring, i.e., fair, brown and dark" – yielded the "surprising" result that "the fair skinned group proved unexpectedly resistant." Even apart from the ethical issues raised by testing chemical weapons on human subjects, the inclusion of photographs in the files to illustrate the different "racial" types showed the implicit assumptions being made about the susceptibility of racialized categories of human beings to chemical arms. The report then further subdivided the Indian men subjected to the burning of their skin with differing strengths of mustard gas solution, according to their "classes," listed in the report's terms as "Punjabi Muslamans, Ghurkas, Pathans, Dogras and Sikh." However, "no true comparison was possible" because of the small numbers involved.[49] Other than proving that mustard gas did cause visible damage to human skin, every aspect of this scientific inquiry asserted differences in fitness to withstand the tools of modern war based on racial categorization.

The 1933 study then became the baseline for further research to determine the consequences for using mustard gas in various atmospheric conditions and the "sensitivity" of different types of individuals. A "Memorandum on the Sensitivity Test," issued in November 1936, justified the study on the basis of needing to prepare better methods for addressing chemical arms. It succinctly explained, "it is evident that fairly accurate information with regard to the sensitivity of humans to mustard gas is of great importance in deciding many chemical defence problems." As this memorandum elaborated, data from tests conducted both in India and at Porton Down would allow researchers to determine "an empirical test for assessing the sensitivity of any given individual" to traces of mustard gas left on clothing, for example. The report then listed

six categories in descending order of such sensitivity to mustard gas:
"1. British troops in India in hot weather; 2. Indian troops in India in
hot weather; 3. Porton hypersensitives [individuals identified as having
an acute sensitivity]; 4. British troops in India in cold weather; 5. Indian
troops in India in cold weather, and 6. British normal personnel in
England." It is noteworthy that the only category deemed "normal" is
in Britain and involves nonmilitary personnel. This suggests that concern
about "normal" Indians would not factor into the proposed aim of
establishing how to protect populations from chemical weapons.
Further assumptions about the intermingling of alleged race (nature)
and climate (environment) suggest a readiness to prepare either chemical
weapons or devices to defend against them (or both) in a variety of
settings. Not to be overlooked, and indeed underscored in the report,
is unease that if these results are accurate, "a somewhat serious situation
as regards chemical defence in the tropics" arises.[50] The relationship of
these experiments to those conducted on "normal" populations in the
British metropole merits further exploration.[51] What was clear is that the
state was investing in both chemical arms and the means of protection
against them on a broad scale despite having ratified the Geneva Gas
Protocol, and embedded in such experiments were attempts potentially
to safeguard marginalized populations in part by defining the "normal."
    Meanwhile, the work that previously had been taking place behind the
scenes became increasingly public. Newspapers began to report on first
aid volunteers and others practicing in gas masks, such as during drills in
London in November 1934. Accounts appeared in April 1935 about an
exercise at Kent's Chislehurst Caves, which stretched for twenty-two
miles and had been converted into gas-proof shelters, in which 100,000
Voluntary Aid Detachment and Red Cross volunteers participated in a
demonstration of anti-gas defense.[52] To show how all members of the
population regardless of age or gender could be prepared to face chemical warfare, reports of children and women practicing with gas masks
began to appear in the spring of 1935. The front page of the *Daily Express*
featured photographs of groups of women in gas masks and protective
clothing, and other major papers like the *Times* also printed such images,
revealing the extent of preparations in terms of first aid for chemical
warfare and the still jarring sight of women in gas masks readying themselves for active participation in a war to come.[53] At the Empire Air Day
celebration that May, schoolboys practiced with gas masks.[54] However,
images of women in gas masks became a more regular feature in the
press, for example in articles about future drills in which volunteers,
"many of them business girls[,] will face the terrors of gas warfare during
the next three weeks."[55] A *Daily Mirror* headline in late June, "Woman

Unafraid in Gas Horror Test," expressed succinctly the growing public awareness that a future gas war would not discriminate on the basis of gender and that all should be prepared for it by having a physical object (a gas mask) and the correct attitude.[56]

Not all the coverage of potential anti-gas protection was positive. In June, the *Manchester Guardian*'s Saturday Competition – where writers competed for a first-place prize of two guineas – asked for a child's thank-you letter for a gas mask in no more than 100 words. Publishing the responses, the paper noted the potential for irony and dark humor, but admitted surprise at just how grim, adding that they thought government officials might like to take a look to see just what the public felt. For a left-leaning paper, perhaps the tone of submissions such as the following was to be expected: "Dear Auntie: I am writing this in hospital because our house has been blown up. Mummy said you were mad to send me a gas mask but it was ripping fun. I did some war experiments in the bath room." Other entries also remarked on the potential for fun in the bath with somewhat less destruction; one spoke of the present inspiring a naughty sibling to draw "gas masks on all the children in a picture in his bible." The winning mock letter from a Miss Maxwell in Edinburgh thanked an aunt for giving her a present that would be "such fun" to wear, adding that Daddy had dug a "lovely deep hole to hide in when the nasty foraners who were not born at Little Pudsey come and bom us." The runner-up, written by Mrs Peacock in Fallowfield, struck a more poignant note:

Thank you for my new gas-mask, but I'm afraid it won't be much good, because you didn't send one for Peter (that's my dog) and if Peter dies I'd rather die too. But Daddy said it didn't matter, because if it ever came to using gas-masks we might as well be dead as alive.[57]

Along with the new visibility of gas masks for civilians came reminders of the limits of what they could offer.

Revealing the Official Policy for Civil Defense

By July 1935, a sense of urgency about the lack of war preparations (civil and military) both inside the government and externally spurred the issuance of the ARP Circular, the government's first official statement on civil defense measures, including those against chemical weapons.[58] Even here, however, the language on gas masks was entirely in the future tense: "protection against gas *will* need separate treatment." It was then hardly surprising that when Geoffrey Lloyd, the Undersecretary of State for the Department in the Home Office under whose authority ARP had now been placed, appeared in Parliament to answer questions about the circular, he was asked whether the government "know of any gas-mask which is capable of giving to the wearer complete protection against any probable concentration of every poisonous gas which is known to the Government; and are such gas-masks available to the public?" In response, Lloyd could only (and accurately) say that "the whole subject of the arrangements to be made for the provisions of respirators has been under close examination for some time past" and that the government "hoped it will be possible to make a full statement on this subject in the near future."[59] The development of a final standard model for civilians, and modifications for all inhabitants including infants, soon preoccupied the scientists at Porton Down, the planners in Whitehall, and many others as debates over anti-gas protection played out in public.

In the *Lancet* in July 1935, an article on "Air Raids and Poison Gas" summarized the prevailing debate. It cited, on the one hand, the work of Davidson Pratt, who, in a recent lecture to the British Science Guild, had claimed that the dangers of gas attacks had been greatly exaggerated and asserted that if the British public could learn not to panic, then they could survive in gas-proof rooms in their own homes. On the other hand, it referenced the pamphlet *Poison Gas* issued by the antimilitarist Union of Democratic Control (UDC), insisting that adequate defense against gas was "an insoluble problem." It concluded that the injuries caused by chemical agents represented a "man-made" ailment, which, like others of its ilk, would be far easier to prevent than to cure.[60]

The UDC was vocal in its opposition to chemical warfare. *Poison Gas* begins by stating its central complaint: "The public has not enough information to decide whether the whole of the British Government's Air Raids Precautions Policy is a sinister and horrible hoax or whether it is a genuine attempt to protect the public from aerial attack." The pamphlet would then help the public to decide. It did so by graphic descriptions of the horrifying wounds produced by all chemical weapons, noting that "war preparations to-day demand the mobilization of the whole nation. In chemical warfare, attack and defence are indivisible." Civilians faced the same risk as soldiers in the field. The pamphlet further offers chilling visual reminders of the horrors of modern war delivered by portraits of an undistinguishable population encased in masks. It argues that the preparations for surviving a chemical war, such as gas masks, offer only an illusion of safety. Moreover, "a population militarized beforehand is far less able, and probably far less likely to protest, let alone organize actively against war. They are already part of the war machine." The great danger with ARP and the gas mask was the political effect of making all citizens complicit in, and willing to accept, this new

Figure 3.3 This photographic spread of a crowd all wearing gas masks
lay at the center of the Union of Democratic Control's *Poison Gas*
(London: Union of Democratic Control, 1935). Public Domain

wartime condition. For the UDC and its supporters, the celebrated
public gas drill at Chislehurst was especially dangerous because it
ignored the painful reality that most in Britain lived far from caves that
could function as shelters. The suggestion that any comparable shelters
could be built without such natural geologic features was "as fantastic as
the suggestions that every man, woman, child and animal could be
equipped with an efficient gas mask" (Fig. 3.3).[61]

Some of the public reaction to the ARP Circular focussed on the
absence of specifics about individual anti-gas protection for the general
population and on the limits of anti-gas measures generally. The UDC
responded by holding a conference in London on August 9, as reported
in the *British Medical Journal*, where leading scientists, including J. D.
Bernal and Dr. J. W. Marrack, condemned proposals that would mitigate
the effects of a poison gas attack on a crowded urban area filled with
civilians. They attacked these as either inadequate (gas-proof rooms,
substandard gas masks) or prohibitively expensive (effective gas masks
and training).[62]

Figure 3.4 This image of a family in gas masks illustrated an article questioning the investment in both air power and civil defense, appearing in *Labour*, August 1935. By permission of the People's History Museum

An immediate example that encapsulates some of the tenor of the public reaction to the circular can be found in the editorial "Uncivilised War" that appeared in the *Daily Mirror* in the aftermath of its release. It found the ARP Circular to be

a reminder of the peril that hovers above. There used to be a specious phrase 'civilised' war. After the first bombs fell in 1914, after the first gas attack, common sense would no longer believe in it. ... The invention of the aeroplane has made war unspeakably barbarous. Women, children, the aged, the sick, the animals, all are now in the line of fire. War has less conscience to-day than at any other time.[63]

The war being planned for did not discriminate, but the fundamental question remained: Would *all* who were "now in the line of fire" receive adequate protection?

Later that summer and autumn, discussions of the ARP Circular continued to appear in a variety of contexts. In August, an article by Francis Williams in the magazine *Labour*, with a chilling illustration of a family in gas masks, questioned who would profit from the new focus on air power and air defense (Fig. 3.4). The *Woman Teacher*, the organ of the National Union of Women Teachers, published in its September 1935 issue a lengthy discussion of ARP by J. D. Bernal, a member of a group of Cambridge scientists who would shortly issue their own highly critical response to the government's plans for ARP.[64] Bernal points out the inadequacy of government plans and proposes disarmament as the only viable option. What the government proposed, according to Bernal, was a "psychological mask," which "has very considerable value. For those people who do not happen to be in an area where there is any gas, this mask is extremely effective. In this way it will preserve the morale of the population. That is all that is offered."[65] If, as asserted, the greatest danger of gas is panic or fear, then a psychological aid is not unreasonable. But the value of this safeguard is undermined by its ineffectiveness in actually saving civilians from being poisoned. Bernal insists, "there is no material possibility of providing a gas mask adequate to deal with modern gases in quantities sufficient for the whole of the population." Thus the whole enterprise was flawed as the government had yet to make provisions to supply the population in its entirety with the very devices that could save their lives.

Bernal was also among a group of leading scientists from Cambridge, Edinburgh, Glasgow, London, and Oxford who issued a public statement in September reiterating these views. They highlighted the shortcomings of what the government proposed: "the purchase of cheap gas masks and the organization of casualty rescue services are grossly inadequate, though they are calculated to produce a dangerous illusion of security." They stressed that the ARP Circular was designed cynically to reassure the population that the government was going to protect them, whereas any truly effective measures against gas weapons (such as closed-circuit-oxygen gas masks and complete vesicant proof suits) would be practical impossibilities.[66]

Longstanding feminist opposition to chemical warfare also reemerged in response to the policies announced in 1935. The British Section of the Women's World Committee Against War and Fascism published *Behind the Gas Mask: An Exposure of the Proposed Air Defence Measures*, which sold for one penny. Its cover featured a cigar-smoking man in a top hat offering gas masks to a line of young children; one has put on the gas mask completely covering his face with something akin to an animal's visage resembling an elephant's trunk. It denounced the idea that there might be compulsory drills to train inhabitants to accept the war to come, as was now the case in fascist countries. In its view, the only purpose of such drills was to keep "the population on the jump," but this ignored the devastating impact of the drills themselves on children. What would be the reaction of sensitive children? They would be "terrified by the masks and the idea of sudden or horrible death, and … would have a cloud of terror over the whole of their lives." As for babies who could not use

AN EXPOSURE of the PROPOSED
AIR DEFENCE MEASURES

PRICE ONE PENNY

Figure 3.5 This cover of the *Behind the Gas Mask* pamphlet (issued by the British Section of the Women's World Committee Against War and Fascism) used the increasingly familiar image of a baby in a gas mask to criticize the recently issued government statement on its preparation for civil defense. London: British Section of WWCAWF, 1935.
Public Domain

regular masks, "they can be put into rubber bags and, it is hoped, kept alive by pumping filtered air." Yet it was still not certain that such "babies' gas bags would be cheap enough for the general population." The only solution to such inadequate, horrifying measures was to resist them and the militarization of daily life that they represented (Fig. 3.5).[67]

Carl Heath, a Quaker leader, weighed in on the arrival of ARP from a religious pacifist perspective.[68] In an article in *The Friend* in July 1935, which was later reprinted as "Christians and Anti-gas Raid Drill," Heath claims that "there is something very specially evil in a spiritual sense" about the government's proposed drills and "gas mask parades." It is, he adds, a terrible condemnation of "Christian civilization" but has the advantage of offering a stark choice to all who claim to adhere to Christian values. They now face following either a "way of life" or one of death. They could stand for mutual aid and friendship among nations or they could surrender to fears by taking "the way of the gas-masks and preventive drill and running for bomb-proof and gas-proof shelters ... of reciprocal massacre and revenge."[69]

All of this reveals the ongoing vocal opposition to the anti-gas provisions being suggested. At this moment, ARP constituted a set of proposals not yet enacted. However, this was also the moment when the international situation began further unraveling as war between Italy and Ethiopia began. The evolving decision to provide state-sanctioned individual anti-gas protection coincided with increasingly widespread reports of Italy's use of chemical arms in its war against Ethiopia. It was thus the imperial context of chemical weapons that started to shift the policy into one that put the civilian gas mask at the center of preparations for the war to come.

Responding to the War against Ethiopia and Anti-gas Protection in Britain

The worsening international climate of the mid-1930s provided an impetus for an acceleration of civilian anti-aerial and anti-gas war preparations both in the metropole and in the colonies. Reports of Italy's plans to use chemical weapons against civilians appeared in the British press during the summer and autumn of 1935. A sensational headline in the *Daily Mirror* in August, when tensions were mounting between Italy and Ethiopia, claimed that Italy possessed "400 Death-Spray Planes," which it was prepared to use. The article also promised "death rays" and "liquid fire," but the claim that "the nations of the world may see in a few weeks a rehearsal of all the horrors of modern warfare" speaks to what the ARP Circular had helped to unleash: an acknowledgement that the war to come would feature "modern warfare" against civilians.[70] Reporting on the eve of war, under the heading "If War Comes," the *Manchester Guardian*'s military correspondent spoke of Italy's war calculations as follows: "no one denies the moral effect, particularly on an untutored population, of gas."[71] It remained unclear what impact this would have on the work of the British Ambulance Service, and particularly of Dr. T. A. Lambie, who had worked in Ethiopia for sixteen years. The *Manchester Guardian* mentioned that he and his colleagues were hurrying back to Africa and that their preparations in London had included buying gas masks.[72]

The first accounts of chemical warfare in Ethiopia appeared in the British press in October. The *Daily Mail* reported on October 10 that the Ethiopians had alleged that the Italians had undertaken aerial chemical warfare which had "caused agony to the wounded" as a "strange chemical irritant ... rained from the skies."[73] Other papers recorded that month that while the Italians insisted that they were not deploying chemical arms, the Abyssinian Legation in London was repeating its complaint that the Italian forces had been using poison gas.[74] Later in October, a short article mentioned that there were "fears for Britons," reporting on how the wife of E. A. Chapman-Andrews, the British consul in Harar, was insisting on being at her husband's side, even if this meant altering a gas mask for her infant son.[75] The full impact of this anecdote was left to the reader, but it was a reminder of all who were vulnerable to chemical warfare.

In the midst of these initial reports from Ethiopia came the British general election of November 14, 1935. On the eve of the election, Edith Ayrton Zangwill delivered a talk on "Abyssinia and the Air" in Edinburgh on behalf of the Women's Peace Crusade. The organization urged electing the party most committed to peace, starting by recognizing that any measures to defend civilians against aerial and chemical attack were futile, especially since "masks could not be worn by very young children."[76] More infamously, the Labour Party issued a poster featuring a blond-haired baby in a gas mask floating against a black background. Only four words formed the poster's stark message: "Stop War Vote Labour."[77] It was a reminder of Labour's support for ongoing efforts at disarmament as well as a critique of current government efforts to promote civil defense as its remedy against the damages that might be sustained in a future conflict. It also followed in the antimilitarist tradition of juxtaposing the emblem of innocence (the infant) with the horrifying evidence of the next war (the gas mask). Critics in the Conservative Party accused Labour of "scaremongering," but an article in the *Observer* on "the campaign by posters" described it as "effective," noting that one of the main targets of such appeals was "that most important person, the woman in the home."[78] It is impossible to know whether such an image produced the desired reaction among women, but the poster raises a further question: Would it have been scaremongering if such devices offered safety against an actual rather than an anticipated threat? Neither Ayrton Zangwill's talk nor this more noteworthy use of the gas mask in popular imagery directly referenced the first rumors of poison gas in Ethiopia, but the reality of gas warfare was increasingly moving from background to forefront in the British press (Fig. 3.6).

By January 1936, other media were turning public attention to the use of poison gas in Ethiopia. A cartoon in *Punch* that month mocked notions of European superiority – the tradition of military chivalry – by depicting Italy as a "knight" spraying poison gas against a racialized, defenseless African, armed only with a spear. The caption, with its suggestion of

Figure 3.6 This Labour Party campaign poster from the general election of November 1935 again used the figure of the baby in a gas mask to urge measures to prevent, not prepare for, war. By permission of the People's History Museum

justifying this as a "civilization" protecting itself, is ironic on multiple levels and, indeed, echoes the propaganda poster making fun of the "knights of the air" used against aerial attacks in the First World War (Fig. 3.7).

A turning point for public awareness came in March 1936 when Princess Tsehai, the daughter of Emperor Haile Selassie, called on the Women's Council of the League of Nations Union to defend Ethiopia. In a telegram that would be often quoted in newspapers and pamphlets, and cited in parliamentary debates and other branches of the British government, she pleads for help as follows:

For seven days without break enemy have been bombing armies and people of my country, including women and children, with terrible gases …

Against this cruel gas we have *no protection, no gas masks, nothing.*

This suffering and torture is beyond description. … Many … are unrecognizable since the skin has been burned off their faces. These are facts.

The Ethiopian Women's Work Association decided to appeal to the women of the world to use their influence against the use of these ghastly methods

WHEN KNIGHTS ARE BOLD.
"IT'S YOUR OWN FAULT. A CIVILISED MAN MUST PROTECT HIMSELF—AND
WHAT'S MORE, IT'S BEGINNING TO RAIN."

Figure 3.7 An early reaction to the exposure of the return of poison gas in Ethiopia came in this cartoon, "When Knights Are Bold," appearing in *Punch* in January 1936. Punch Cartoon Library/TopFoto

With all the power that is in me and with the greatest appreciation for what the women of England and Scotland have done to help … , may I appeal to the Women's Council of the League of Nations Union to protest against this criminal breach of the 1925 protocol?[79]

This powerful message offered a candid and vivid description of the damage that chemical weapons could do, and it cites Italy's breach of the major piece of international disarmament legislation against poison gas. Given the ongoing debates over ARP at that time, reports of the damage inflicted on women and children because of the lack of defensive measures resonated among the British public.

Groups representing women responded powerfully to reports of the use of chemical weapons and the March appeal from Princess Tsehai, with its immediate impact rooted in the following claim: "We are only a small race, but I am 17 and its leading daughter, and I know as you know, that if mankind lets armies and gas destroy my country and people, civilization will be destroyed too."[80] In April 1936, the National Free Church Women's Council wrote to the Secretary General of the League of Nations to communicate its resolution condemning "with much earnestness" the attacks on women and children and especially "the cruel use of poison gas," urging Free Church women to protest vigorously against this inhumanity. It would follow this with another letter in June 1936 to condemn the wrong done to Ethiopia and urge support of Princess Tsehai.[81] In May, the British Section of WILPF wrote to urge action, sharing its resolution that its members were appalled both at the invasion of Ethiopia and "at the barbarous weapons of warfare employed."[82] The Women's Peace Crusade similarly wrote to share its executive committee's protest to the British government at the use of "barbarous methods of warfare," urging it to bring to Geneva, where the League of Nations was frantically trying to resolve the conflict, a call to vigorously condemn Italy's use of poison gas, outlawed in the protocol of 1925.[83] A group of prominent British women, including the MPs Nancy Astor, Eleanor Rathbone, and Ellen Wilkinson, as well as representatives of the Association of Women Clerks and Secretaries, the British Federation of University Women, National Council for Equal Citizenship, and the National Union of Women Teachers, also signed a public letter in response to Princess Tsehai's appeal. In it, they protested against the "inhuman use of poison gas" and called upon the women of Britain to condemn "the cruelty inflicted by a ruthless aggressor" and proclaim "their detestation of such wanton inhumanity."[84]

The potentially larger consequences for Britain as well as the world of ignoring the dangers of poison gas warfare were further laid out in contributions to the *Times* in the spring of 1936. More wartime "atrocities" had, by now, been laid at the feet of the Italian military, including the bombing of a Swedish Red Cross hospital in late December and of an Egyptian Red Cross unit and Red Cross ambulances less than six months after the original reports detailed the use of chemical weapons in Ethiopia.[85] A telegram from the Executive Secretary of the Ethiopian Red Cross, Dr. T. A. Lambie, appearing in the *Times* on March 25, mounted an official protest on behalf of that organization against the indiscriminate bombing with mustard gas of "country villages," which had resulted in "the permanent blinding and maiming of hundreds of helpless women and children." For Lambie, the issue that this should signal to his audience was "how dreadful an unscrupulous enemy can render war with this monstrous weapon, which surpasses in fearfulness the wildest dread of a disordered imagination."[86] As his final clause makes clear,

To-day a few thousand peasants in Wallo will be groping their way down the dark years because of a dictator, whose name they have never heard of, but whose decree of ruthlessness has put out their eyes. Wallo is a long way from Charing Cross – yes, but not for aeroplanes.[87]

From beginning with a description of the sites of attack as "country villages" to making explicit reference to the heart of London (Charing Cross) as being vulnerable to the airborne unleashing of chemical agents, Lambie suggests that what was at stake was as much a question of the threats posed to those in Britain as about the mistreatment of some distant, less fortunate population. Like the rhetoric used to describe First World War gas attacks and to predict the war-to-come earlier in the interwar period, this account helped spur anxiety about gas and thus potentially the expansion of anti-gas protection.

A second contribution in the form of a letter to the editor from Sir Hesketh Bell in response to Lambie's account suggests that a failure to respond would have dire consequences for the empire and for relations between Europeans and Africans, Blacks and Whites. He starts by taking Italy to task for being "uncivilized" in using this method of warfare against women and children:

One may imagine that even the most humane of European armies might be tempted to terrible excesses in retribution for unspeakable acts of cruelty done by savages, but what excuse can the Italians offer for the deliberate blinding and maiming of women and children merely because they are the wives of and offspring of the men who are bravely dying in scores of thousands in defence of their country and liberty?

Moreover, in addition to chastising Italy for having no excuse for employing such methods, Bell continues,

Is the voice of collective civilization going to remain silent in the presence of the horrors that are being perpetrated in Ethiopia? Are the coloured peoples throughout the continent of Africa to be allowed to believe that the latest war-methods of the white man are all that they may expect whenever a European nation covets the lands that have been the[ir] homes[?][88]

The "nemesis" that may come to haunt all Europeans if this conduct is allowed to stand is the further loss of legitimacy of the whole enterprise of imperialism. Lord Halifax (Lord Privy Seal), responding to Viscount Cecil's reading of Princess Tsehai's appeal in the House of Lords, echoes Bell's concerns about race and empire. Halifax states that the reports of poison gas, if documented, "would have a gravity which could not be exaggerated ... upon the whole relations now and in future of the white and coloured races."[89] The use of poison gas tears asunder any claim of Europe acting to benefit its colonized Black subjects.

In more official circles, debates in Parliament that spring focussed on the recurring accounts of Italy's use of poison gases against unarmed civilians, with MPs demanding action from the British government and the League of Nations. And as the *Times* editorial noted, "public opinion

THE DAWN OF PROGRESS.
"BUT HOW AM I TO SEE IT? THEY'VE BLINDED ME."

Figure 3.8 By the time this cartoon ("The Dawn of Progress" by Bernard Partridge) appeared in *Punch in* April 1936, evidence of the use of chemical arms in Ethiopia was more widespread and provoked strong reactions condemning Italy's use of such arms. Punch Cartoon Library/TopFoto

in this country has been deeply stirred by the persistent reports of the use of gas by the Italians in Abyssinia." Furthermore, as it commented upon debates on the issue in the House of Lords, "this violation of the Geneva Protocol must be regarded as an outrage, not only upon the unfortunate Abyssinians who have been its defenceless victims, but upon the whole world." The editorial was especially approving of the speech of Lord Mottistone in calling the use of gas "a crime against humanity."[90] The *Manchester Guardian*'s editorial page similarly noted that a triumvirate of "inhumanities of warfare," including the disregarding of the Red Cross emblem, bombing civilian towns, and the use of poison gas, had been proved to have taken place in Ethiopia. It found Italy's violation of its signing of the Geneva Protocol of 1925 to have been intolerable for a "State that claims to represent civilization against barbarism."[91]

After this renewed publicity about the use of chemical weapons, in April 1936, *Punch* published a second cartoon, "The Dawn of Progress," with its stark depiction of poison gas sufferers, portraying the Africans (now plural and including women and children) as defenseless victims (Fig. 3.8). At roughly the same time, a David Low cartoon appeared in the *Evening Standard*, again showing how "barbaric" Europeans had become with their use of poison gases. Low's drawing featured Mussolini, arms filled with poison gas canisters and his own gas mask gesturing at dead Africans lying on the ground behind him, claiming, "they were savages, without ideals."[92] Both of these cartoons emphasized the "otherness" of the targets of chemical weapons, delivering a message that using them is a terrible thing, unworthy of "civilized" states – something echoed in responses directed at the League of Nations itself and in letters to the editors of British papers. Mary Toulmin wrote as a concerned citizen to the *Manchester Guardian* in early April that she was "driven by ... anguish" to ask how Britain could do nothing "when we hear, day after day, of innocent women, little children ... being killed from the air or suffering the agony of gas poisoning?"[93]

The horror of poison gas compounded by the lack of masks shaped other contemporary accounts of the conflict after its conclusion. The *Time*s journalist George Steer's account of the war, *Caesar in Abyssinia*, appeared in 1936, a year before he would go on to fame as the reporter on scene at the bombing of Guernica in April 1937. He himself had been expelled from Ethiopia in May for anti-Italian propaganda and, specifically, for "transporting gas-masks to Abyssinian troops."[94] His narrative of the Second Italo-Ethiopian War echoes the *Punch* cartoons and other public voices: What did it mean that the "civilized" European state was the one committing an overt atrocity? Steer tries to stress the unprecedented nature of this use of chemical arms by hyperbolically proclaiming, "On Sunday December 22 ... for the first time in history, a people supposedly white used poison gas upon a people supposedly savage. ... The moral effect was even more terrible than the material."[95] Steer offers detailed and sustained reports of the use of poison gas against both Ethiopian troops and civilians, stating categorically that the Italians deliberately bombed Red Cross units to drive away witnesses "from the front while the Italians were employing illegal methods of warfare," including the mass spraying of mustard gas (280–81). He even recounts in detail the press campaign in England to expose the persistent use of gas warfare so as to condemn government silence on the issue.

Steer then tells of local efforts to provide some means to protect the civilian population – the incident that presumably led to his expulsion. Since no external help was forthcoming, the same Ethiopian Women's Work Association referenced in the princess's global appeal – an outfit run by Lady Barton, wife of the British minister to Ethiopia, Sir Sidney Barton – set to work. By using a basic First World War respirator as a model, the members experimented until they devised a gas mask that they could make themselves. It consisted of "head bags of flannel, done up in little canvas cases … [with] mica slits for eyes" and tied around the neck with tape (286). For camouflage, the masks were "coloured a rich chocolate brown," and a dozen "experts" using only sewing machines were able to concoct 1,800 such gas masks (286). The imperial connections that might sustain the making of gas masks further emerged in an article in the *Irish Examiner* in March 1936, which reported on a cable from the Ethiopian Women's Work Association to South Africa "to resist the first use in history of poison gas by whites on blacks" by sending funds to make "masks to combat the cruel and unrestricted gas warfare." According to this cable, some £370 had already been raised to aid the construction of masks.[96]

Yet, by the time Steer set out to deliver them, it was too late.[97] In his introduction, where he presents the lessons to be drawn from this account of war, he emphasizes that the final defeat – the sack of Addis Ababa – was made possible by "the threat of gas from the air that demoralized its people." His proof is "the crowds that gathered round Lady Barton's committee rooms for masks." (9) Here, as during the first uses of chemical arms in 1915, the making of the gas mask becomes the province of women, as a domestic task that belies the modernity of the mode of warfare against which it is being used. It is also perhaps in the aftermath of this use of poison gas against defenseless colonial subjects that the idea of imperial civil defense including anti-gas protection as a kind of defense of the imperial enterprise itself becomes clearer. If attacked by an external foe with poison gas, the imperial state could now offer to come to the rescue of its colonized population by providing the devices to face this threat. Certainly, if the British government was going to sustain imperial populations in a war to come, it needed to do better than Lady Barton's improvised "chocolate brown" gas masks.

The tragic lessons of Ethiopia and the victory of those willing to wield chemical weapons should not, Steer states, be lost on Britons, and he ends his book with this cautionary reminder: "Ethiopia is nearer to Europe" than those choosing to ignore this crucial aspect of the war would think.[98] The numerous treatises, novels, essays, and other public voices discussing what might occur in a future war that were published after 1935 could take note of the ways in which, despite everything that was being done to develop the gas mask, the use of poison gas in Ethiopia blindsided civil defense planners and advocates for disarmament alike.

There were lessons drawn here by military strategists as well. Rightwing Major General J. F. C. Fuller, in articles such as "The Italo-Ethiopian War: A Military Analysis of an Eye-Witness Observer" and then in his 1936 book *The First of the League Wars: Its Lessons and Omens*, asserts that poison gas won the war for Italy. According to Fuller, special sprayers were installed on aircraft so that they could vaporise over vast areas of territory a fine death-dealing rain ... It was thus that as from the end of January 1936 soldiers, women, children, cattle, rivers, lakes, and pastures were drenched continually with this deadly rain.

The very refinement of barbarism consisted of carrying ravage and terror into the most densely populated parts of the territory. The object was to scatter fear and death over a great part of the Ethiopian territory. These fearful tactics succeeded. Men and animals succumbed. The deadly rain that fell from the aircraft made all those whom it touched fly, shrieking with pain.[99]

The lesson that Fuller drew was that war was now "totalitarian" and that gas was its weapon, as dangerous in its demoralization of the population as in its killing impact. He assumes therefore that poison gas will (and even should?) be used; he has an aside about how if Britain were inclined to use it, "we could, even with a raw militia, subdue the whole of the barbarians on our Indian North West Frontier in a few weeks."[100] One conclusion, then, was that Britain must be prepared to face this threat that extended to an entire population, not just to troops. If gas, as the Emperor Haile Selassie, Fuller, and many in public concluded, had won the war, however dishonorably, Britain had to be prepared to face down this threat and win.[101]

Indeed, government planners had been working out in secret whether or not providing civilian respirators for everybody was possible or even advisable. They had initially decided that supplying masks for those under age five was unfeasible, and took until the autumn of 1935 to conclude in secret that gas masks would need to be free of charge and available to every British subject. They began to redouble their attempts at anti-gas protection for children and infants as the decade progressed.[102] Such efforts increasingly came into public view and with a somewhat warmer reaction.

All of this helps explain some of the shifting tone of the British press coverage of anti-gas civil defense by the summer of 1936, such as the headline "£850,000 for Civilian Gas Masks" in the *Daily Mail* with its claim that the "perfect" gas mask had been discovered and would soon be available "at convenient centres all over the country ready for issue to the public in an emergency."[103] Columnists in British newspapers were encouraging readers to accept the promised gas mask, as in an article in the *Daily Mirror* in July 1936, which featured a woman wearing a version of the civilian respirator. Readers should celebrate rather than fear the gas mask's appearance, for, it continued, if "it's not the average woman's idea of a saucy hat," then it should nonetheless inspire gratitude and calm rather than horror (Fig. 3.9).[104] Instead of being terrified by such photographs, the author urged his readers, they should see them as

Figure 3.9 Hugh Cudlipp, "Don't Be Horrified – Be Thankful." The message behind an increased circulation of images and information about civilian gas masks aimed to reassure the public that the government was ready to protect them against the horrors of modern war. *Daily Mirror*, 1936. Mirrorpix/Reach Publishing Licensing

evidence that "we are no longer afraid to make ourselves safe … Isn't it on the whole far less disconcerting to be a little scared now than to be suffocated when that war comes?" The feeling of being ready to face the worst should triumph over the disturbing visual (and tactile) qualities of the device.

Conclusion

Much of the discussion in this chapter has focussed on state preparations and public – rather than personal – responses to the shifting circumstances of the 1930s. The state was facing a crucial set of questions in this increasingly fraught international climate: What was its responsibility to protect its noncombatant subjects and citizens? These issues seemed less acute at the start of the decade, when hopes were high that the long-awaited Geneva Disarmament Conference of 1932 could offer a good chance to halt the aerial delivery of chemical arms. Advocates for disarmament were clear that this was the only way to stop the deliberate lethal poisoning of populations en masse from being the future of war.

When those efforts collapsed, advocates did not stop their work, nor did the government, which effectively discounted the viability of international agreements to control the new weapons of war and proceeded to prepare to give anti-gas protection to civilians. When it decided to go public with these plans and announce the arrival of civil defense in the summer of 1935, it envisioned a population prepared voluntarily to accept an apparatus that would make them able to withstand aerial and chemical arms.

In the midst of these plans and public debates came an international conflict that involved chemical weapons. Italy's use of poison gas in Ethiopia did more than raise the stakes of civil defense planning and the invention of the civilian gas mask. It highlighted the dangers that such weapons posed both to the populations subjected to them and to the states that might lose a war because of such weapons. The public conversation surrounding this return of chemical arms and then the return of air war to Europe accelerated the process by which the gas mask came to be seen as the solution. It had to be ready for the public by the time the next war came.

The last straw came with the outbreak of the Spanish Civil War in July 1936. This conflict soon generated substantial evidence of the damage inflicted on European civilians from the air. For government officials and antimilitarist activists alike, the news from Italy and Spain heightened the urgency of proposed civil defense measures. Throughout the latter half of the 1930s, British preparations for war – and resistance to such preparations – increasingly focussed on the gas mask, a device that by decade's end became the most tangible and widespread form of state action to protect civilian life from the horrors of modern war.

4   Unveiling the Gas Mask
Designs and Dissent, 1936–1938

Introduction

Britain faced a profound set of challenges in the second half of the 1930s. As German aggression became increasingly overt and international conflicts intensified, its government had to prepare civilians for a war that could inflict enormous damage on their bodies and belongings while convincing them that somehow everything would carry on normally, that there was no need to panic. For over a decade, civil defense planners had focussed on the potential for aerial chemical war to cause devastating harm if the civil population did not respond to it correctly.[1] At the same time, political leaders had to contend with some public criticism that the government was not doing enough to protect civilians, while others accused it of "scare mongering" as it gradually revealed its work to provide civilian gas masks as well as beginning ARP drills.[2] All of this culminated in an intense two-year effort to produce, distribute, and publicize gas masks.

What those advocating disarmament and resistance to preparing for war shared with the war planners and advocates for accepting the likelihood of aero-chemical warfare by the late 1930s was a recognition that the gas mask had come to epitomize the state's efforts to protect civilians. Plans for civil defense would stand or fall with the gas mask. As a shorthand to convey both the terrors of the war to come and the potential for a scientific response to scientific warfare, the gas mask placed the civilian body at the center of conversations about what it would mean to wage modern war (Fig. 4.1).

Government discussions continued about whether or not there would be acceptable limits to who would receive gas masks, on the basis of factors such as geography, age, and status. The stated goal was reassurance, but as international conflicts multiplied after 1935, decisions about protection served to designate those who most mattered to the nation and the empire and, at times, reflected biases that included overt racism and classism. As designers worked to ensure types for specific

Figure 4.1 The finalized version of the general civilian respirator on display in July 1936. Keystone-France Contributor/Getty Images

populations such as the "abnormal" and the elderly, the choices about who should get gas masks reflected debates about the state's ability to protect everyone.

The return of devastating aerial warfare to European soil in the Spanish Civil War had intensified the sense of danger and the need for action on civil defense in Britain. In particular, the aerial bombing of Guernica in April 1937, which became the best-known atrocity of the war, caused public voices to note the connections between the devastation that the conflicts in Ethiopia and Spain wrought upon the defenseless. An editorial in the *Daily Herald* condemned both actions: "If the Abyssinians fight for their homes and country, they shall be tortured with poison gas. If the Basques fight for theirs, their towns will be razed and death will be rained upon their women and children."[3] Both air power and chemical weapons had badly injured civilians in these conflicts, even if only the conflict in Ethiopia had used poison gas.

Against the backdrop of German aggression toward Czechoslovakia, Britain's nascent civil defense regime encountered its first public test when civilians across the nation lined up to be fitted with gas masks on September 25, 1938. As much as the government may have sought to assure all observers – both foreign and domestic – that it was prepared for

Figure 4.2 The anti-gas protection for pets such as dogs and cats
available in 1938. Fox Photos/Stringer/Hulton Archive/Getty Images

war, Gas Mask Sunday quickly revealed the limitations of its efforts. One
of the startling realizations for those lining up for protection from poison
gas was that not everyone would be able to receive it immediately. This
soon gave rise to dark humor, such as the *Daily Mirror*'s report on a
conversation overheard in London's Smithfield Market the following
Monday: "Wotcher mean, War? I ain't even bin fitted wiv me ... gas
mask yet."[4] On the following Wednesday, the *Daily Mail* reported that
although protective devices for infants were still in development, the
People's Dispensary for Sick Animals had "perfected" gas-proof kennels
for dogs and cats.[5] Clearly, there was work to be done in order to be
prepared when war did come (Fig. 4.2).

As international politics and conflict came into public prominence,
behind the scenes, the development of a standard model gas mask for
civilians of all ages (and workable under specific circumstances) had
become the centerpiece of efforts by the scientists at Porton Down,
spurred on by the planners in Whitehall and the MPs in Westminster,
who passed the first major related piece of legislation, the ARP Act, in
1937. The government had, for instance, begun to test gas mask models
that would allow employees at telephone exchanges to keep working, but
protection for the very young was still a work in progress. One sign of

new public efforts can be found in January 1937, when the first government gas mask factory opened in Blackburn.[6] It was against this flurry of political action that efforts to imagine the war of gas and flame in the literature of the late 1930s appeared and contributed to the increased demand for anti-gas protection until Gas Mask Sunday. The gas mask offered a solution to ever more fraught representations of what war might inflict upon domestic spaces and bodies in Britain.

Popular Culture and the Normalization of Anti-gas Protection

By 1937, the prospect of everyone needing a gas mask in the event of war was widely circulating, thanks in part to the attention paid to the violence in Ethiopia and Spain. It also emerged as a result of the increased presence of gas masks in popular media. In the context of current events at that time, it was not surprising that the gas mask was the main feature of the first ARP publication, *Personal Protection against Gas*, which became available in March 1936 and had 477,000 copies in circulation by August of that year.[7] It also contains numerous advertisements for anti-gas protection, although the cover notes that the government does not accept responsibility for any nonofficial statements or devices. This handbook offers a set of illustrated instructions about the new gas mask, how to use it, and how to care for it, including step-by-step photographs of how to put on the gas mask: by thrusting one's chin into the device and then adjusting it. Its general preface stresses that the "use of poison gas in war is forbidden" but that the risk of its use remains a possibility. The tone is dryly informative and matter-of-fact. Although the *Daily Mirror* article mentioned earlier suggested in July 1936 that a gas mask was not "the average woman's idea of a saucy hat for summer," that same paper reacted to the new handbook by asserting, "don't be horrified, be thankful." The gas mask was going to save lives: "the finest thing the British Government could do at the moment would be to frame this picture and present it to every woman in the land ... not as a warning but as a reassurance that we are no longer afraid to make ourselves safe."[8]

In the official pronouncements of 1936, the formal design for the general civilian respirator presented to the public featured a wide window over the eyes and a filter covering the face from nose to chin. Expanding its outreach beyond those giving first aid as volunteers, the government contacted the British Medical Association and a range of medical schools in order to ask that their students be trained to work with the medical personnel ready to address the injuries caused by chemical warfare, since the general public would turn to doctors and nurses first if they were injured.[9] One reason why they might need to do so would be the anxiety stoked by representations of poison gas warfare in popular culture.

The prospect of chemical war featured in a range of 1930s media. Novels such as *The Gas War of 1940* (1931) portrayed the destruction of London from chemical arms, in this case a vision narrated by the nation's dictator from the safety of his airship.[10] One of the strangest of such texts was Simpson Stokes's 1935 *Air-Gods' Parade* (both written in response to the ARP Circular and dedicated to the new ARP Department of the Home Office). It reenacts debates about the utility of gas masks among its main characters, but it also vividly describes the impact of a gas attack upon those without protection.[11] Not only literature but cinema, such as the 1936 *Things to Come*, at that point the most expensive British film ever made, depicted the dire effects of chemical warfare. *Things to Come* opens in what is labelled "Everytown" (the stand-in for London) and shows it quickly succumbing to flame and poison. All such imaginative depictions emphasized the ultimate failure of the gas mask. Taken together, these cultural works promoted disarmament as the better alternative to any preparations for war, but they also helped to make anti-gas protection a topic of broader public conversation.[12]

A *Punch* cartoon illustrating an imagined "Gas Drill Day at Westminster" in January 1937 raised further doubts about the government's civil defense efforts. Showing a room of MPs, all wearing gas masks, it depicts the speaker gesturing broadly and announcing, "I think I may confidently say judging from the expression on the faces of honourable members, that the house is in unanimous agreement with the views I have expressed." In this "vision of the political future," the gas mask, of course, has erased individual facial features and anyone's ability to communicate nonverbally. This was one of the many ways in which the gas mask horrified and amused the public, but also in which the gas mask became increasingly normalized.[13]

One of the most powerful fictional evocations of gas warfare and the gas mask came in Sarah Campion's 1937 *Thirty Million Gas Masks*. Like many interwar fantasies about the war to come, the novel begins with the First World War. In its prelude, a young girl – Judith, one of the protagonists – gives her account of this war, a combination of marching feet, khaki uniforms, and the death of her brother Clement, which have turned her home into a "house heavy with sorrow."[14] The scene then moves forward in time to a thirty-year-old Judith, now a committed pacifist sitting in a darkened cinema, watching images of thousands of Japanese schoolchildren allegedly enjoying a gas mask drill as "the roar, the clatter, the insane and maddening din of the peace-professing, war-preparing world of 1937 went steadily on" (34).

During the weekend that follows, Judith and a group of friends gather in Cambridge. At one point, Judith and her friend Conrad (a Jewish, socialist, pacifist, German émigré professor) engage in a heated debate about pacifism and how to respond to the new types of warfare ushered in with the First World War: "In your day Daddy kissed his family, went away to the war, and either got killed, or survived and came back again rejoicing. ... Now someone drops a bomb and wipes out the whole family before poor Daddy has time even to *start* for the war" (116, emphasis in original).

Suddenly, the scene shifts forward in time to 1939. The BBC announces that negotiations have broken down and that the government is about to issue free gas masks, encouraging everyone to prepare gas-proof rooms. Still adhering to her pacifist principles, Judith cannot take action: "Dead, gas, bullets, machine-guns, bombs; mere words; they brought an image with them, but an imagined, not an experienced image" (140). She truly has no "inkling" of what would happen if bombs fell tonight.

And fall they do. Judith is taking care of her friend's child, Griselda, and as she hears "a crash, a rumble, a very crack of doom" (168), she has Griselda put on her gas mask:

Her round face vanished horribly: there was nothing but a blank incurious snout, a grotesque khaki snout with an awfulness worse than idiocy upon it. The snout paraded the dairy, Griselda's body incongruously supporting it. It peered at the guinea-pigs, poked into the food basket, snuffed at the fallen white-wash, came back at last to bed and thrust itself, an obscene caricature of the human face at its beastliest into Judith's.

"Don't" said Judith, sharply, sickened.
Griselda came out and blew exaggeratedly. "Phew," she said, "it's hot in there."
"Put it on again."
"You put yours on too. Gosh, you do look a sight." (169)

The gas masks in this setting reduce the human child to a horrible, "obscene caricature" of a human face and render her and Judith as less than human.

Then the two await the gas. Judith finishes fastening Griselda's mask, and she senses that "sickliest sweet smell which drifted faintly up her own artificial nostrils was, she supposed, imagination: speak to the scared human being about poison-gas, and he at once finds it in the purest air" (169). Yet the sickly smell is not imagined but real. As Judith waits with Griselda, the child snuggling against her, she visualizes the nightmare that has now descended upon them all:

thousands upon thousands of khaki snouts with glassy eyes alongside, clustered hopefully in lower rooms and cellars ... in the open, perhaps, under that brilliant and indifferent moon –

For what could be more absurd, more bitterly laughable than these rows without number of blank hygienic head-shelters devised by man to protect himself against man; hopefully devised, manufactured, and pronounced safe only because man so desperately wanted them to be safe, not because any facts at his disposal made them inevitably so? (174)

Slowly Judith realizes that the "sweetish suffocation" she senses is gas, because the guinea pigs have died (174).

As a result, Judith makes a significant choice. Raising her arms, she "untied the clasps, tapes, buttonings of her mask. She had always hated waiting. If she must be gassed, she thought, struggling with a buckle which seemed swelled to a monstrous shape under her fingers, it had better be quickly" (175). Given the moment when she faces the prospect of a death that she can only delay but not escape, Judith rejects the gas mask's promise of protection. She chooses to go quickly and to enact a final agency against the insanity of what has just occurred.

In the novel, what has happened to Judith and little Griselda is then narrated as history: "Something like ten thousand Cantabridgians were wiped out (as every schoolboy knows) in the Air Raid of 1939. There are memorials to the Cambridge dead all over the rest of Great Britain." But this narrator has a snarky sense of humor, noting, "It was, say the memorials (not from personal experience) a Glorious Death." And it is "all the more glorious" because of a mistake: the result of releasing the deadly new gas GZHQ by accident before the bombing plane could reach London. It is in this postwar future, a forever-ruined Cambridge that is haunted by the ghosts of the gas raid dead, that the novel spirals to its conclusion. The spirits who haunt Cambridge may think of themselves as inhabiting a pacifist state, laughing at the creatures from the outside who drift in, "uncouth figures with gas-masks and all sorts of laughable apparatus, sent by the Government to test once more the poison-laden country, appeared every now and again" (208). They look around, then "got once more into their aeroplanes, and went back finally to the lunatic world to report: 'Gas still lingering dangerously in the marshes' or 'unfit for habitation' or 'the opening up area of Central Cambridge not advisable'" (208).

The London Mercury's Christmas issue of 1937 reviewed the novel, finding it "inconclusive as argument, and hard reading for a work of fiction," and leaving the ultimate judgment of Judith's pacifism (unmitigated even after she dies in the great gas raid) undetermined. Thirty Million Gas Masks shares with its many interwar speculative fiction counterparts a complete awareness of the changed stakes of modern war, waged indiscriminately against civilians of all ages and sexes, and of the grotesque futility of the apparatus (the gas mask) designed to protect against such horrors. Its protagonist would rather die of gas poisoning than wait to suffocate in a mask or live in a chemically ravaged landscape.

Opposition to ARP and vocal fears about the next war coalesced around the gas mask in other forms of media. The Peace Pledge Union (PPU), among other antimilitarist groups, called upon the public to respond to the issuing of "Anti-gas Precautions" and the promise of gas masks with skepticism. In its early 1937 pamphlet "Anti-gas Precautions: Some Facts They Did Not Tell You," it called upon experts to explain that the simple-sounding rhetoric of official ARP pronouncements hid basic facts, such as these:

A respirator cannot be worn by children under five, by invalids, or by old people with weak lungs or hearts. Apparently gas-proof "tents" have now been invented to fit over cot or pram. But how long will a child allow itself to be so enveloped. And what of poor families with one pram between half a dozen children?

Once again, it was the inadequacy of measures to protect the most vulnerable bodies that made the government scheme unthinkable.

In case this point-by-point critique of the government measures did not persuade readers, the PPU issued another, simpler pamphlet, "Burn the Babies." Here it explains that there are some things "no one would do – not even in the name of Patriotism. For instance, no one, however loyal, would put his neighbour's baby on the fire at the suggestion of the Secretary of State for War." Yet that was what preparing to accept government measures for a coming war meant: preparing to allow babies to be set on fire.[15]

Despite this vocal opposition, preparations for such a war in the form of anti-gas protection proceeded apace. It was in January1937 that Geoffrey Lloyd, hailed as the "First Gas Mask Minister," presided at the opening of a government gas mask factory in Blackburn.[16] Yet, by the end of that year, as an editorial in the *Daily Mirror* noted, despite all the talk of gas masks, of there being "twenty million ready," no one seemed to have seen one. It elaborated:

1) The Inspector General of ARP says there are twenty million of them ready ("canned like fruit")
2) The same authority says there are already plans for their distribution
3) The same authority says that warning of an air raid in the next war might be as brief as ten minutes
4) Are twenty million gas masks going to be distributed (after canning) in ten minutes?
5) Or perhaps *you* have already received your gas-mask?

We haven't.[17]

As the ARP Sub-Committee had predicted, if the government raised the expectation that the population would receive gas masks, then it had better deliver. Otherwise it risked disillusionment or an unwillingness to take the matter seriously when it became vital.

Behind the scenes, plans were fully underway to develop anti-gas protection for infants and children and to prepare to distribute gas masks to the entire population, but public skepticism was also growing. We can see this in the rhyme that won a contest sponsored by the *Daily Express* in December 1937:

> Here lies the body of Citizen John,
> Who went to bed with his gas-mask on,
> Beneath his bed his bucket of sand
> His shovel gripped firmly in his hand
> To find the enemy when they came
> Used bombs of neither gas nor flame
> But just the straight explosive stuff
> Poor John has paid: they called our bluff[18]

Like many such public expressions concerned about the looming war in the late 1930s, this poem reflected the perspective that government preparations – especially the gas mask – offered misguided protection against the horrors of what awaited civilians. Despite the state's best efforts to manage expectations and appear to be doing something to keep its population safe, the measures promoted thus far seemed ludicrous in the face of both the rising foreign dangers and the visible limitations of the government's efforts.

Gas Masks in the Empire after the Second Italo-Ethiopian War

The working-out of civil defense and anti-gas protection in this fraught moment was not restricted to the metropole. The government of Britain had been exploring the need for ARP within the United Kingdom since 1924 and passed the first major piece of legislation in December 1937. However, the potential needs of its empire, at least those serving its military, had been evident in its testing of gas masks and chemical arms upon populations in India. That its other colonial subjects might also need gas masks on a large scale became apparent as a result of the use of chemical weapons in the conflict in Ethiopia as well.

As accounts of the use of poison gas by Italy became public knowledge, British officials in Aden (a colonial space where Italy had bases a mere 150 miles away) began to ask for instructions about protecting the civilian population from potential gas attacks. At the same time, Malta also emerged as another potential site for poison gas attacks, but officials in Aden were much more vocal. Correspondence between those on the ground in Aden and the Secretary of State for India and for the Colonies began as early as August 1935 to raise questions about what anti-gas measures could be taken. The British authorities indicated a willingness to send gas masks and asked for the numbers needed. The lists that came back were subdivided between Europeans and non-Europeans, with a note added in September: "we have not mentioned wives and children." The prioritizing of particular bodies was here left implicit. The government then agreed to send 5,000 gas masks for "essential personnel." What of the others? Additional requests came in for another 20,000 civilian masks, which those in Aden planned to offer for sale at a reasonable price to members of the general population. One notable factor arose in the course of discussing the supply of respirators: It took too long to get the gas masks to Aden. The first shipments of any civilian gas masks arrived only in late December (almost six months after the initial request). Since Aden was spared any direct danger resulting from the nearby war, the gas masks ended up being unnecessary. Yet the incident certainly alerted the government that advance planning was crucial if it wanted to extend protection to those in the empire.[19]

Planning for civil defense overseas was complicated. For example, the India Act of 1935 granted some autonomy to particular areas of the subcontinent. Since much of official civil defense in Britain was left to local authorities and volunteers, initiatives along these lines in India had to incorporate this arrangement, and it was not until an order of the Executive Council dated August 25, 1937 that planning for civil defense in India arrived. This order, moreover, merely set up an exploratory committee whose purpose was to report on the need for ARP in order to protect civilians, industries, and essential government services in India against gas or bomb attacks, "and to make from time to time recommendations for the initiation and coordination ... of Departments of the Government of India and Provincial Governments of such protective measures as may be considered necessary."[20] Once the Government of India Committee inquired into the *need* for civil defense, it quickly concluded that something should be done.[21]

In the meantime, queries from a variety of other imperial sites reached the Colonial Office regarding the provision of gas masks, especially for civilian family members of military personnel. A November 1937 memorandum from the Committee on Imperial Defence's Overseas Defence Committee noted that the Colonial Office "were prepared to accept the view that the Colonial Governments must be responsible, in normal circumstances for the provision of respirators for the families of service personnel as part of the civil population." However, "a special degree of protection" might be needed under "special circumstances," although what this meant in practical terms was left unclear. An attached list stated where such respirators would potentially go, including the West Indies, West and East Africa, and colonies in Asia, such as Burma or Singapore. By May 1938, the Army Council was asking for gas masks for family members of those serving in the military in Aden, Gibraltar, Hong Kong, Malta, and Singapore, and here again, calculations came in two headings, "European" and "non-European," in terms of the numbers to be provided in each locale. The very existence of these separate categories plausibly suggests that Europeans would be granted a more favorable status for getting such initial protection.[22] Who received a gas mask said something about their value to the state.

Overall, imperial bodies and spaces remained tangential to calculations taking place in London throughout the decade. Other limits as to whom the gas mask would reach in Britain's far-flung empire also emerged in the final years of the interwar era. Outside the metropole, plans developed for potential gas mask factories in India and Singapore. Gas masks for military purposes had been manufactured in India since the start of the decade, but the need for civilian gas masks – and in large quantities – had led to expansions by the late 1930s.[23] The wives of naval officers in Singapore, for instance, had begun practice drills with gas masks in the summer of 1936, demonstrating their commitment to do their bit to prepare for war as a "Women's Anti-Gas Brigade," but this group did not include local inhabitants.[24] There were some further moves to start anti-gas civil defense in places like Singapore and Malaya by the middle of 1937, in conjunction with groups like the St John Ambulance, but there was no indication of how gas masks might be provided beyond the few available for practice.[25]

While the supply of masks to colonial inhabitants remained uncertain, the role of the colonies in supplying the resources necessary to make gas masks became ever more apparent. As early as September 1936, the Singapore *Straits Times* wrote of how the provision of gas masks for civilians in Great Britain offered a great boon to rubber-producing countries, since it was "an entirely new use for rubber" on a mass scale.[26] Sri Lanka (Ceylon at the time) was also utilizing its coconut crop to provide coconut charcoal for use in gas masks, selling this core component to France and Germany as well as Britain by the end of 1937.[27] Some of the crucial raw materials for making gas masks for everyone in Britain, above all rubber, would come from its empire, but it was never the case that all those living in the empire would benefit from the anti-gas protection to which they contributed these resources.

By 1938, British colonial officials were regularly asking about the status of anti-gas protection for all. Officials in Hong Kong in January 1938 corresponded with the Colonial Office about the supply of gas masks to those in the empire. Could Hong Kong make its own gas masks? In response, the government stated its intent to maintain factory production in Britain (presumably to keep those jobs in the metropole), and it was therefore "desirable that Colonial supplies should continue to be manufactured in this country," i.e., Britain. Hong Kong officials then asked whether they should begin making gas masks on their own that could be available for sale to the general population in such locales, assuming that there would be service gas masks for police and other ARP personnel, civilian duty respirators for essential civil service workers, and approximately 72,000 regular gas masks for the families of those vital workers. The unsatisfying answer to the question of what to do about the remaining population was that it was "now under active consideration."[28]

Elsewhere, the *Times of India* reported on plans for a civilian gas mask facility near Cawnpore in February 1938, and the *Straits Times* claimed that the Singapore Rubber Works was about to establish another gas mask factory in Bandeong by year's end; this company had been producing gas masks for nearly a decade at that point.[29] Despite some efforts to protect certain colonial populations, more paramount concerns lay with keeping the production (and presumably the workers employed therein) going in Britain itself while not being willing and/or able to provide gas masks for all colonial subjects.

As the Second World War's outbreak in Europe loomed, there was, at least on paper, a commitment to provide some means of protection against aero-chemical war to some select colonial subjects. This included the transfer of civilian gas masks, a state-sanctioned and state-supplied device against some of the most feared weapons of the next war, albeit in a very limited way. As ARP, gas drills, and especially the gas mask further entered into public consciousness in the troubled years of 1938 and 1939, the tension between preventing panic and fostering a sense of preparedness was ever present, even in the empire. However, the calculations of who could or should get gas masks, the lists separating populations of colonial inhabitants between "European" and "non-Europeans," show how certain criteria (notably race and class) could distinguish who was worth protecting.

Finalizing the Gas Mask's Design

By the start of 1938, the scientists at the CDRD at Porton Down had established the basic contours of a gas mask that would be appropriate for civilian use, but they had some more work ahead of them in order to develop suitable models of respirators for specific groups of people.[30] They had focussed their energy on the "general civilian respirator," the main gas mask for those not in military service; whether such masks would work for most women and older children was not yet clear. Civilians who performed vital ARP duties would receive a "civilian duty respirator," a higher-quality gas mask designed to enable the wearer to do more strenuous work for longer. The general civilian respirator came in three sizes – small, medium, and large – but the quantity that might be necessary in each size remained in doubt. In the final stages of development, researchers turned to populations that could be easily exploited in order to test the gas mask's limits and potential. One of these early attempts to see how gas masks fit and what sizes might be required was conducted on boys at a Dr. Barnardo's home for orphaned and destitute children in Essex in the autumn of 1937. Here, CDRD staff realized that the transition between small and medium was around the age of eight or nine but that the small size did not work for those younger than four or five.[31] A crucial aspect of civilian gas mask development thus involved adapting the basic design for those whom it would not automatically fit and thus protect.

Those in need of an adapted gas mask might include, for example, people whose faces were too small for the standard model, especially children and infants, as well as those who wore glasses, who had prior breathing difficulties, or who had what the records deemed "abnormal" faces. Porton Down scientists brought a precise attention to detail as they tested prototype gas masks. A group of girls was one subset for a third report on fitting in December 1937, and a group of boys was the basis for a fifth report in August 1938; here a helpful notation confirmed that fitting gas masks on boys was much easier than fitting them on girls since they lacked hair ornaments.[32]

Between these studies and as evidence of their commitment to making sure they provided adequate protection, the scientists tested five children between the ages of five and six-and-a-half at Porton itself to determine the volumes of air breathed in by children at rest and those exercising. Although noting that this was a small sample, they concluded that children needed one-third the air of an adult and that designs should take this into account. The photograph accompanying this test offers a startling snapshot of the uncanny nature of the apparatus in question. The five children are lined up together, not all facing the camera, but in the center is a boy in short pants and a mask that completely obscures his face. The CDRD provided no comment about who these children were or about the use of them as experimental subjects, nothing on the

Figure 4.3 Children participating in a breathing test for the Chemical
Defence Research Department in 1938. Photograph and permission
from The National Archives

discomforting implications of what they were testing and how disturbing
it looked (Fig. 4.3).[33]

On the other end of the age spectrum, scientists conducted tests on the
elderly and infirm at a county hospital in Kent, where they had twenty-
four men wear gas masks while resting for ten minutes and then after
walking 100 yards at a regular pace (no photographs accompanied this
file). Here they found that while most could tolerate the gas mask, "the
discomfort experienced by these old people was naturally greater than
that usually observed in individuals in the prime of life." They further
noted that some had to remove their glasses and could not see well, and
that this might be a problem for other elderly persons. Moreover, the
medical officers at the hospital were convinced that those suffering from
cardiovascular ailments were more "distressed" after exercising while
wearing gas masks than without them, although the scientists detected
"no markedly adverse effects." The report concluded that it was now up
to the Chief Medical Officer of ARP to determine whether the findings
were sufficient to proceed.[34]

In May 1938, a series of tests of the general civilian respirator in Bristol
occurred at a parking garage, a tobacco company, a brewery, and a clinic.
At each location, a variety of people were fitted with gas masks and asked
to carry out their regular tasks. These ranged from those persons conducting "very strenuous work" to the men, women, and children at the

health clinic who were asked to sit in a room and then walk down a hallway and up and down a flight of stairs. The conclusion: in "the majority of cases ... under more severe conditions than are envisaged," the respirators achieved "generally satisfactory results." However, the testers were startled that so many women needed the large size of gas mask, and they were concerned that those with "awkward angular faces" might require special fitting.[35]

CDRD officials understood that a gas mask's effectiveness relied heavily on its fit. Responding to complaints that those working at the Metropolitan Police Nursing Home in Denmark Hill, South London, could not wear the gas masks without "extreme discomfort and distress," Major J. C. H. Walker and a colleague visited the site in May 1938 only to find that the staff were not wearing masks that fit. Further, the staff did not know how to wear them correctly: the head harnesses were so tight that they produced severe headaches. All of this could be corrected with proper fitting and instructions, but Walker's report warned that this was the third time Porton's workers had seen civilians wearing respirators of the wrong size despite the masks having been distributed by allegedly qualified personnel. They worried about inhabitants who received gas masks of an incorrect size, fearing that this would lead to a "disinclination" to wear them. They thus pointed to a need to ensure that the fitting procedures were standardized throughout the nation. Everyone needed a gas mask that fit, but fitting relied on volunteer civilians, and the government had to be confident that regardless of whether the civilians fitting and distributing masks had gone through the relevant training at the Civilian Anti-Gas School, they knew what they were doing.[36] The issue of the correct size was seen as paramount in assuring not only the ultimate utility of the gas mask but also that people would actually wear them when needed, which was just as important.

Size and fitting may have been even be more of a complicating factor in Britain's overseas empire. In another summation from May 1938 of the development of standardized gas masks thus far, researchers acted on reports from Hong Kong that the standard gas mask did not seem to fit well on Chinese inhabitants in the territory. A team at Porton Down noted in response that the standard gas mask incorporated special shaping at the temples and cheeks, "arranged for British faces." This might not work for Chinese faces with their "very long heads accompanied by very small chins," according to the report. Although they acknowledged a limited knowledge of Chinese facial structure, after testing a sample respirator manufactured in China, they found it satisfactory.[37] Again, this reveals how racialized ideas inflected the design of individual anti-gas protection.

These sorts of concerns led those planning ARP anti-gas protection to consider the potential limits of the standard model for the civilian gas mask. After looking at those with "abnormal facial contours," designers turned their attention to "those persons who could not readily wear any existing type of respirator." In initial proposals, such persons included those with "distorted" heads and faces – deemed too large or asymmetrical for the regular gas mask – as well as post-operative cases and those with diseases of the chest or with chest wounds in addition to potential limits due to age. Porton Down considered utilizing designs that did not require something strapped on the face, an approach similar to the preliminary ideas about designs for infants being developed at the time.[38]

While it continued its efforts to make respirators work for civilians with a variety of special needs, the government also had to contend with emerging challenges surrounding the production and distribution of the quantity of gas masks needed for the entire population of Britain. The factory in Blackburn tasked with making the approved general civilian respirator had been publicized to great fanfare at the start of 1937, but as production continued to be ramped up there, concerns emerged about the inadequate supply of components. Reports also raised questions about the effects on workers who made the masks, such as the health consequences of charcoal dust in the factory air as well as rising complaints about dermatitis among the workers at a Birmingham rubber company. After investigating the latter, Porton scientists concluded that wearing the gas mask might irritate the skin of "hypersensitive individuals in the general population" if worn for a long time. They recommended that tests be carried out on women and children to determine how widespread this risk might be, though they also cautioned that alternative fabrics had not yet been identified. That manufacturers were experimenting to find alternatives was clear by the middle of 1938, when they claimed that production had also become more efficient since "the removal of secrecy from the assembly" of certain components of the gas mask. Prior to the public unveiling of gas mask production, it seems that workers had to be kept ignorant of what they were making, leading to wasted space due to partitions within the factory, but these could now be abandoned.[39]

Concern about how to modify the basic civilian gas mask to meet the needs of populations that would have difficulty with the standard model continued through 1939. That November, scientists selected sixteen persons of both sexes, ranging in age from five to eighty, from the large number whom the Home Office had identified as unable to wear the regular mask. Among these special cases were people with asthma and nasal obstructions as well as some who had had a tracheotomy. While it proved difficult to find a solution for tracheotomy patients, designers claimed that simple modifications to add an "expiratory valve" solved the problem for adult women and young children who were otherwise unable to breathe in a mask.[40]

Thus, even as the investment in the gas mask heightened during this time, the central question of civil defense still remained: Would it be possible for the government to protect everyone? As it increasingly became evident that total protection of civilians within Britain and its empire was impossible, the government focussed on identifying which bodies (and places) mattered most. The government's expanding interest in the protection of civilians of all ages in the United Kingdom led to it frantically developing anti-gas protection for children and infants; this was a sure sign of its commitment to safeguard lives of no immediate military purpose. Another sign was its acceptance of the need to investigate protecting those with "abnormal" faces or breathing difficulties. Yet it was becoming obvious, at least among the planners, that only a small number of colonial subjects would get a gas mask and that the prospect of supplying masks to other populations – like nonresident aliens, criminals, refugees, and those in transit – raised questions about the extent to which the state could or should offer this device to all. This issue would only become more acute as war drew closer.

Preparing for the Gas Mask to Enter Daily Life

As soon as some gas masks became available to populations other than those performing specialized medical, military, or civil defense services, communities began to arrange for gas mask drills. In some cases, children had earlier been excluded from such activities for fear that they might prove too damaging to their psyches. By early January 1938, efforts to shelter children from such drills were now facing criticism. As an editorial in the *Daily Mirror* pointed out:

Little Dot has made herself a paper gas mask so that small Tom can bomb her in an air raid with his Christmas aeroplane … (this is true, we've seen it).

But the Board of Education decides that our five and a half million school children mustn't have gas drill because of the "adverse psychological effects."

We don't dispute the decision; but it conflicts with our experience of tender minds

While you are anxiously protecting the babes from knowledge of the world's ways *they* are arranging a rehearsal of horrors they don't realise as such.[41]

This acutely sums up the challenges and dangers of extending gas masks and civil defense to the entire population. Opponents of widespread civil defense measures, especially in the absence of an actual declaration of war, may have been worried about the psychological health of children, but others asserted that such approaches discounted their ability to cope. It is also evident that everyone's mental and physical health would be at risk once the airplanes and gas masks were no longer merely toys. The mounting incursion of gas masks into public life was apparent throughout 1938, building on the articles and photographs that had begun to appear in print in 1936, which tried to call attention to gas masks and alternated between the serious and official, the seemingly comical, and the bizarre aspects of anti-gas protection.

In February, an editorial in the *Daily Mail* endorsed increasing government expenditure on ARP, declaring that "every householder must know, as quickly as possible, where to get a gas mask" as well as where and how to take shelter. A large photograph in the *Daily Mail* later that month showed MPs in a gas mask drill outside the Foreign Office, and photographs of everyone from dock workers to female telephonists in gas masks appeared in March. By April, headlines read "Gas Masks for All," celebrating the fact that the Home Office had announced the distribution in that first week of April of 30 million gas masks to the facilities that would dole them out in an emergency.[42]

Such public announcements reflected the fact that a circular from the Home Office had gone out to all local authorities in England, Wales, and Scotland with detailed instructions and blueprints for how to set up a depot in order to distribute civilian gas masks to the public. Step by step, the circular outlined the significant amount of space and resources that each locale would need, starting with regional storehouses in several locations in London as well as provincial centers such as Bristol, Cambridge, Coventry, Gateshead, Leeds, Liverpool, Manchester, Nottingham, and Reading. Since gas masks would not be distributed to individuals until a crisis, the essential feature for depots would be speed: how quickly local areas could assemble and give out 30,000 respirators at a time. The government thus recommended that storing the components for gas masks in too large a group would lead to congestion and delay during an emergency, but that smaller depots might not make economic sense, given that the estimated space was 1,000 square feet per 30,000 gas masks. Moreover, "some modifications will be necessary to meet the case of rural areas and districts where the population is widely scattered." Once space for a "local respirator store" was identified, officials had to determine the estimated number of the three main adult sizes, as well as those for children two to four years old and for children under two. Carefully laying out the schematics, the government predicted that each local store would then supply distribution depots serving about 4,000 inhabitants – e.g., eight ARP warden posts, assuming that each post would be distributing about 500 gas masks.[43] As the images accompanying these plans suggest, the government's calculations extended from mapping out where to place respirator stores and depots to precisely where workers should stand around a table when assembling masks. They outlined the process of distribution of gas masks and provided standard forms to record the size needed for every inhabitant in every locale (Figs. 4.4–4.7).

This set of instructions specified that ARP wardens would be the main conduit between the government and the individual in terms of fitting, distributing, and explaining the use and upkeep of gas masks. As such, wardens might encounter some reluctance and even some instances "in which persons refuse to allow themselves, or those for whom they are responsible, to be fitted with respirators." While hoping that few would respond in this manner, the guide recommended that in such cases, the wardens should note the refusal but still record the number of persons in a household and their sense of the sizes of gas masks needed; "they should do this in the presence of the householder, who should be informed of the fact, and that the refusal and its possible consequences are the responsibility of the householder." In this way, the government would attempt to persuade those reluctant to have gas masks that they were putting themselves at risk and that the state would still have these devices on hand in order to keep the civilian population safe.[44]

As discussed earlier, the international context of such publicity was also significant. While not so dramatic as the news from Guernica in 1937, the escalated bombing of Spain, and especially of major urban centers such as Barcelona, had prompted some newspapers at the start of 1938 to ask what the British government was doing to prepare for airborne attacks on civilians: "Barcelona's appalling massacre makes you wonder where are our own bomb shelters. ... Then again, have you ever seen a gas mask or met any of your neighbours who have had that experience?"[45] Having raised expectations about its preparations, the government had to respond to expressions of anxiety that its efforts were falling short of the mark, especially as "the chief terror of war in the minds of millions of ordinary citizens [was] ... gas."[46] In a lecture on ARP, a Colonel Garforth recounted receiving a letter "from an anxious old lady" asking where she could purchase gas masks for her Orpington hens, presumably including this for comic relief in a grim presentation.[47] Yet when she received no satisfactory answer, Mrs. Perkins of Kenford (near Exeter) made her own and sent in the picture to the *Daily Mirror*; it looked like a miniature version of the First World War gas mask complete with eye holes and tiny filter. Aside from its startling visual effect, it

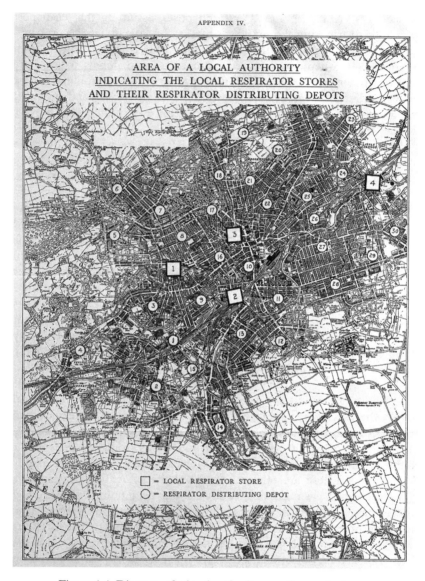

Figure 4.4 Diagram of a local authority map for use in the mass distribution of civilian gas masks by locating both regional places for storage and local depots for delivering them (1938). Image and permission from The National Archives

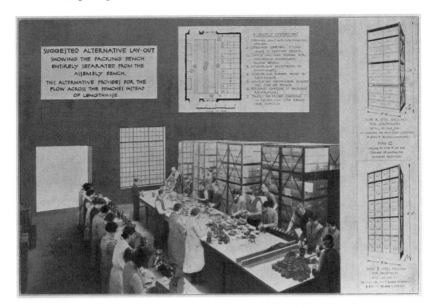

Figure 4.5 Diagram illustrating the ARP official plan for the rapid assembling of civilian gas masks for delivery to the public (1938). Image and permission from The National Archives

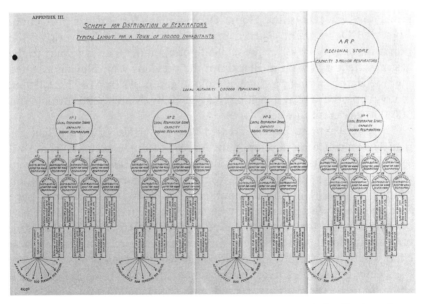

Figure 4.6 Diagram outlining the local storage and distribution of civilian gas masks for a town of 120,000 inhabitants (1938). Image and permission from The National Archives

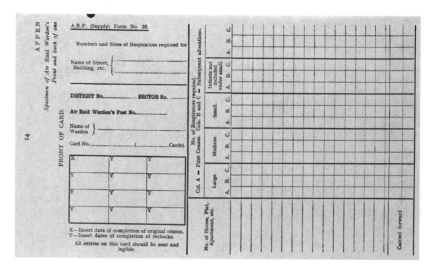

Figure 4.7 The ARP gas mask census and supply form (1938). Image and permission from The National Archives

testifies to genuine concern about the vulnerable nonhuman animals that people cared for and that the government had no plans to safeguard.[48]

Efforts to publicize growing supplies of gas masks for humans were evident that spring. In early April 1938, the press reported on the self-proclaimed success of the Home Office's plans for anti-gas protection. The ARP Department claimed that Britain now led "the world in the provision of gas masks for the civilian population," thanks in part to the gas mask factory set up in Blackburn the previous year. Having asserted that the factory would produce 30 million gas masks by March 31, 1938, it now boasted about reaching that goal by March 29, turning out 500,000 gas masks a week.[49]

The popular press largely stressed that the arrival of the civilian gas mask was a welcome development. As part of the response to the April 1938 ARP directive to all local authorities, the *Daily Mail* sought to assure its readers that gas masks would be ready for general distribution "within 8 hours" of the declaration of a crisis.[50] Its editorial page heralded the "efficient speed" with which gas masks had appeared as offering a model for every other aspect of civil defense, noting that from now on, the local authorities could ensure that "every man, woman, and child would be promptly safeguarded against gas attack."[51]

In daily newspapers, reassurances about the coming of the gas mask abounded, and these often focussed on the consequences for women and children. In response to a father who doubted that his young daughter would ever willingly wear a gas mask, an ARP worker wrote to the *Daily Mail* that after fitting hundreds of children with gas masks, their response was that it was "good fun."[52] Another sign of how gas masks were increasingly taken for granted can be seen in a spread on fashion in the *Irish Times*: "There is no better tonic in the world for any woman than a new hat. And, with things as they are, it may be that next year these gay bits of femininity may have given place to wretched gas masks, so why not be pretty while you may?"[53] Concern about women's vanity emerged in other accounts of the slow fitting of gas masks. A July 1938 *Daily Mail* column focussed on a Marylebone air raid warden who complained about householders generally not taking the gas mask seriously. To illustrate his point, the warden described women who were fearful that their gas masks would spoil their hairstyles.[54] When six nuns from London convents gathered together with another thirty middle-aged women to learn about gas masks, they confronted a unique problem. How could they fit on gas masks if they couldn't take off their veils, especially not in front of men? One of the event's organizers, Lady Victoria Hope (daughter of Earl Haig), solved the problem by leading the nuns to a room where they could remove their headdresses, "leaving little caps on to cover their hair."[55] Again, the hint at comedy in discussions of the gas mask seems to have become part of normalizing it.

When the milestone of producing 35 million gas masks was reached in July 1938, local newspapers quickly publicized this accomplishment. The *Western Daily Press* called attention to the arrival of the masks in regional stores across Britain, while the *Dundee Courier* elaborated that this meant that the government was fulfilling its promise that no population center with more than 5,000 inhabitants would be further than twenty miles from a respirator storage facility.[56]

One local reporter went on rounds for a gas mask census in Derby to determine the numbers of each size of gas mask needed, an act that the article proclaimed would make civil defense measures apparent "as never before in individual homes." The wardens encountered a variety of responses, including householders who claimed to be "too busy" to be fitted and others whose initial reluctance could be overcome. In one home, the parents called in their children, and "even the smallest toddler was not omitted and although near to tears was persuaded by his older sisters to undergo the test." The father at this home recollected the masks that he had worn during the Great War and how glad he had been to take them off, because they were so hot. Overall, the two wardens reflected that they had faced less resistance than anticipated and that it was crucial that wardens were local and not strangers. There might be more opposition in some areas, the article concluded, but on the whole, "the response of the public, although not overwhelmingly enthusiastic, is likely to be satisfactory."[57]

In contrast to such "satisfactory" acceptance, others continued to express their support for disarmament, in opposition to what they saw as the destructive tendency to prepare for war by giving out gas masks. A column in the left-leaning and influential *Daily Mirror* in early June denounced the sight of figures in gas masks inducing panic, and "the pantomime side-shows with villagers in full air-raid costume" as missing the point. The reporter argued that "there are more urgent things in war than gas-masks," such as better airplanes and antiaircraft guns. Gas masks, in this view, were only a costly distraction from the real danger in the war to come.[58]

Pacifist and antimilitarist organizations and communities struggled to counter the prevailing admonitions to support civil defense no matter what. Sometime in early 1938, the following poem appeared in a PPU pamphlet illustrated with a woman cleaner looking at a figure in a gas mask:

> "you got to be prepared" 'e sez
>   "It ain't no use to grouse"
> "Mark off a gas-proof room," 'e sez
>   In your palatial house
> Install your wireless and your books
>   Your larder and your bed
> You'll be snug as a bug in a rug, sez 'e
>   With the raiders overhead
>
> So it's all set fair
>   For the rich and rare
>   But what I fail to see
>   Is what's going to happen when the sirens go
>   To all the kids and me?
>
> "Come try a gas-mask on," 'e sez
>   "And what's the price?" sez I
> "And what's the little kids to wear?"
>   'E ain't got no reply
> So it's all my eye: when the bombers come
>   There's nothing for the poor
> But a pillow or two up the chimney flue
>   And a rag across the door.[59]

Like many such texts concerned about the looming war in the 1930s, this verse reflects the perspective that government preparations – especially the gas mask – offered misguided or inadequate protection against the horrors of what awaited civilians. Despite the state's best efforts to manage expectations and appear to be doing something to protect its whole civilian population, the measures promoted thus far seemed ludicrous in the face of the emerging dangers. The government's claims of being prepared met with dissent. If the maintenance of morale (and the associated management of fear-induced panic) formed an essential element of civil defense, then proponents of disarmament stressed the gas mask's limited ability to help with any of those ends.

That said, the pacifist position on anti-gas civil defense was more complex than at first it may have appeared. Local Quakers in Lancashire and Cheshire had protested the opening of the gas mask factory in Blackburn in January 1937 by offering a "loving warning to our fellow citizens not to put their trust in the provision of gas-mask appliances as a means of safety nor as a method of solving the unemployment problem."[60] Among Quakers nationally, ARP thus raised a number of questions, and the Society of Friends Peace Committee created a subcommittee to determine what Quakers should do as pacifists in the face of ongoing efforts to prepare for war. A report from this subcommittee in March 1938 asserted that ARP relied on an "assumption of the inevitability of war – which assumption we unhesitatingly reject" and that its provisions in general gave only an "illusory sense" of security. However, the Quakers struck a more nuanced tone when discussing the gas mask:

We believe, however that the question of acceptance or refusal (in war time or in preparation for a war situation) of such protection as is obtainable from various devices, including the official "gas mask," must be one for the individual conscience and judgment, and we recognise that for some Friends in positions of responsibility in hospitals, schools, etc., this question brings special difficulties.

Thus, while rejecting ARP as such, it left the decision to use a gas mask to the conscience of the individual, refusing to condemn the use of masks to protect oneself or others. This would become part of the official statement on ARP issued by the Friends Peace Committee in July 1938.[61]

That would not be the last word from Quakers on the subject. Karlin Capper-Johnson, the Secretary of the Friends Peace Committee, began his 1938 pamphlet "Air Raids Precautions: An Appeal and an Alternative" as follows:

What size in gas-mask do you take? One, two or three? That is a question which we shall all of us be asked very soon. And they're asking it all over Europe. Everywhere people are trying them on, seeing how they fit. We are dressing ourselves for the next war – as best we may. As best we may, for we are always being told that they won't really protect us from fire and gas and explosion, and that the first purpose of air raids precautions is to keep us quiet whilst our bombers bomb the other people.

Here, Capper-Johnson takes the government's underlying message of ARP generally, and especially of anti-gas protection, that the most dangerous thing during an attack on civilians is panic, and turns it into something insidious: The government wants you in a gas mask so you will shut up while your country destroys other populations. In this view, rather than demonstrating the government's concern for the well-being of its citizens, the gas mask represents something deeply wrong with society.

Capper-Johnson then concludes by suggesting that gas masks are the emblem of the war-making system under which all now live:

> We can't just get rid of gas masks alone. If we don't want our children living in gas masks and constant fear of war then we must get rid of the things which make war – armaments and empire. It's not just a choice between two gas masks but between two great policies.[62]

Although similar warnings about anti-gas civil defense had appeared earlier, they gained a new urgency as the government was preparing to distribute gas masks widely across Britain.

Feminist antimilitarists also weighed in as ARP took off. The British Section of WILPF held an executive meeting in July to discuss ARP as a likely attack on "civil liberties" as well as potentially traumatizing for children, who could not be kept ignorant of the subject. They noted that civil defense diverted funds from pressing social needs, but whether or not individual members should participate raised questions about the greater social good. Members acknowledged that "the Government is organizing A.R.P. in order to prevent the population from being afraid," but concluded that the measures proposed were not the solution. Better to develop "a spirit of calmness and thus create a far stronger force against fear than any other method of protection," including presumably the gas mask.[63]

The government continued to use the popular press to disseminate its message. After the official statement about gas mask distribution in April 1938, papers such as the *Daily Express* explained that the "Gas-Mask Man Will Visit You Soon," since the "the aim behind the new ARP speed-up is to have every man, woman and child in Britain fitted for a gas mask by the end of the summer or, at the very latest, by the end of the year." In order to do so, ARP workers would visit "every flat, villa, hotel, caravan, houseboat" and ensure that each one of Britain's inhabitants would try on a gas mask. However, there were still not enough wardens to accomplish this task.[64]

This prompted a special ARP autumn recruiting campaign, which the government outlined in August in a policy statement to be issued to members of the press in order to aid their writing articles on the subject. The memorandum first suggested that ARP actions be presented "as part of normal defense precautions," explaining that the government would continue "to examine the consequences to an industrial country of air attack under modern conditions. But in its desire to refrain from any action which might create, anywhere, an impression that this country expected, or was preparing for, war, " Britain's ARP planners had waited until other countries introduced civil defense before doing so. Now its moment had come, and the need for volunteers was acute, which meant that the state had to raise a volunteer force of millions.

The government made clear the centrality of the anti-gas component to civil defense:

> It is often said that far too much attention has been paid to anti-gas measures. It is true that gas has not been used in air attack in Spain or in China, but it was used from the air recently and it might well be used against the built-up cities of this country. It is a peculiarly horrible form of attack and terribly damaging to the morale of any civil population exposed to it. But it can be guarded against. ... It is for this reason that the Government are manufacturing civilian gas respirators for the whole civil population and already the total manufactured is nearing 40 million. These respirators are made in three sizes for the ordinary population and special types are being made for very young children and for babies.

The job of outfitting the population with gas masks was thus a key part of the tasks that fell to ARP volunteers. And "the fitting of a respirator is such an essential and common-sense precaution that it is to be hoped that all members of the public will have themselves fitted promptly."[65] The provision of gas masks was thus presented as an unobjectionable as well as basic part of civil defense. The government was doing its part: It had 40 million gas masks for its population of almost 50 million.[66]

The call for ARP resonated that fall in both the national and the imperial press. The *Daily Telegraph* reiterated the need for wardens and the accomplishment of having now nearly 40 million gas masks ready to deliver.[67] Meanwhile, photographs of gas-mask-clad workers continued to appear, such as members of the Women's Transport Service in a camp in Surrey.[68] An article in the *Straits Times* in late August featured a woman, identified as an ARP volunteer, holding a dog in a gas mask.[69] In these images, the gas mask was something you could joke around with. When the *Daily Mail* proclaimed in August that "Civilian Gas Masks Are Safe," it supported the Home Office's official statement that criticism of the gas mask as ineffective was unmerited. All three types of the government's gas masks worked.[70] In Derby, Mr. Hall, an anti-gas expert, reported that the government gas mask was absolutely fine so long as it was fitted properly. He used the example of his eight-year-old son, who tested a gas mask by staying in a chamber filled with chlorine gas for twenty minutes and came out "as happy as when he went in."[71]

More controversially, late that summer, publisher William J. Brittain asked the photographer Horace Roye for a "startling publicity stunt" to benefit his newly launched paper, the *North London Recorder*. Roye was a famed photographer of female nudes, and his resulting photograph, "Tomorrow's Crucifixion," was, in his own words, "his most sensational." According to his autobiography, Brittain and Roye together dreamt up the idea for the shocking and publicity-seeking photo: "a powerful and dramatic picture of a girl wearing a gas mask and symbolically crucified on a cross by the war-mongers." The photographer further used a special technique to "give a gas-cloud effect across the print," and the image both captures the essence of surrealism and echoes prior (if less exploitative) uses of women as symbols of innocence endangered by the weapons of modern war.[72] This image of a naked young woman wearing a gas mask with two large round eyes holes while posing as if crucified on a large white cross took up much of the front page of the *North London Recorder*'s August 12 issue. Quotations solicited from leading, largely religious figures of the day as well as Roye's own commentary literally surrounded the photograph, thus framing it as a vital antiwar statement. As Rev. J. T. Hodgson opined, it "vividly symbolizes ghastly possibilities of future warfare," a photograph that should call "every citizen" to work for justice and peace.[73] Somewhat hyperbolically, the paper proclaimed that such quotes revealed how "men of god" interpreted "a picture which will live for ever." On the eve of the gas mask's biggest public appearance, this image spoke to its ongoing ability to evoke the horrors of modernity, especially modern war.

In marked contrast to denunciations of the gas mask, a public campaign in conjunction with increasingly specific plans for its use in civil defense had begun to make this object a vivid part of how ordinary members of the public would face the next war. While Quakers and antimilitarists such as members of WILPF criticized the gas mask on the grounds that it helped persuade people to accept war and especially the use of chemical weapons, a government-supported concerted press initiative pushed acceptance of the arrival of the millions of gas masks that started to appear. The increasing output of general civilian respirators was a sign of the commitment of the state to protecting its civilians, but getting them into the hands of the population required thousands of ARP volunteers. Figuring out how to protect young children and infants remained a problem to be solved when the Munich Crisis arrived.

Gas Mask Sunday and Its Aftermath

As ARP, gas drills, and especially the gas mask further entered into public consciousness amid the rise in international tensions throughout 1938, the most concrete threat to European-wide security emerged during the summer. Nazi Germany had already shown its willingness to challenge the terms of the international order in Europe set by the Treaty of Versailles, most recently in the Anschluss in March, which brought Austria under its control. Yet, among the events of 1935–39 that came to be characterized as "appeasement," the Munich Crisis looms large as a pivotal failure of the democratic states of Britain and France to confront Hitler's ongoing aggression.[74] Having rallied elements in Czechoslovakia sympathetic to the Nazis while claiming only to want to protect that nation's German population in the Sudetenland region, Hitler demanded the right to intervene to ensure the well-being of this minority population. The sovereignty of Czechoslovakia was at stake. Would the leaders of democratic states in France and Britain come to its rescue? Between September 12 and the summit of the leaders of Britain, France, Italy, and Germany convened by Mussolini on September 29, which produced the infamous Munich Agreement ending the crisis, Britain's government began to prepare in earnest for war by expanding its civil defense initiatives in highly visible ways.

Gas Mask Sunday – September 25 – took place at one of the most fraught moments of the mounting crisis and underscored the tension between preventing widespread panic and fostering a sense of preparedness when it came to civil defense. It also provided the major public test of the assumption behind the gas mask: that if the state would provide to the public an object that embodied its commitment to keep everyone safe, then the public would accept this promise of safety and refrain from losing its nerve in the face of war. This was the gas mask as security blanket.

As the *Daily Mirror* headline proclaimed, "Britain Queues Up in Millions on Gas Mask Sunday," and this included 102-year-old Mrs. Hannah Kettlewell of Newcastle, who wore a gas mask for several minutes and said that "she hoped to live many years yet." There were boy scouts assisting at fitting stations across the City of London, 800 volunteers aiding the fitting stations in Croydon, 116,000 masks distributed in Nottingham, and another 240,000 in Cardiff.[75] The emphasis in most newspaper accounts was on the range of the ages, classes, and genders found among the participants, all displaying stoicism, humor, and a willingness to cooperate with the government schemes. Across the nation, civilians alone and in family groups lined up to receive or be fitted for gas masks (Figs. 4.8 and 4.9).

Whole families went together to be fitted. Here is one family at Penge, London, S.E., wearing their gas masks ... a typical English family taking precautions and taking them calmly—with faith in Britain Prepared and Britain Strong.

Figure 4.8 A family posing with their gas masks on Gas Mask Sunday. Photograph, *Daily Mirror*, September 26, 1938. Mirrorpix/Reach Publishing Licensing

Figure 4.9 "Britain Queues Up in Millions on Gas Mask Sunday," *Daily Mirror*, 1938. Mirrorpix/Reach Publishing Licensing

In practice, Gas Mask Sunday was very much a test of the nascent civil defense apparatus of ARP. As one ARP volunteer, Allen Newberry, recalled in his record of serving in St Pancras in London, it was at the end of the first week in September when the first floor of Foster Court on Malet Place became the local respirator store and September 12 when the warden service began to call on all householders to fit them with respirators. Sunday September 25 saw him and other volunteers putting together 500 gas masks from their separate components, followed by an order to fit and issue them to the public. With only 5,000 gas masks fully assembled, rapid arrangements led to the reassignment of 200 workers from the highway department to assist with the project. With everyone working full out, night and day, it still took until Wednesday evening for the full quota of 200,000 gas masks at the store to be assembled and ready for distribution.[76] This was far from the earlier promise of the immediate availability of anti-gas protection in case of an emergency, and of course, by that Wednesday, the potential need for the device was rapidly declining, as war had been averted. Nonetheless, during October and November, ARP volunteers in this district went door to door to complete the "respirator census," the recording of everyone who might need gas masks and of what types and sizes would suit them.

Such mobilization of civil defense forces for the assembling, storing, and distributing of gas masks took place across the United Kingdom. In Glasgow, for example, the month of September saw the city's civil defense committee contemplating the storage of 750,000 gas masks before official word came from the national ARP Department to begin the fitting and issuing of them on Gas Mask Sunday. The detailed records of the Glasgow committee reveal the further need for clarification about who would receive the masks. Fundamentally, the government had promised anti-gas protection to every man, woman, and child, but queries came rapidly into the office. Could businesses ensure that those working on their premises would receive gas masks through their employer to enable them to keep working? Were the gas masks available to resident aliens? What about nonresident aliens? Clarification came relatively quickly that all British nationals and members of foreign consuls could receive masks, but not aliens, regardless of whether they were living locally or passing through. The enterprise went into crisis mode; letters came in from local groups looking to help, including the Girl Guides, and by December of that year, there were over one million assembled gas masks in the city.[77]

In London, temporary ARP volunteer Denis Perkins reflected in his journal on the emotional labor that went into the work of fitting gas masks. He writes on Monday, September 19, of being "oppressed by the thought that Rodmell people have not been fitted for gas masks," and he learned more that evening about how to fit such masks. On September 28, he notes how he worked "yesterday evening from 6 till 10.30," fitting and distributing gas masks: "a queer grim evening of pouring rain, candle-lit kitchens, frightened faces peering out of gas mask windows." His door-to-door visits included a stop at the home of Virginia and Leonard Woolf: "I had been chatting cheerfully all the evening ... to combat the nervousness of my victims and when I met the famous Virgy for the first time I went on chatting automatically. ... 'I'm sorry,' I said 'that I should have this honour on such an unhappy occasion.'" But, he continues, it went well, as Virginia was charming and Leonard offered to be an air raid warden if war broke out. Yet, "in spite of this pleasant interlude I came home worn out and nervy beyond all description. I seemed to be half awake all night, refitting every mask, but with great difficulty."[78] Perkins offers a glimpse of the toll taken on the person responsible for giving gas masks to everyone, chattering amiably but terribly "nervy" nonetheless.

What the government had hoped to achieve during the long process of developing civilian gas masks and distributing them to the public came at a significant human cost and with mixed reviews in public forums. In the immediate aftermath of the distribution of masks, one reporter affirmed:

> the people of London displayed to the full the qualities that they do have. They took up the duty to their land in the "decent and dauntless" spirit of which one American has spoken, and which, in the words of another, makes Englishmen, faced by emergency, "melt into one family." ... It has been shown something of what war means now that the air has become its chief theatre, and of the transformation that it enforces upon every branch of ordinary life.[79]

This seems very much the rehearsal of what would become trumpeted as the "Blitz spirit," a mood of unity summoned by adversity and available to all. Yet, like the range of attitudes historians have found during the Second World War, out of the public eye, people were not always so calm and accepting of anti-gas protection.[80]

Writing to her family in America, Sharlie Davison, a pregnant wife and mother living in Surrey, described how her anxiety built as the crisis unfolded: "The gas masks came this morning. We were fitted last week – but never feared they'd be issued so soon. To our horror there's no provision for children 1–5 yrs. A fact which is strengthening Jack's [her husband's] determination that we must leave."[81] In a letter of September 30, 1938, from another British mother writing to family overseas, Helena Britton's account of Gas Mask Sunday offers an alternative perspective to that of the government and media:

a car with a loud speaker, came round and said, everyone was to go to the nearest school to be fitted for a gas mask you can guess how we felt, at first I said I wouldn't go, they were useless, but Dad said we must do what we can to protect ourselves and he would go, so I thought, well if a war does come, Dad will be giving me his & that won't do, so I must go. We had to line up men, women and children, I had never seen so many pregnant women before, my heart ached for the young mothers and fathers. ... We were fitted & given a card, which we had to take, when the gas masks arrived.[82]

This visualizing of the most vulnerable bodies – pregnant women, babies, and small children – in their gas masks did not always lead, as the government had hoped, to a sense of calm and resolution.

One of the most famous public accounts of Gas Mask Sunday came in Jan Struther's columns depicting the fictional Mrs. Miniver's responses to the respirators. As this upper-middle-class wife and mother queues with her young children (and her nanny, cook, and parlor maid), she observes the gas masks "covering the floor like a growth of black fungus." Mrs. Miniver then recalls that "[i]t was for this ... that one had boiled the milk for their bottles, and washed their hands before lunch." Her inability to protect her children is part of what this new warfare brings. Yet Struther also ventures into a moment that reveals how the consciousness of such women may have changed when she has Mrs. Miniver further reflect on the responsibility she has: "the most important of all the forms of war work which she and other women would have to do: there are no tangible gas masks to defend us in war-time against ... [the] slow, yellow, drifting corruption of the mind." When the danger of an immediate outbreak of war ends with the resolution of the crisis, she recounts that her family is "poorer by a few layers of security" but enlarged by a sense of "looking at each other, and at their cherished possessions, with new eyes ... by a sudden clarifying of intentions."[83]

That mothers found the arrival of gas masks difficult also emerges vividly in crime fiction author Margery Allingham's 1941 lightly fiction-alized account of her village at war, *The Oaken Heart*, where she describes the atmosphere of the 1938 crisis: "the incredible descended upon us, and we were suddenly required to take instant precautions in case of an attack on our lives by poison gas." When gas masks arrive on that fateful Sunday, writing retrospectively, Allingham comments that "now that we are all so used to gas-masks all their visual horror has gone" but at that moment, "the obscene elephant-foetus effect of the thing burst in on us for the first time and its obvious efficiency brought home the reality of the situation with a jolt like the kick of a mule." Even more powerfully for Allingham, despite having seen antiwar illustrations of children wearing gas masks, watching her daughter try on her mask shook her to the core:

"the sight of Chrissie in one … her eyes which I have known for so long, looking truculently out at me … turned my stomach over more sickeningly than anything else in that whole unbelievable day." Yet despite her personal distress, Allingham insists that the lesson of the arrival of gas masks – despite the alarm of the lack of protection for babies – is that the village came together, unified. Still, "if the main purpose of the distribution was to allay panic … it might possibly be a highly mistaken policy," as "the sudden present" of a gas mask could not wipe away decades of fear surrounding the next war.[84] The gift from the state remained dual-edged.

Other immediate responses to the distribution of gas masks on this fateful day can be found in the reports sent to Mass Observation, an organization founded in 1937 to capture the experiences of ordinary people. It solicited a group of volunteers – men and women of varying ages across the country – to send in regular diary entries about their everyday lives, and it soon began soliciting responses to specific questions or about particular circumstances. Over the course of both the buildup to and then the experience of the Second World War in Britain, some in the government thought that Mass Observation responses might be useful in trying to gauge morale and people's reactions to ARP.[85] Between 1937 and 1938, a group of volunteers also recorded their daily experiences in "day surveys." Many of these surveys reference the distribution of gas masks during the crisis and people's reactions to receiving them. While the diaries and surveys were anonymous, Mass Observation kept a record of the gender, age, occupation, and location of each participant.

For instance, in this entry from September 29, 1938, Respondent 032 (a single woman in her early thirties) reveals contradictory emotions about going to receive a gas mask at a polling station with a number of her neighbors. First, she expresses a concern similar to that voiced in public by the iconic Mrs. Miniver: "It seemed so dreadful to see the tiny children being fitted." Yet then she switches to emphasizing that the general atmosphere was "cheerful," an insistence mirrored in public accounts: "a good many jokes went about, about trimming the gas masks with feathers & ribbons etc. One warden told a little boy he 'looked like his father playing at Father Christmas' (in a false beard)" – this last parenthetical then crossed out. The entry concluded that while gas masks were still being distributed, few other preparations were being made.[86]

Sometimes, diarists recorded conversations with others to fill in a broader sense of what those surrounding them were thinking. Such views reflect a span of opinions, ranging from anxiety about gas masks and government measures to outright rejection of them. An actress in her mid-twenties notes the views of a barmaid on her way to the theatre that Sunday, who shares her nervousness: "I think it must be getting very bad if they have to make us try gas-masks on on a Sunday." When asked later in the day whether she herself had been fitted, she said, "no, I'd almost rather be gassed." She was not alone; another woman was blunt, saying, "I'd rather be dead than live the way ARP says" – i.e., with a gas mask on.[87] A housewife in Laindon (Essex) found someone with a similar view about gas masks, but this time based on politics, recalling a woman in her mid-thirties who told her: "I refuse to further the war machine by accepting my gas mask." And her own reaction to this: "I had great difficulty with the sentence about the gas mask. I meant she *refused to accept a gas mask*." This respondent clearly found the idea of rejecting this aid unthinkable.[88]

The emotions of the diarists sometimes appear more explicitly, as in the case of a bank clerk in his mid-twenties in Essex who noted that his jottings of conversations were made "under conditions of fear and despair" and that he himself was neither "calm" nor "dispassionate." He found that "events are becoming more personal," with people asking lots of questions about whether they had been fitted for their gas masks, talking about their sizes, and making jokes: "they'll never fit you. It's that mouth of yours that'll be the trouble." Amid the jokes and his own purchase of a guide to ARP by Haldane, he heard one person say, "I kept mine [i.e., his newly arrived gas mask] on for a quarter of an hour last night. You get used to it."[89] Getting used to it was exactly what the government wanted, and the role of the media was seen as crucial to this acceptance. As one respondent put it, "only by continued appeals in the newspapers has it been possible to rouse public interest in the distribution of gas masks."[90] That, of course, assumed that there were gas masks to be had.

Even as the crisis ebbed, the *Daily Mail* proclaimed that two-thirds of the country now had their gas masks, although babies, or more precisely children under four, had only been registered for their anti-gas protection; this was still forthcoming.[91] This would not suffice if there was an actual need of them. As the immediate danger dimmed, the absence of gas masks for all remained a concern, as did people's seeming lack of basic information about what having a gas mask meant. A letter from a reader to the *Daily Mirror*, for example, asked if it was true that there was a fine for not wearing a gas mask, as a friend had told him. In response, the paper made its view of the query and of the mask clear: "Your friend has been telling you fibs. ... There's nothing compulsory about it, but if anybody is damn fool enough not to get a mask, which is supplied for his own protection, then he ought to have his brain examined."[92] While the question of the lack of compulsory gas mask wearing would return during the war, by stating that wearing a gas mask was simply common sense, the paper helped to normalize this state of war preparation.

Later that fall, other newspapers pointed out that Britain's policy stood in stark contrast to that of France, where a new civil defense decree stated that any French civilian who failed to keep his or her gas mask in good working order would face a fine.[93] Some British press accounts of the aftermath of Gas Mask Sunday called out those civilians who were not taking the prospect of war seriously, such as mothers who viewed respirators "as an easy way of amusing the children. In Notting Hill, children played with them in the streets, and were seen trying them on the dog."[94] The cultivation of the proper emotional state combining fortitude, calm, and optimism – all bolstered by government devices like gas masks – was not going to be accomplished overnight.

Another perspective on the lessons to be learned from Gas Mask Sunday came from Britain's empire, where newspapers published in the colonies showed keen interest in civil defense in the metropole. The *Times of India* had a full headline with photos of "London Day by Day – Queues Outside Churches – Summoning Parliament – the Crisis – Britain's A.R.P."[95] About six weeks later came a longer reflection on the events of that Sunday for India in "A Letter from London." Here the article stresses that "[t]he most visible sign of civilian protection is the gas mask. But candour compels the admission that it is psychological rather than material; everyone agrees that the danger from gas is exaggerated." Still, it continues, "It is obvious that effective measures for the safety of the civilian population are going to necessitate changes in our lives and institutions of which only the glimmerings can now be discerned."[96]

Even if the dangers of what poison gas delivered aerially might do had been exaggerated, the arrival of the gas mask provoked fears that could be manifest in the unconscious, in people's dreams. In early November, a regular *Daily Mirror* column interpreting dreams for the general public sought to reassure a Mrs. R. A. Miles, who reported dreaming of being at war, hiding in a cellar, and emerging to find herself fired upon by dozens of bullets. In Mrs. Miles's dream, she then proceeded to go to bed and felt as though she was being gassed. Columnist (and dream interpreter) Pamela Rose explained that this dream was undoubtedly a response to the recent crisis, but that there was a hopeful sign, "the belief you held that if the worst came to worst Britain would not go under," since, after all, the bullets missed her. As for the feeling of being gassed, "it was not unnatural ... when lately you had tried on a gas mask."[97] Mass Observation also collected accounts of nightmares and bad dreams and issued a report on how these might be used to manage the population if war came. Although its summary report found comparatively few dreams relating to the war, it did include one by a young woman of twenty-three who dreamt of being in an air raid. It became a nightmare, because her gas mask was upstairs in a chest of drawers when the attack came. She tried to rush up the stairs "but stumbled a lot and … I could see the gas coming after me in waves like smoke" until finally when she reached the drawers, "all sorts of clothes and bits of stuff entangled with the mask and I could not get it out."[98] In this instance, possession of the object has provided some reassurance – it is going to make this woman safe – and the anxiety derives from the fear of not being able to get to it.

Whether in the realm of dreams or in memory, as the gas mask physically entered into ordinary people's lives, it marked a vivid prelude to the outbreak of war. In his memoir, James Payne, who later served as a member of the Royal Engineers, recalled his boyhood in Manchester and when he felt the war encroaching on his life:

I was still at school, 1938, and the clouds of war were gathering. We were fitted with gas masks in anticipation of the dreadful things that might befall us if Hitler continued his blitzkrieg on everyone in sight. I well remember my 12-yr-old face being thrust into the rubber cocoon with its little plastic eyepiece and the advice that it might someday save my life; then the ramming of a piece of cardboard across the air inlet which blocked any entry of life-giving oxygen to my lungs, to check if there were any leaks. If she doesn't move that piece of cardboard soon, I thought, this so-called life saving device will kill me off before the war even starts.

The detail in this memory is consistent with those of others who experienced the arrival of the gas mask as children and saw it as a vivid marker of the movement from peace to war.[99]

The *Times* summed up the implications of the crisis and the way forward for civil defense in a set of articles on "A.R.P. To-Day" that December. The articles began by talking about the "the symbol of the gas mask" in a world where ARP policy had caught up with public opinion. Moreover, if one of the popular reactions to gas mask distribution was that it was "just a bluff to reassure people," such comments "entirely miss the point." The use of poison gas in war remained uncertain, but it was clearly better to be safe than sorry. Moreover, figuring out how to distribute gas masks in the recent crisis had laid bare to the government other problems in the vast apparatus of civil defense. The main objective of civil defense in light of Gas Mask Sunday was to coordinate efforts so that everyone could be made as safe as possible. The gas mask remained central to this plan.[100]

Conclusion

By the later part of the 1930s, international crises in Ethiopia and in Spain and the responses to these developments in parts of the British Empire such as Aden had forced officials to take more seriously the prospect of the widespread use of poison gas in the next war. The acceleration of civil defense was one manifestation of these international tensions. From the first legislation passed in 1937, the set of policies and procedures by which the civilian population could be made safe was slowly coming to fruition. Central to this development was the gas mask, the object that would serve as the emblem of government efforts to protect individual civilians by ensuring they could breathe despite deliberately poisoned air and to shore up their mental fortitude by helping them avoid panic and carry on.

Yet, as this chapter showed, regardless of extensive preparations, many aspects were far from ready during these crucial years. There were no gas masks for small children or infants; there were modifications to be made to ensure that the full range of the population could be protected, even those with "abnormal faces" or breathing difficulties. The variety of tests conducted so that there would be protection theoretically for all is a remarkable story of the commitment of material, expertise, and money to solving the problem of how to keep civilians safe from poisoned air. The elaborate details of how to set up the centers and depots that would rush gas masks to everyone during an emergency testify to this.

Nonetheless, while the designers of ARP could now offer a model civilian gas mask and detailed instructions about how to wear it, Britain was still debating its responsibilities to global colonial populations. It was unwilling to pledge itself to the same level of protection of civilians in its empire should war occur. The government's efforts to show its commitment in principle to safeguarding civilians from grave wartime dangers coalesced during September 1938 around an event throughout England, Scotland, and Wales that soon came to be known as "Gas Mask Sunday," but there was no equivalent in the empire.

When the first test of ARP in the metropole took place during Gas Mask Sunday, Britons responded in a variety of ways. Some were eager to have their gas masks, others saw them as useless, and still others were outraged that there were, as yet, no devices to protect babies. The entire apparatus of civil defense provoked reactions that those who had been planning its contours for years could not anticipate, and in a society with a robust press, these played out in public. Although the government was still not ready to fulfill the promise of anti-gas protection for all civilians in September 1938, by the time the Blitz commenced two years later, there were indeed gas masks available for the vast majority of inhabitants of the United Kingdom. Tracing how the adult general civilian respirator, the small children's gas mask, and the baby's anti-gas protective helmet became part of everyday life in the next chapter will help to illustrate just how central these objects were to the management of emotions as well as bodies when the bombs began to fall.

5   Curating the Good Citizen
The Gas Mask Goes to War, 1939–1941

Introduction

"It can be momentarily comforting to regard the history of the present as a chapter of absurdities." So began an article in the *Manchester Guardian* in late August 1940, on the cusp of the sustained and harrowing German aerial attacks on the United Kingdom that became known as the Battle of Britain. In this instance, the absurdity was the sight of an unaccompanied woman carrying a large baby doll on a bus across the city. She was on her way to an office where she would place the doll in the baby's anti-gas protective helmet and, as part of an ARP exercise, train local women in how to use the helmet. This particular group of women "from small congested streets ... had walked a long way on a very wet evening in order to have a simple training in ways of helping their neighbours during air raids." Silently, they took turns working the device, and when the training was over, there were cries of "Eh, dear!" and the voice of one grandmother saying, "We've come to something when we've to have things like this ready for the babies." Everyone murmured their agreement. While the nation had gotten used to many things, "a baby's gas helmet – a handsome thing in itself – is too much for our understanding to cope with."[1]

Yet, as the demonstration continued, the women began to share reactions that diverged from the initial discomfort. One began to joke about twins, given that the helmet could fit only one baby, or what to do with someone who had a baby and two toddlers. Then the conversation turned to the government's spending £3 on each helmet, an object that was "beautifully made" of good materials, "and it is evident that the provision of so expensive a piece of baby's outfitting to any poor mother is regarded as weightier proof of the Government's munificence than is ever signified by less tangible social services."[2] The account of the event ends with the hope that there will never be a need to use the helmets.

This one meeting on a rainy evening in August reveals competing ideas about the gas mask, its intended purpose, and the varied reactions of those who engaged with it. Unlike the responses of other mothers, it portrays these women viewing babies' anti-gas protection not solely as horrifying or dismaying but as a sign of caring. They might be disquieted by the idea of needing such objects and what that says about the state of the world, but the overall reaction reported in a left-leaning paper is gratitude to the government for demonstrating, in this small way, that it cared about poor mothers' children enough to provide such an expensive thing to keep them safe.

The period of time between the dress rehearsal for war (September 1938) and the moment at which aerial bombs began to inflict serious damage in Britain (September 1940) saw the reach of gas masks (including the new small child's respirator, a variation of which was sometimes nicknamed the "Mickey Mouse" gas mask, and the final version of infant protection, the baby's anti-gas protective helmet) to growing numbers of the British population. Not everyone could get a gas mask in the early months, and not everyone who could do so accepted one. Both the development and the issuing of anti-gas protection for infants in particular – the devices were both more expensive and more complicated to produce than other types – had proceeded more slowly than the official statements had indicated. Even when attacks on British civilians remained more theoretical than real, this object was slowing entering into ordinary lives and on its way to becoming a centerpiece in accounts of the war ever after.[3]

As civil defense measures accelerated after the Munich Crisis, the Home Office's ARP Department began to outline the unfolding of its full range of measures to safeguard civilians from aerial attacks, continuing to assume that these would include chemical arms. When discussing precautions for businesses, officials were clear that there would be no need to supply industry with gas masks, because everyone would receive a general civilian respirator.[4] Behind the scenes, it was also now confronting further questions that the trial run of issuing of gas masks during September had raised, in particular, what exactly was the life expectancy of the gas mask? Porton Down scientists began to determine whether and how the devices distributed now could last until they might be needed.[5]

In the meantime, critics of the whole civil defense enterprise denounced not only the government's efforts but also the entire protocol. In Northern Ireland, an area deemed less likely than England to be bombed, there were delays in getting equipment to the population, and then after the Munich Crisis, according to official reports, "a clamour for gas masks arose." Yet when the government was on the point of distributing them, the Irish Republican Army in Belfast went from door to door collecting them and burning them in public, proclaiming that gas masks had been issued to people in England "to wean them over to her side if she happened to be involved in a conflict." According to the unpublished official history, this was an inconsequential act; only a small number of gas masks were destroyed.[6] However, a few months later the public nature of the burning of gas masks led to questions in the Northern Irish Parliament about whether delays in the implementation of civil defense measures were related to the gas mask burning and the Irish Republican Army broadcast that accompanied it.[7] That resisting the gas mask could be publicly stated as resistance to Britishness and to imperial control in the case of Northern Ireland is revealing about the symbolic, political meaning of accepting the gas mask, something that would play out during the war's arrival on the British mainland, not to mention the empire.

When the government decided to mass-produce gas masks and distribute them free of charge, part of the rationale was the management of emotions and actions. It wanted people to see the gas mask as a gift from a benevolent state to which was owed appropriate behavior. Carrying a gas mask in public and undergoing training in its proper use registered as signs of an individual's willingness to follow regulations about civil defense, to be a good wartime citizen. This was evident in the wartime government's commissioning surveys of gas mask carrying and creating a large-scale publicity campaign in 1941 to support gas mask carrying, including a film about the gas mask revealingly called *The Guardian of Your Life*, and then trying to assess the success of this effort. The government gave gas masks to civilians above all to keep them alive in a chemical attack. In so doing, it also sought to reassure everyone that they would not need to worry that persons incapacitated by poison gas might slow down other needed actions in response to air raids. Those who embraced their masks thus validated the state's extensive, ongoing investments in individual anti-gas protection as the civilian gas mask came to symbolize the new state of being in a total war.

Progress and Dissent: The Babies Get Their Anti-gas Protection

One sign of this increased civil defense activity was the further distribution of ARP pamphlets and public information leaflets in the spring and summer of 1939, but the critiques of ARP, especially from the left, also continued. These critiques included a pamphlet from the Hampstead Communist Party, *A.R.P. for Hampstead*, with a foreword by J. B. S. Haldane himself, where readers could learn that the party at this local level was taking note of what the government had failed to provide, adequate shelters. Although the text praised the local ARP workers for having gas masks delivered door to door, "saving the waiting in queues experienced in other boroughs," it pointed out that this only underscored how totally unprepared other sections of London were in comparison. It also offered this damning criticism: "no gas masks were provided for children under three, and even now we are only promised gas masks for babies in the future."[8] As the immediate threat of war lessened after the Munich Agreement, the challenges of getting gas masks and information about them only intensified.

Others signs that some in Britain were rejecting outright the government's efforts to inform them about steps they should take, including instructions about how to prepare for chemical war, can be found in the files of the ARP Department of the Home Office. Several copies of "Public Information Leaflet No. 2," issued in mid-July, which provided detailed instructions about how to maintain and use a gas mask as well as how to black out windows at night, were mailed back to government officials. One bore the phrase "returned with disgust" and a signature, with the added message, "money and gain for the rich is at the bottom of all wars. Its time people learnt better." Another copy of the pamphlet came back with this message scrawled across the cover: "No use to us we refuse to assist in war and war preparations," signed "Family man Leigh on Sea." Handwritten across the text inside were the words, "Feed the Starving Children. We Refuse War. We Demand Peace. We Demand Friendship Not Gas Masks." Winifred Grace Toby wrote a more formal note to Sir John Anderson to accompany her returned leaflet. She began by stating, "I refuse to accept the enclosed leaflet which was delivered to my house by post this morning. As a Christian British citizen, I cannot accede to this anti-Christian request." One recipient went so far as to annotate the leaflet's content, adding to the heading "Your Gas Mask" the words "or practical experiment in Euthanasia." Others wrote to say that the pamphlet might have been more useful if the recipient had actually been able to obtain a gas mask.[9] All of this suggests that the government's desire to persuade the population to accept the gas mask generated a potent counter-narrative with roots in both Christian and humanitarian pacifism.

This left the government with two challenges. One was practical: It had to try to fulfill its promise that there would be anti-gas equipment for all, an issue that involved production and distribution. The other, and perhaps greater, challenge involved making sure that its citizens accepted such protection and would therefore use it if the worst should come. In terms of the first, seemingly easier task, the 1938 crisis accelerated movement toward the one major segment of the population that had thus far been left out: babies and young children.

Figure 5.1 Photograph of men looking at the Labour Party poster featuring the baby in a gas mask in March 1938. Keystone-France Contributor/Gamma-Keystone/Getty Images

Such protection had frustrated Porton Down for some time because young children and infants could not wear anything like a conventional gas mask.[10] Plans also had to contend with the ways in which representations of the baby in the gas mask had been so central to antiwar campaigns. From cartoons to pamphlets to novels to poems, the full horror of chemical war came from imagining its impact on young children, with a particular emphasis on light-skinned and light-haired babies as emblematic of a racialized innocence.[11] Writers such as W. H. Davies had asked in September 1937 whether "life on Earth [is] a viler thing / Than ever was known before" and suggested asking "the Baby, three weeks old / That wears a gas proof-mask" for its verdict.[12] From the images circulated during the First World War discussed in Chapter 2, the idea of placing an infant or young child in a gas mask evoked feelings of fear and repugnance. Perhaps unsurprisingly, the infamous Labour Party poster showing the baby in a gas mask from its campaign in 1935 resurfaced in March 1938, provoking the Conservatives, who declared the poster again to be in "bad taste," even as Labour claimed it was "intended as a warning of 'things to come'" (Fig. 5.1).[13]

Government scientists had tried a variety of solutions to the problem of anti-gas protection for babies, including a failed attempt at a gas-proof pram in 1935. This did not stop efforts to forge alternate solutions. One device was hailed in the *Daily Express* as offering a new solution: "Babies to be Sealed in Gas-Proof Bags." It reported on a test carried out in public on the green lawn outside Dr Barnardo's Babies' Castle in Hawkhurst, Kent. Four-year-old Cyril Wilkes, "a flaxen-haired little fellow," was, the reporter declared, the first of "3,000,000 British toddlers to wear a gas mask. His eyes peered wonderingly through the mica." And Cyril proved "a lucky first choice," having played with his mask by swinging it around beforehand. When he came out of it, he wanted to put it on again. The article concluded by noting that the staff "paraded him round the other toddlers as a good example." This suggests that perhaps not all young children or infants would be happy in these masks, but that the state was assuring its subjects that it was going to look after them (after first using them as guinea pigs).[14]

Despite these ongoing experiments, in public and private, the absence of infant anti-gas protection during Gas Mask Sunday was troubling, and as a result, the issue became a focal point of the national media. Some reassurance could be found in articles suggesting that a "blanket" might make a good makeshift sort of anti-gas protection if children could not be sent to relatives in the country.[15] Behind the scenes, in July 1938, several different devices were tested at a maternity and child welfare clinic in Southampton. In August 1938, scientists conducted tests on babies at Holborn Town Hall to see whether the baby bag, protective stretcher, or anti-gas protective helmet appealed most to babies and their mothers.[16] The events of Gas Mask Sunday and the stepping up of ARP work prompted a letter from Mary Smith of the WVS for ARP to the Home Office ARP Department in October to ask whether their services were needed, "i.e. to provide you with babies to have bags tried on them."[17]

By the end of November, officials were publicly touting the near-availability of a device that would keep babies safe, although some may not have been comforted by press releases that described them as "anti-gas cages for babies."[18] Yet those anticipating being able to put their babies in such devices would continue to wait. Meanwhile, in the absence of government-issued devices and despite the unsuccessful government efforts to produce a gas-proof pram in 1935, the *Daily Mirror* displayed the image of a privately developed anti-gas apparatus for infants on December 9, 1938, under the heading "Your Baby Can Be Safe Now." This object, developed by Edward Mills and using wood and unbreakable glass, looked a bit like a rolling coffin. The gas-masked woman pushing the object, her own face obscured, seemed potentially

Figure 5.2 This photograph of a mother wearing her gas mask while pushing an innovative gas-proof pram appeared in the *Daily Mirror* on December 9, 1938 with the caption "Your Baby Can Be Safe Now." Chronicle/Alamy Stock

to be a vision from a nightmare rather than someone meant to reassure women and/or babies. Alternative designs were also being sent to officials; an extensive correspondence developed between ARP officials and engineer Alice Leigh-Smith, who claimed that as a mother, she had a far better design, since those developing infant anti-gas protection had not considered that this was "a mother problem as much as a baby problem."[19] Mothers did not like placing their babies in containers where they could not be readily comforted (Fig. 5.2).

British families would not have to make do with such cumbersome rolling protection for their babies. On February 3, 1939, Sir John Anderson, in his role as Lord Privy Seal with responsibility for civil defense, announced the arrival of the baby's anti-gas protective helmet, stating that production was going forward rapidly. The *Daily Express* proclaimed, "Gas Mask for Babies Found," explaining that "the new product is believed to be designed like a helmet, cannot be torn off and allows complete bodily function."[20] It was also made clear that this device and any other gas masks would remain government property. Having now finally developed anti-gas protection for all ages, the government still had to contend with ongoing resistance to gas masks and to civil defense. While giving a speech in Glasgow announcing the baby's gas mask and other ARP measures, Anderson was shouted down and pelted with pamphlets and gas masks. According to news accounts, the cry from the man who threw the gas mask that landed at Anderson's feet was "we don't need these. Give us real protection."[21] The challenge of getting the entire population to accept gas masks remained, especially because the counter-narrative, largely articulated by J. B. S. Haldane at this moment, stressed that the danger lay not in gas bombs but high explosives, for which the government needed to provide deep shelters.[22]

Nonetheless, a kind of bleak awareness of the need for, and thus inevitability of, the new baby's gas mask emerged. On February 20, the *Daily Mirror* offered an editorial reflecting on the "modern child," whom it did not envy, "being born almost complete with gas masks into a world where not to live dangerously is hardly to live at all." The hard lesson was that such a child had to learn "to adapt to its time and environment."[23] And scenes of such adaptation began to appear in the press. By early March, babies' anti-gas helmets were advertised as being available in Holborn Town Hall, where mothers of the district would learn how to fit and use them on babies of between six months and two years. The article helpfully noted that "no gas will be used in the demonstration which is intended to show the correct method of fitting the masks."[24] This was followed by an illustrated article showing how mothers learned to rock babies in the device. The process of making this disconcerting device normal was beginning.

Yet not everyone was willing to accept the new circumstances that this heralded. A few days later, the *Daily Express*'s James Agate penned a lullaby to the child entering this dreadful new world, the baby wearing a gas mask:

> What though nasty bombs come whirling
> Mustard gas all round is swirling
> Go to sleep, my boy or girling.
> Baby's gas-mask's on!
> Refrain:
> Hush-a-bye, baby,
> Cosy and warm –
> Mummy's got something
> To keep you from harm!
> …
> Though the world with war is seething
> Calm and peaceful be your breathing.
> Concentrate upon your teething!
> Baby's gas-mask's on![25]

Figure 5.3 "Blind Babies Do Gas Drills" read the headline of this photographic spread appearing in the *Daily Mirror* on April 13, 1939. The baby in the gas mask had gone from imagined fear to reality. Mirrorpix/Reach Publishing Licensing

This was one more sign of the unease rather than reassurance provoked by the infant anti-gas protection that was now on offer from the government for the next generation.

Perhaps the most vivid example of how far the world of childhood had changed with gas masks placed on every child can be seen in a two-page spread showing that "Blind Babies Do Gas Drills." Even more striking than the account of how blind toddlers in Sussex were learning how to wear gas masks was the accompanying photograph of a line of small children at a school for the blind all holding on to each other and all wearing gas masks. It is an image that vividly evokes the famous painting *Gassed* by John Singer Sargent, which shows a row of First World War soldiers with each man's outstretched arm on the shoulders of the man in front of him, bandages around eyes injured by poison gas. Only this time, chemical weapons are potentially going after babies and not soldiers (Fig. 5.3).

The publicity given to the arrival of the anti-gas protection for young children and babies signaled the full incorporation of civilians regardless of age into the calculations required to wage war against chemical agents and air power. Having a functional object was the first step; now came distribution and, in the case of this device, a strategy for instructing those caring for babies in how to use it. It was far from an intuitive device. When officials had developed plans in December 1938 to launch the baby's protective helmet, they had agreed that the training of "Mothers in the use of the device" required careful consideration, and "for obvious reasons the demonstrations [of how to use the device] should be given by an individual in the Medical Officers of Health Department, accustomed to handling babies," rather than by the local civil defense instructors.[26] *A.R.P. Newsletter* No. 3 from May 1, 1939 noted that now that the baby's anti-gas helmet had come into being, demonstrations of how to use it were taking place in Kent, Sussex, and South Wales.[27] By early August, British families were still being given assurances that there would be one baby's gas mask for every 7,000 people, even if none had materialized. While many had been manufactured, they would not all be ready for another month or two, and unlike regular gas masks, including those for young children, the baby's anti-gas protective helmet required an external person to operate it. As the article announcing the new, albeit limited, availability of the baby's gas mask elaborated, the general idea was to start distributing it at maternity homes "so that a mother's last duty before leaving for home with her new baby will be to learn to put him in a six-pound helmet and how to manipulate the pumping apparatus."[28]

The government's unveiling of the official baby's anti-gas protective helmet did not come until the summer of 1939. Still, the government had answered the question about gas masks for infants posed in September 1938, and the new baby's anti-gas helmet was available nationally by the onset of the war. Once the mothers of Britain learned how to use it, they did not always find it comforting or reassuring. In her memoir of her wartime childhood, Hilda Casey recalls her mother's reaction to the baby's gas mask:

Mum wasn't adverse to accepting gas masks for us but she was dismayed when shown the peculiar contraption offered for her baby's protection against gas attack. About the size of a large suitcase with mica porthole, it was impossible for her to consider putting our baby into it. She burst into tears.[29]

A few months after the baby's anti-gas helmet appeared in Britain, it made its way to certain parts of the empire and to key communities in strategic locations. According to a chart compiled in January 1940 to show where babies' anti-gas helmets and small children's respirators were being sent as well as left in store for distribution via local authorities, out of an estimated 2 million orders, only 91,000 made it around the globe. The numbers are quite small even in relation to the populations of these locales, so that a place like Aden, despite its pleas for protection during the Second Italo-Ethiopian War, received but one baby's helmet and 200 children's respirators. Gibraltar merited 850 helmets and 800 children's gas masks, whereas Hong Kong was due 10,000 of each; and the "British Community" in Egypt was granted 725 devices for babies and 1,025 for children. Both Malta and Northern Ireland appear on the list under "Colonies," although, of course, Northern Ireland was officially part of the United Kingdom, but perhaps this is less strange than the treatment of Ireland (Eire), which received, or was meant to receive, the same number of babies' anti-gas helmets as went to Northern Ireland (20,000).[30] Despite the array of imperial spaces left out, the journey of this object around the globe offers a vivid emblem of the militarization of domestic life embodied by the gas mask.[31]

The Gas Mask as War Begins

As the crisis leading to Britain's entry into the Second World War approached in August 1939, the government issued another wave of pamphlets, articles, and other media designed to inform the public about civil defense, and particularly about the care and keeping of one's gas mask. Evidence that this was not restricted solely to the metropole can be seen in the report issued that June by an expert committee advising on India's defense, which stated matter-of-factly that anti-gas equipment and training for troops were "axiomatic." It noted the lack of action by the civil authorities in India to offer "corresponding measures for the protection of the civil population in vulnerable centres," and while this fell beyond the purview of the committee, the committee felt that "in certain cases the complete absence of protection" for civilians, especially those living near military sites, might "produce a state of panic" that would impair troops from taking any action.[32] The fitting of Indian women in June 1939 in order to determine what sizes of gas masks might be needed for them, discussed in Chapter 1, suggests that some measures were under way to determine how to protect civilians in this vital imperial space. Yet determining what might be needed to safeguard civilians in the empire was far from actually providing such protection.

In the metropole, a flurry of public statements aimed to inform the public about what to do. *A.R.P.: A Complete Guide to Civil Defence*, prepared by William Deede (the *Daily Telegraph*'s ARP correspondent), introduced the fitting and distributing of gas masks as a key part of the warden's role: "They have the difficult and often unpleasant task of imparting unwelcome information about gas masks, shelter and other precautions to householders; and they are often and foolishly accounted of no importance."[33] The danger of a possible gas attack – the potentially most deadly feature of aerial warfare – could be mitigated by household refuge rooms and by masks. As the guide further claims: "There is, however, much to be said for the official viewpoint to-day: 'If the nation is prepared against gas, gas is less likely to be used; if gas is not used by our enemies, these precautions are not wasted, but abundantly justified'" (58). This distills the essential message of anti-gas protection and the mask in particular – and it has little to do with the actual threat of chemical arms. The gas mask's utility lies in its deterrent effect; but this can be achieved only by full cooperation with the state's new regime of gas discipline: having, carrying, and practicing with the mask.

Moreover, Deede also seeks to mediate the "public misapprehension" (61) caused by the existence of three types of official masks. Both the Service Respirator and Civilian Duty Respirator equip active personnel, such as firemen and decontamination squads in the case of the former and ambulance drivers and wardens in the case of the latter, to perform vital functions. By contrast, the ordinary "General Civilian Respirator" serves a specific purpose: "its design has been simplified so that large numbers can be mass-produced without diminishing its reliability." Since ordinary civilians

will not normally be required to move about or remain long in contaminated areas[,] accordingly their masks are lighter and less elaborate. It is absurd to suggest that these respirators are useless against gas, because they have been well-tried in gas chambers, and have been found more than adequate for their purpose. (61)

A similar defense of the gas mask can be found in other guides, such as Evelyn Thomas's *A Practical Guide to A.R.P.*, which emphasizes that in order to prevent gas attack from shattering morale or terrorizing the population, Britons need to know some basic elements of anti-gas protection and, above all, to make use of their gas masks. Thomas's section on the gas mask offers photographs to show how it should be worn, including a model of the baby's protective helmet. It offers a few suggestions for children too: Since "small children do not, as a rule, take well to respirators, it is best to arrange for their evacuation to safe areas" or for a shelter where a gas mask will not be necessary. As for babies, once placed in the helmet, they will be "absolutely safe from gas for any length of time," so long as someone is operating the bellows used to circulate air; "otherwise the child will suffocate."[34] One can commend Thomas for being thorough and matter-of-fact, but the message here seems to suggest an encouragement to flee rather than face chemical weapons head on.

Using a slightly different tone, Major-General Sir Henry Thuillier's *Gas in the Next War*, which appeared in 1939 in a renowned military expert's series on the next war, provided not only details about the effects of gas war, but also reassurance. Thuillier unequivocally states that the government has "perfected a form of respirator which can be truly said to be 100 per cent. Efficient against every gas that has been used up to date ... it is beyond question that entire trust can be placed in the gas respirator of to-day." As far as the general civilian respirator specifically is concerned, he is confident that the six hours or so for which it could provide protection would be sufficient to endure a gas attack from the air.[35] He concludes that the prospect of using such weapons may be alleviated by two factors. The first is that the provision of gas masks to the civilian population would make using chemical weapons not worth the effort for the enemy. The second is that the greatest danger from gas lies in "panic through fear and ignorance." Avoiding panic requires preparation so that "discipline, courage and well-conceived measures of defence" will prevent poison gas from affecting the outcome of the war by avoiding or reducing suffering and death. This was the essence of "gas-mindedness," the ability to be fully prepared to survive a chemical war.[36]

All the effort, at this stage, to defend this device as not being "useless" illustrated the need to combat the ongoing public skepticism about civilian gas masks. Two features of this argument in support of gas masks stand out. One is that the somewhat lukewarm assertion that they are "more than adequate" would probably not suffice when one's own life or the lives of one's family were at stake. The other is the assumption that the inhabitants subject to a gas attack would not "normally" need to move about or remain in poison-filled areas for hours and could somehow flee such spaces readily. After a mass air raid, would they be able to do so? After all, the lives of those relying on this official version of a gas mask – the majority of the population – were at risk here. The special pleading to rely on the gas mask for safety does not seem to address underlying questions about its efficacy.

As individuals acquired gas masks, the masks also quickly took on a largely symbolic meaning, denoting the imminent arrival of war. Londoner Vera Reid volunteered as soon as the war began and found herself helping to assemble gas masks to distribute and fit.[37] Writing in her diary on August 28, 1939, a nurse described how "During our off duty, we help to put Gas Mask together. ... We are just living from day to day, waiting for the fatal moment which we all realise must come. ..."

Figure 5.4 Gas masks in their cardboard boxes carried by children during their evacuation from London in September 1939. Hulton Archive/Stringer/Getty Images

And when war was officially declared, she spent one of its first days, September 3,

fitting gas masks on the poor T.B. patients, whose breathing is so distressed at the best of times, that the idea of putting the mask on is almost too much, but they realize how grave the situation is, and after one or two have put them on, we have no further trouble, for the rest can see that it is possible to breathe.[38]

The gas mask was deployed on the very sick in hospitals and became one of the objects that children being evacuated from London carried with them. Among the many accounts in the press, one from the *Daily Mail* on September 2 spoke of the tens of thousands of children in London who each had a label on their coat for identification, food for the journey, and a gas mask. The sight of children with signs hanging from their necks and the cardboard boxes containing their gas masks as they were evacuated was one of the vivid indicators of the war's early days (Fig. 5.4).[39]

The appearance of gas masks heralded the arrival of war, signaling this not only within the country but also outside it as the embodiment of

Britain in a state of war. In her first letter from London as the chief correspondent for the *New Yorker* on September 3, 1939, Mollie Panter-Downes wrote: "Gas Masks have suddenly become part of everyday civilian equipment, and everybody is carrying the square cardboard cartons that look as though they might contain a pound of grapes for a sick friend."[40] Despite the doubts, they were suddenly everywhere, even if the mask with its strange substitute for a face lay concealed in cartons and containers.

By September 1939, most inhabitants of Britain's metropole now had gas masks, and as the text above reveals, many were carrying them around with them. The creation of decorative objects – containers and cases – designed to carry the gas masks was quick to follow. This set of objects that grew around the original device shows how quickly certain segments of the population who had received masks in Britain, mainly women, began to domesticate this strange new thing, to make it familiar and presumably less discomfiting. A mere month after the official outbreak of war, a photographic spread of a variety of gas mask cases appeared in the *Illustrated London News*. It assured its readers that "the official exhortation to 'take your gas-mask with you' loses much of its grimness when it is possible to stow the unaesthetic-looking object away in such well-designed, not to say *chic*, containers as these." The ten designs ranged from a full disguise of the object to mere coverings of the cardboard box with colorful fabric. The caption, in fact, highlights the case that most closely resembles a handbag – something in which to carry one's "handkerchief" beside "the gas mask" – the ordinary and the seemingly impossible-to-make-ordinary placed alongside one another (Fig. 5.5). This same design element was featured as one adopted by the queen herself in another image, where a photograph shows that she is wearing "a coat of steel blue with hat of same shade. ... Notice Her Majesty's new gas-mask bag. Of fawn corded velvet, it's a gas-mask container and handbag in one."[41]

Through the desire to hide the gas mask, an object that had been used to alarm if not terrify people in the decade before the war, turning its container into an object of fashion led to a variety of responses in the media. On September 11, 1939, a *Daily Mirror* column provocatively invited readers to discern the "new use for your swim suit." First noting that "the best gas mask notice I have so far seen is in a Kingsway tailor's window," which reads "Gas mask cases tailored in blue serge," it continues: "Many girls, however, have solved the case problem by turning their bathing suits into cases. I saw one pretty girl with the white cords of her bathing suit round her shoulders and the rest of the costume in a pack on her back, holding her 'snuff box.'" The same paper later reported on

Figure 5.5 "The Dernier Cri in Gas Mask Containers," photographic spread of gas mask carriers in the *Illustrated London News*, 1939. © Illustrated London News Ltd/Mary Evans

the case of a bride at Manchester Cathedral who had her gas mask case covered in the same material as her wedding gown.[42] There was nowhere the gas mask could not go. Commercial establishments quickly began to advertise both practical and fashionable gas mask containers: "'Stormgard is your safeguard': Gas Mask Container, Guaranteed Waterproof."[43] If one was asked to carry a gas mask everywhere, then incorporating it into everyday life led to creativity and commerce.

In the diary entries of thirty-one-year-old Vivienne Hall, who was living with her mother in Putney and working a secretarial job in central London, we can see the appeal of something that combined the handbag and gas mask case. She comments on September 11, 1939:

still the war goes on and still our office goes on and still the A.R.P. goes on. … All the girls are ordered to parade about the building with their gasmasks slung over their shoulders and handbags – so when anyone rings to give us letters we have to be armed with gasmasks, handbags, notebooks and pencils and pile of papers.[44]

Consolidating the handbag and gas mask case was practical. A few days after this entry, she notes: "The little cardboard boxes which contain our gasmasks are slowly losing their 'sameness' as the most fantastic and colourful covers are appearing everywhere. It doesn't take a woman long to ornament even that nasty little necessity."[45] The prevalence of gas mask cases as desirable consumer items throughout the first months of the war can be seen in everything from a letter from two evacuated children, Margaret and Muriel Shean, to their parents, thanking them for "the letter, Gas-Mask cases ... and Cigarette Cards," to a recent college graduate, Eileen Alexander, writing to her beau that "I bought myself a beautiful gas-mask case" and to a war worker, Rose Cottrell, writing a letter from her home in Kent to her married sister in Zurich and noting that her Christmas presents included "a brown suede gas mask carrier."[46]

The gas mask itself was carefully designed, marketed, and distributed so as to be "generic" in order to offer a standardized form of protection that could be easily transported and used; the ultimate aim was reassurance. Yet, almost instantly, its case became something to be individualized and incorporated into daily fashion – to hide this object's "grimness" inside something pretty. That this was a highly gendered reaction, in Hall's words, that it did not take women long to transform into something "colourful" and "fantastic," may speak as much to assumptions about the feminization of domestic skills as to associations between gender and aesthetics. The leather, luxury, or waterproof gas mask containers for sale could also signal class status, but the capacity to decorate a box does not seem to have been fundamentally restricted to any particular class. Rather, deploying feminine domestic arts – sewing, knitting, embroidery – to cover up the gas mask case shows the civilian respirator's transformation into something familiar, something whose decorative outer manifestation could conceal the purpose of the object within. And this was not restricted to women; an article in the *Daily Mirror* referenced how a tailor hard hit by lack of demand for regular men's clothing turned his hand to gas mask cases: "I used to make a dozen suits a week. Now all I have to do is to make gas mask containers [to match suits] out of odd bits of material. I sell them for Is. and Is. 6d." As war began, the gas mask became an object seemingly located everywhere, and yet invisible behind its case.

As the war got underway, yet with limited effect in Britain itself, new problems with the availability of gas masks and their use both within and beyond the civilian population of the United Kingdom were starting to emerge as well. In addition to earlier concerns about fitting gas masks on "abnormal faces," the war brought new questions.[47] For example, police superintendents wanted to know what should be done for prisoners. Presumably, a memorandum began, "in the majority of cases prisoners would have their own civilian respirators." The superintendent at the Cannon Row Station of the Metropolitan Police pointed out that there might be people – "especially drunken persons" – who would not have them, in which case "the responsibility of affording such persons some means of protection against gas must be ours." It was a moral responsibility, if nothing else. While they could be supplied with service respirators (the type given to policemen) from reserve stocks, it would be desirable to have the Home Office supply them.[48]

Other unanticipated issues arose. Letters came to the Foreign Office at the outbreak of the war from Poland, France, and Belgium. What about the provision of gas masks to British subjects located or, indeed, living elsewhere at the outbreak of war? Other queries came in from Istanbul, where the majority of British subjects in the area were Maltese and unable to afford their own gas masks. The official response: "supply of respirators to subjects abroad not been seen as an obligation of His Majesty's Government." Such subjects were on their own, another sign of how the state prioritized the value of some bodies over others.[49] The distribution in the colonies and other parts of the empire and, as will be discussed in Chapter 6, the later provision of gas masks to internees, continued to reveal the core of civil defense: to determine who could or should be protected, who mattered.[50] War had arrived, and with it the gas mask, although some inhabitants did not receive their gas masks until several weeks into the war. Reactions continued to vary. Twenty-six-year-old Esther Bruce refused to leave London and return to her father's native Guyana when war broke out, and according to a later memoir, she was given a gas mask at the start of the war, but hated it: "It smelled of rubber. I only wore mine once."[51] When Muriel Green, living in a rural village in Norfolk, picked up masks for herself and her mother and sister only on October 23, she wrote in her diary: "Have not had one until now, surprised to find not too unpleasant to wear as everyone else said they could not breathe. Have practised wearing it in private and think I could keep it on any length of time if necessary."[52] When it might become necessary, where it could be found, who wore it, whether they would do so with the acceptance of someone like Muriel Green, and thus what it all meant were still being determined.

Reacting to Gas Masks before the Bombs Fall

Despite the immediate issuing of wartime civil defense measures, including the distribution of gas masks, during the so-called Phony War from September 1939 through the spring of 1940, inhabitants of Britain's metropole remained almost entirely insulated from the most violent effects of the war taking place at sea and on the rest of the continent, and of what had already been underway in Asia.[53] That changed for those serving in the British army with the escalation of violence in Norway and the Netherlands and, ultimately, with the invasion and fall of France in May and June. Yet the almost complete absence of bombs falling in England, Northern Ireland, Scotland, and Wales meant that some semblance of regular life continued for British civilians. One of the more visible reminders of the ongoing aerial threat was the population's carrying of gas masks to the extent that it retained enormous symbolic importance. That this read as indicating one's full commitment to the war effort became increasingly evident in the attention ARP officials and ordinary volunteers paid to this simple act.

Alongside the Home Office's official reports, Mass Observation regularly conducted surveys of gas mask carrying to determine how many Britons of all ages and in all locations took seriously this aspect of ARP.[54] It tried to establish who was likely to carry a gas mask, when, and why, thus attempting to trace the rise and fall of gas mask use during this period. It occasionally offered some speculation as to the extent that gender, age, class, or even emotional state determined gas mask carrying. It is clear throughout the reports of these surveys that unlike other features of civil defense, carrying a gas mask was "the only voluntary civilian war-activity in which everyone was recommended to join," as one of Mass Observation's wartime studies put it.[55] Thus carrying the gas mask could be read as an important sign of national unity, and the failure or refusal to carry a gas mask could send a message that one was not committed to following the government directives that were intended to sustain the war effort.

An initial report on gas mask carrying from London, issued on September 4, 1939, noted that of 100 men and 100 women observed, 62 men and 71 women carried their masks; 47 men older than forty but only 15 women in the same age cohort had masks with them. The tendency of women, and of younger women in particular, to be more likely than men to carry masks remained notable, although a marked drop-off occurred as the war continued without air raids taking place. An overview in May 1940 summarized the previous eight months, noting that gas mask carrying had risen steadily, peaking at about September 6, 1939, when two-thirds of the population consistently (or at least visibly) carried their masks with them. This fell to 50 percent in October and 33 percent in November, reaching about 10 percent in mid-January and falling well below 5 percent in March. Not until the news of the invasion of the Netherlands and Belgium reached the country in May did the carrying of masks rise to about 20 percent of the observed population, according to these records.[56] Even the launching of sustained heavy aerial attacks on Britain pushed gas mask carrying up to only 35 percent by late September 1940.[57] Another summary analysis of gas-mask-carrying data concluded that women were always a bit more "mask-minded" and that Londoners exhibited a greater propensity than those in other locales to carry masks before the bombs fell.[58] Whatever these findings about the small differences between genders, ages, and regions were (by this point in 1940 indicating that more women, more older people, and more in the south of England carried masks), the reports reveal an overarching concern: How could the state get people to adopt the first step of anti-gas defense, i.e., simply taking their gas masks about with them?

That this posed special problems for Britain was noted in the summation of Mass Observation's 1940 report *The War Begins at Home*. While the government *required* certain behaviors, such as honoring the blackout, the initiative to follow instructions to carry gas masks was left to the individual. There was no "attempt to create a strong and long-term mentality capable of facing any terrors or despairs."[59] Yet the gas mask had been designed, at least in part, to help people to face the worst terrors of modern warfare. According to the report, one of the problems with persuading people to adopt the habit of carrying a gas mask lay in the posters and public information that could be ignored. What seemed to work was visual evidence of prominent people, such as the queen or MPs, carrying gas masks in public; images of Prime Minister Winston Churchill toting his gas mask appeared in the press as well, although he himself was not pictured wearing one.[60] When they saw such high-profile individuals doing this, "the masses were helped to feel that if this was a new kind of war, it was their war too. The gas-mask was, for a time, the best of any propaganda to uplift civilian morale ... a participation between You and Us, the civilian and the soldier. Everybody was armed."[61]

How did individuals feel about their gas masks and about carrying them? Even if gas masks were not the overt subject of its studies, Mass Observation's directives to its respondents, such as one in November 1939 asking them to comment on the "inconveniences of wartime," provided diarists with opportunities to reflect on their encounters with, and thoughts about, these devices. An unmarried nineteen-year-old male shop assistant in Essex focussed on the annoyance of gas mask carrying: "Gas masks are a great nuisance, as they get in the way, are difficult to manoeuvre in certain positions, and several times I have forgotten mine when going out. Valuable time may be wasted in going back to fetch them." This soon became linked to what the mask signified, as this same diarist noted on September 4: "Practically everybody is now carrying a gas mask. What a reflection on our civilisation!" On September 9, there was "nothing of much interest to note. Except for gas masks and newspaper placards one would hardly think there was a war." Midway through that first month of war, the gas mask emerged as one of the few signals that something had changed:

In fact, life goes on much as before, except for carrying gas masks, obscuring lights, and talking about the war. Of course, the war is much talked about and rumours float about rather vaguely. To-day I went out without my gas mask again. I don't seem to be able to get used to taking it with me.[62]

He was not alone; in this early phase of the war, carrying a gas mask invited comments. Despite the pretty cases and the pressure, a substantial group of Britons had not yet made this a part of their everyday activities. A seventeen-year-old clerk in an undated entry for September 1939 recorded the following anecdote:

For the first time I took my gas mask (why "gas mask" surely it's an anti-gas mask) Percentage of pedestrians with gas mask about 40. I hadn't been out ten minutes before a lorry driver, taking a smoke yelled "Whatcher got there mate? Box o'chocolates?" I joined in the joke and said it was a camera. Hearty laughs on both sides.[63]

Much as in the initial encounters with these objects on Gas Mask Sunday, humor was one recurring way in which people made the gas mask palatable and covered up what acknowledging its real purpose might mean.

There was an unspoken presumption that gas mask carrying was linked to fear of actual attack, and that the device therefore worked to manage this emotion. So it is not surprising that those involved in ARP work noted that the longer Britain went without facing an aerial attack, the less fear existed and the fewer gas masks appeared in public. ARP warden W. A. Rodgers recorded in April 1940 that "less than 5% of the people now trouble to carry gas masks."[64] That seemed to correlate with Mass Observation findings that saw diminished carrying after a peak in September 1939.

As the so-called Phony War was coming to an end, the government introduced a new filter for the general civilian respirator in late May 1940, which coincided with signs that Britain's war had entered a more active phase. Having already been called upon to aid the government by offering feedback on the state of morale indicated by how many people were carrying their gas masks, Mass Observation reporters took to the streets to record how ordinary civilians across the nation responded in their local ARP depots when their gas masks were upgraded. At St. Peter's School in London, the warden made the following comments: "There is no panic – most people take it as a joke – if they ask 'what is it for?' They are quite satisfied with 'it's a specially fine filtre' or 'it's just an extra precaution.'" But then he added that "some people are annoyed because fancy cases are useless" since the new filters would not fit inside them, suggesting perhaps that "makers of the cases invented the new filtre."[65] One observer concluded that the overall atmosphere was one of "Quiet apathy – few questions asked. Most people putting the mask on the table in silence." In contrast, another report from elsewhere in London recounted: "The Chief Warden told me they had been constantly busy without being rushed & there had been no nervousness except in the case of one or two elderly ladies who complained that they could not breathe in their masks and were inclined to be hysterical."[66] "Hysteria" was a highly gendered term, hearkening back to earlier fears about some members of the nation, women in particular, being unable to exhibit the "gas discipline" necessary to use gas masks effectively for themselves or for their children.

That some regular ARP volunteers were coming to view gas mask carrying as showing one's good citizenship can be seen in a letter sent to the editor of the *Daily Mail* in early June 1940, just after the evacuation of British troops from Dunkirk had occurred. Writing as an air raid warden in North London, the letter writer was clear: "I think it should be realised that the person who does not habitually carry his or her gas mask is an ally of the enemy." He urged that the government orchestrate "severe penalties" on people not carrying their gas masks, attributing the lack of gas attacks on troops until then to the knowledge that soldiers all had masks. Yet if the enemy discerned that civilians at home – who had been given "real protection" – were not carrying their masks, then it would deploy gas. The resulting large numbers of casualties in such a raid would hinder the work of defense forces and of persons who, instead of contributing to the war effort, would be "occupying valuable space in hospitals (and mortuaries!) through their own fault." In this writer's reasoning, the gas mask is a deterrent, and failure to carry it invites attack, demonstrating one's disloyalty to the nation and support for the enemy, a perspective that echoed the official narrative about gas masks.[67]

Refusing to carry or, worse, to accept the gas mask was becoming a sign of dissent, of unwillingness to aid the national community fully. Some of the tribunals to determine the status of conscientious objectors indicated this clearly. Conscientious objection emerged when Britain introduced conscription during the First World War, but part of the legislation that allowed this break with the tradition of the volunteer army permitted those whose beliefs would not allow them to fight to receive this designation. It represented a minority stance during that war and was largely unpopular, even when those seeking such status came from Britain's pacifist religious orders such as the Society of Friends (Quakers).[68]

For those applying for conscientious objector status, their decision whether or not to have a gas mask became a critical piece of evidence. For instance, the choice to accept a gas mask became a crucial issue for the London tribunal evaluating the case of Ian Forrester-Paton, a former head of the Oxford Union Pacifist Association. He declared himself a pacifist who refused to do any ARP, agricultural, or defense work. Yet, when asked why he had a gas mask if he disapproved of ARP, he responded, "It is a compromise." The tribunal decided that he could be exempted from military service only if he got a job in farming, forestry, or the mercantile marine.[69] Another case of a conscientious objector who accepted a gas mask attributed this to his mother: John Prince of Prestwich had refused the gas mask, but when his mother obtained one for him, he took it so that he could get into the cinema (by this point cinemas and theaters had started to exclude those who showed up without their masks).[70]

The Lancashire tribunal confronted the decision of what to do about David Coleclough, who refused even to recognize the "right of the State to establish any tribunal to try a man's conscience," at a hearing in April 1940. Coleclough instead wrote a letter, which was delivered by a friend who testified to his honesty. Explaining the determination to grant him conscientious objector status, the chair noted that "when they read the statement in his letter that he had refused the gas mask," the members of the tribunal became persuaded that he was indeed someone who conscientiously objected to doing anything to support the military efforts underway in the country.[71] Refusing the gas mask sometimes accompanied the rejection of other wartime measures. Mr. C. S. Murphy of Mearns appeared before the Aberdeen tribunal for refusing to accept either a gas mask or a ration book. He stated clearly that he was not afraid of gas and, in response to a question, claimed that he would not wear a gas mask under any circumstances.[72] The Manchester tribunal granted Arnold Morrey of Blackburn an unconditional exemption from military service, for in addition to his spiritualism and vegetarianism, he had refused a gas mask and stated that he would not use an air raid shelter. The tribunal found him suffering "from the great handicap of not being a realist."[73]

Some conscientious objectors pointed to the longevity of their refusal of gas masks as evidence of the sincerity of their beliefs. Lorry driver

William Naughton from Bolton told his tribunal that he had refused to accept a gas mask and that, in case of an attack, he would put a wet handkerchief around his mouth. This prompted the chair of the tribunal to call him "a silly ass. ... You should laugh at yourself" while still registering him as a noncombatant.[74] Naughton's case was not yet resolved, for he appealed six months later for an unconditional exemption from military service. Among the testimony recorded in February was his statement that he had "failed to enlighten" the initial tribunal about the "principles involved in not accepting a gas mask." To support the sincerity of his convictions, his now estranged wife, Annie, sent a letter to the tribunal in which she noted that his pacifist beliefs had alienated their friends as well as herself and that as long ago as 1938, he had quarreled with the local ARP warden because he refused a gas mask. When war broke out, Naughton rejected demands from his employers that he carry a gas mask in his lorry. His belief, she explained, was that pacifists should not take part in ARP but instead do their utmost to avoid any aspect of it. Naughton's refusal to use a gas mask had contributed to his dismissal from the job he had held for eight years, and he had now found work driving a heavy truck transporting potatoes. The tribunal decided to allow him to register as a conscientious objector, provided he kept this job or found another in hospital, ambulance, or land work.

The duration of the refusal to use a gas mask seems to have been important. The following spring, after some of the more devastating air raids of the war, nineteen-year-old Donovan Welch stated that since 1938, he had refused to be fitted with or to accept a gas mask. According to the dictates of his conscience, he was willing to do fire watching voluntarily but not if compelled, and he was then ordered to perform noncombatant duties.[75] After the 1941 National Service (No. 2) Act extended conscription to unmarried women between nineteen and thirty-one, women could also claim conscientious objector status, and Kathleen Wigham (née Derbyshire) also noted that she refused to have a gas mask at her tribunal; she was sentenced to prison.[76]

Gas mask carrying mattered to the government for more than just ensuring that the civilian population could survive a chemical attack. It offered one of the most visible signs that the individual would adopt fully the behaviors now required to help ensure the survival of all. Every effort was made to showcase this object as a vital component of wartime civil defense, so much so that when an ARP alphabet appeared in July 1940, "G" stood "for Gas-mask, which you always carry with you."[77] When the devastating air raids on London that lasted for nearly two months began in early September 1940, there was an uptick in gas mask carrying, but the government had to remind ardent ARP volunteers that even those without gas masks should be admitted to public shelters. Once the worst air raids largely subsided by the spring of 1941, the British government could have concluded that since gas had not been used, it should emphasize even more its preparations to cope with high explosive and incendiary bombs. Instead, the spring of 1941 saw it launching a new public civil defense campaign that put the gas mask fully at its center.

Hitler Will Send No Warning: The Gas Mask Campaign of 1941

As the German air campaign now known as the Blitz raged on, and as the British government touted the nation's resilience and its capacity to survive the blows of air war, there was still a sense that the worst might yet come. A January 1941 article in the *Times* reported on how inhabitants of Britain were coping with the war after the first serious aerial attacks. Its author noted that a female reader in Winchester, believing that invasion was ever more likely, had suggested that "the civil population should be urged to make a daily practice of wearing their gas masks for at least half an hour. 'Very few have ever put them on since being fitted by their A.R.P. wardens. ... while the Forces have constant and regular gas mask drill.'"[78] The message delivered by official sources and experts remained that it was important to practice using gas masks. This woman's statement went a bit further, however, suggesting that civilians should act like soldiers by having regular gas drills and developing a familiarity with their masks. All of this was in keeping with the militarization of civilian life under the renewed regime of total war.

Concerned by the intensity of bombing raids, the Home Intelligence Department of the Ministry of Information reached out to Mass Observation for a study of civilian morale. In response, in February 1941, Tom Harrisson submitted a report describing "the condition of the public mind at present, the conditions that have led to this present condition and the possibilities of future development." The report signaled that opinions about what Hitler would do next had shifted between September, when such queries began, and December 1940; the number who worried about invasion had dwindled, but the small percentage expecting a gas attack had gone up.[79]

In public, the start of 1941 saw the announcement that special gas masks were now available to those who had breathing difficulties or a facial deformity that prevented them from using a general civilian respirator. Two models had just been approved after much testing and would be sent to local authorities for distribution.[80] The news was heralded in the tabloid press alongside photographs of the "new gas masks for invalids."[81] Thus did the promise of protection for all – seen in the range of testing that predated the war – continue to motivate provisions.

By the time gas mask tests and gas drills began in the months ahead, there was no excuse not to have a gas mask, and increasingly members of the public were alternately shamed into carrying their masks or praised for having remembered to do so. A large photograph in the *Daily Express* in early February was accompanied by the question "Are YOU still not carrying your gas mask?" It had arrows pointing to the only two people who were following the official request. The newspaper followed up with another photograph taken at the same place a week later in which only one person carried a mask.[82] Clearly, something had to be done, and so a series of public gas tests began.

In mid-February, Brighton became the site of the first general town "gas alert" in which a mild form of tear gas was released outside a local cinema. Inhabitants had been warned for two days by loudspeaker that on February 17, they would need to carry their gas masks for a scheduled gas drill. Everyone with a gas mask was fine, but a few were caught unprepared and had to be treated at the local first aid depot.[83] One observer of the drill noted seeing "gas-masked shop girls … watching gas-masked pedestrians go by." According to a local ARP official, some found it challenging to carry on polite conversation, some grumbled, and some were self-conscious, but mainly there was good-natured cooperation and the children were "magnificent."[84] The sight of people going about their daily tasks while wearing gas masks was novel enough that it inspired a photographic spread in the *Illustrated London News* that featured school children in masks crossing a street, a milkman serving customers, and a policeman giving directions to a motor coach driver. Despite the mayor of Brighton heralding the test as a great success, with citizens behaving as if it were normal to carry out "their ordinary occupation" in gas masks, a contemporary observer might still find something uncanny about images of daily life in which no human features can be discerned (Fig. 5.6).[85]

The *Manchester Guardian* cautioned its readers a week later that while many civilians considered the gas mask to be an optional accessory, it offered "security" and a "quiet mind" just in case the enemy chose to poison the air. Indeed, a recent count had found that only 467 out of 7,480 people were carrying gas masks in Manchester. This was a poor record that showed "dangerous carelessness." The enemy relied on human weakness and forgetfulness, but the British government had outsmarted him by providing gas masks. To defeat him, civilians were

Figure 5.6 Images from the gas alert test in Brighton showing children and others proceeding with life in gas masks. Photographic spread in the *Illustrated London News*, February 22, 1941. © Illustrated London News Ltd/Mary Evans

reminded to "take them [gas masks] about with us and not waste a wise and costly precaution."[86] In that same issue, a letter to the editor suggested that everyone should be compelled to wear a mask in public on specific occasions, practice using it during tear gas demonstrations, and "learn the value of ... respirators." It would be too late when poison gas was actually used; the moment to prepare was now.[87]

An editorial in the *Daily Express* offered its own take on why some refused to carry their gas masks; some might be careless and some did not want to be thought alarmist, while others were skeptical that the Nazis would use gas. None of these reasons were deemed adequate. The message was clear:

From this day forth it would be a point of honour for all people of good will as part of their service to the nation, to carry their gas masks with them wherever they go. A person caught without his or her gas mask during a gas attack would be an immense liability, a source of alarm and embarrassment to the rest of us.

This powerfully distills the reason for gas mask carrying as not being solely about safety and avoiding tempting Hitler to use poison gas. It is a sign of being a person "of good will," a responsible citizen, and someone willing to obey and thus to serve the wartime nation.[88]

The Ministry of Home Security launched a multi-pronged propaganda offensive in spring 1941 to encourage Britons to take the gas menace, and thus their gas masks, seriously. The War Cabinet Civil Defence Committee had approved of this initiative in late January, and it amounted to, in the words of one of the officials seeking funding for the endeavor:

a carefully devised campaign of increasing publicity designed to familiarise the public with anti-gas precautions. ... As gas has not so far been used by the enemy we are faced with the necessity, firstly of rousing the public to the need for preparation, and secondly, of retaining their interest in correct methods of protecting themselves should the emergency arise.[89]

The campaign to be orchestrated by the Public Relations Department of the Ministry of Home Security had agreed to make use of several different methods of publicity, appearing at regularly timed intervals to keep the topic in public view for a long period. Deploying leaflets, press advertisements, news reel films, and "admonitory" as well as "instructional" posters, the effort began with an £11,000 budget.[90] This helped pay for the printing of 15 million copies of a leaflet titled "What to Do about Gas." The campaign also included posters and reprinted content from the posters as advertisements in the press.[91]

The posters featured a stark new message: "Hitler will send no warning" read one, featuring the official vivid gas mask in contrast to

Figure 5.7 "Hitler will send no warning." Poster for the gas mask
campaign of the spring of 1941. © Imperial War Museum

an earlier poster exhorting the population to "Take Your Gas Mask
Everywhere" that featured only the cardboard box (Fig. 5.7).[92] The goal
of this new poster was to get public attention, and that of the associated
"What to Do about Gas" leaflet to help citizens be better informed about
what to do if faced with a gas raid, from recognizing the warning sound of
the gas rattle, a device that wardens would sound by walking through the
streets, to taking steps to keep food safe. The whole campaign had one
overarching point, which was that poison gas was not a great danger if
one was prepared. It thus repeatedly emphasized, "in your gas mask you
have the best possible protection. ... It is a sure defence if you use it
properly and in time." This required having it fit correctly, taking care of
it, knowing how to put it on quickly, and, above all, carrying it throughout the day and keeping it close at hand at night.[93] At the same time,
papers like the *Daily Telegraph* could, in an article on science and war,
quote the proceedings of the House of Lords, where Lord Mottisone
denounced efforts to get people to carry their gas masks as likely to terrify
the population when anyone with common sense knew that a gas attack
on a breezy day could not possibly do harm. Competing views about gas
mask carrying continued to be aired despite the new campaign.[94]

As part of this latest publicity campaign, Minister of Home Security Herbert Morrison spoke on the radio in March 1941 to reassure his audience in Britain that "against a well-prepared population which knows exactly what to do and does it, gas can be rendered little more than a serious nuisance."[95] Morrison stated that there was not yet a decision to make gas mask carrying legally required, but that the government hoped the population would see it, in contrast to Mottisone, as "common sense." He also announced plans for more gas drills in order to encourage civilians to carry their gas masks at all times. On April 2, the *Daily Mail* featured a photograph illustrating the government's "drive to make Londoners gas mask 'conscious.'" It displayed a car using loud-speakers to ask, "Where Is Your Gas Mask?" on Regent Street in London, where many pedestrians appeared not to have their masks with them. As well as being asked where their own gas masks were, readers were told again of the dangers of not carrying this vital thing: "What would you do if there were a gas attack now?"[96] Such patrols continued in the West End. This may have been among the first signs of a new official effort to call attention to gas mask carrying and maintenance.

The timing of the initiative raises a question: why now, in the spring of 1941, the moment when the worst of the initial aerial raids associated with the Battle of Britain had passed? By the end of March 1941, the intensity of attacks had diminished in terms of location, duration, and damage. There were bodies to count and horrific stories arising from places like Clydebank in Glasgow, but the bombs used had been incendiary and high-explosive devices: The long-anticipated, greatly feared German poison arsenal had not materialized.[97] However, some public forums indicated that Morrison had warned the country that the threat of a gas attack had increased.[98] A possible motive behind the government's campaign was the desire to ask ordinary civilians, who now understood what air war could mean for their lives, to show that they would do their utmost to keep themselves safe by following orders.

Some inhabitants had already begun to take the prospect of a gas raid seriously. Irene Fern Smith, a thirty-nine-year-old wife and mother living in Wolverhampton, who kept a diary for the first half of 1941, began attending Red Cross gas lectures in the middle of January in an effort to be better prepared for her other wartime volunteer work. Her diary entries treated this activity as no more unusual than her comments on the weather, the films she attended, and the presents she bought for her young daughter. By February, however, she finally noted something of what took place at these lectures, where "we were told that the threat of gas is becoming plainer. Told never to go without our Gas Masks from now on. Information has come through from our Secret Service of huge supplies of Gas at the French Ports."[99] Rumors about the use of gas are not surprising, but that Irene Smith attributes them to an official course on how to prepare for gas attacks is significant. Smith's diary does not discuss how she felt about such information or about the gas mask as an object of safety, but she does note when the gas mask became a nuisance because of the several occasions when her daughter was in trouble at school after another child took her gas mask. She notes other rumors about "the likelihood of gas being used in the near future" and that there was more agitation in the press about the need to carry masks always, placing such observations alongside comments on the likelihood of invasion.[100] The diary gives a sense that Smith's attention to gas and these potentially frightening suggestions of chemical raids or invasion was not all-consuming. One week she skipped the gas lecture to attend a performance by the London Symphony Orchestra, but she was pleased to note that she answered 85 percent of the questions correctly in an examination on her anti-gas training.[101] Yet the government worried that too many citizens lacked Smith's commitment to civil defense.

One way to engage members of the public was to let them experience a mock gas raid themselves. In early April, a "Gas Drill Test" at Esher (Surrey) was extensively publicized, including being recorded by Mass Observation, and featured in a British Pathé newsreel as a "Mock Gas Attack." The nearly two-minute silent film shows how ordinary scenes can be transformed by the release of (tear) gas and the wearing of masks. We first see a group of boys putting on their gas masks before the film cuts to a group of women in masks beside a bus stop. Another scene shows smoke, or visible white-colored gas, escaping from a home as well as from a stand pipe in the road. The next scene cuts to a warden in full anti-gas protection, including the civilian duty respirator, using the gas rattle to warn of an attack. The scene then pans along an ordinary street, where three girls, all in masks, are pushing a wheelbarrow full of scrap metal, then shifts to men in their civilian duty respirators, to a woman and a small boy, both in their masks, outside a store, and finally to a police officer directing traffic in his mask. The next bit of footage shows a little boy, surrounded by women in masks, being helped to pump the bellows for a baby's anti-gas helmet, and then it cuts to a woman in a white uniform, presumably a nurse, holding a baby in an anti-gas helmet, with an unmasked woman and child beside her. There is even a scene of three men in what appear to be uniforms, demonstrating the brand-new mask for those unable to use the standard one; they walk along manipulating the bellows for these special and particularly odd-looking masks. By including a variety of ages, genders, and masks, this film asserts the

Figure 5.8 During the April 5, 1941 mock gas attack drill in Esher, Surrey, air raid wardens wear the new gas masks designed for the elderly and those with lung complaints. A. Hudson/Stringer/Hulton Archive/ Getty Images

willingness of an entire community to behave responsibly. Such behavior was not meant to be exceptional, but typical (Figs. 5.8 and 5.9).

That this filmed drill was carefully staged emerges clearly in the records of Mass Observation, which sent three observers to view two tests in Surrey, one at Esher and another one at East Molesey (just outside Greater London). In its evaluation of the entire episode, the report comments that "the photographers added unreality by getting people to pose for them and indeed moulding the whole shape of the occasion." Yet not everyone responded in predictable ways: "a large number of children were present at both tests and found them great fun. But some mothers pulled their children home when the test began, apparently frightened that the children might be adversely affected."[102] In both areas, a sense of the episode being artificial also came from the fact that the drills started later than scheduled, which made participants uncertain about what to do. In East Moseley, no wardens were out sounding the gas rattles after the first tear gas was released, and it was

Figure 5.9 Women wait at a bus stop during the mock gas attack drill in Esher, Surrey, in April 1941. George W. Hales/Stringer/Hulton Archive/Getty Images

similarly unclear when the tests were over. As a result, the Mass Observation reporter noted, "This rather confused and random organisation accentuated an already present tendency on the part of the civilians to treat the whole thing as a sort of free show and great fun."[103] There is a marked contrast between the sense of "fun" at a "free show" and the lack of organization for what was, at least in intent, a drill for preparing for chemical warfare. This emerges vividly in the account of mothers who kept their children home for their own safety, both physical and emotional.

"Gas preparedness" was the intent of the entire spring 1941 campaign, but the government always had to balance the seriousness with which it wanted the population to take the prospect of chemical war with the need to prevent them from feeling fear or panic. The government wished to motivate people of all ages, genders, classes, and life circumstances to carry the state-sponsored object designed to keep them safe. The sense of fun during the gas test rather than fear displayed by a population that had just survived devastating air raids appears powerfully in some of the news reel footage and photographs of these public gas drills. But this led to condemnation of the entire exercise as being beside the point. The Mass

Observation reporters were brutal in their evaluation of the behavior of some of the participants: "as for preparing people against gas attacks this mock raid was an absolute fiasco; but considered as an opportunity for idle middle-class women to show off their importance, as an opportunity for photographers to photograph ... it was perfect."[104]

In this critique, the observers see a potentially serious exercise descend into spectacle, which the behavior of these women encapsulated. The attack on women of a certain class is interesting but not surprising. On the one hand, there was an implicit sense, while the gas mask was in development, that its effectiveness required the proper attitude as much as an understanding of its value. Civil defense overall, and the gas mask in particular, were conceived of as something that responsible middle-class inhabitants would grasp but that working-class members of society might struggle to adopt. Yet civil defense campaigns also targeted the "idle," singling out middle-class women as those likely to thwart rules that guaranteed equality of sacrifice and working for the good of all, whether by trying to subvert rationing or by refusing to accept evacuees. The wartime state asked a lot of women, but this also created opportunities to critique them [105]

Government officials sought to balance motivating the population to take seriously the directive to be prepared (always having the gas mask at the ready) with not alarming them unduly. The spectacle of the gas drill as bringing out people to gawk and laugh also had the effect of normalizing the gas mask. It could become part of ordinary life. What the government desired was the reaction of the three-and-a-half-year-old boy described in the *Daily Mirror*, who insisted on testing his gas mask when a portable gas van came to Wembley. When he left the chamber, he asked, "Where is the gas[,] daddy?" The boy's reaction was proof that the child's gas mask was efficient and safe because he didn't even know he needed it.[106] The real proof of such tests would be that members of the public responded by increasingly carrying their gas masks and demonstrating their willingness explicitly to be part of the war effort.

Other elements of the government campaign now started to appear in the media such as the *Manchester Guardian*, including advertisements that made it clear that the response to the sound of the gas rattle was to put on your gas mask wherever you found yourself. One image featured a middle-class couple putting on their masks.[107] Other advertisements directly addressed mothers by holding them responsible for "mak[ing] sure your family have their gas masks with them night & day." The illustration above these words featured a woman using the baby's anti-gas protective helmet.[108] When devising this set of "Hints for Mothers" as part of the campaign, officials concluded that since there was not space to convey the full set of instructions, it was crucial to give emergency guidelines. Even though the ARP advice was that during a gas alert "no woman and her baby should be out of doors" and the best thing would be to get to a shelter before putting the baby in the anti-gas helmet, the advertisement instead urged that the mother learn to put her baby in a helmet anywhere and that she allow toddlers to practice putting on their own gas masks. The final advice was to "first put on your own mask, then you will be better able to help baby."[109] The message, under the heading "What to Do about Gas," was clear in every variation of the campaign: Always have your gas mask with you and ready to use.

Internal records show that the government officials working on this campaign paid attention to every aspect of the messaging. They developed slogans and made sure that the illustrations accurately reflected the proper way to carry the gas mask, remove it from its case, and wear it. As they were drafting one set of these designs, Gertrude Williams, a member of the Public Relations Department and the official who seemed to be in charge of this aspect of the campaign, wrote back to the designer with a suggestion:

> Could you persuade the artist to take the look of terror out of the lady's eyes? We are anxious to convince the Public that there is no need for any apprehension if you have your gas-mask with you and know how to put it on. As this lady is putting her mask on we should like her to be shown wearing an expression of calm confidence.[110]

Altering the woman's facial expressions was a key change for a poster that was going to replace the "Hitler will send no warning" message on the London Underground and other venues, and it speaks to the purpose of the gas mask campaign as being about the managing of emotions. The gas mask was meant to instill feelings of safety, tranquility, and faith in the object and the government that stood behind it. The portrait of the lady in this poster, like that of the man beside her, could show no fear (Figs. 5.10a, b, 5.11, and 5.12).

Newspapers also promoted the government's view of civilian gas masks by reprinting specially devised quizzes. The first newspaper gas raid quiz appeared in the *Daily Express* on June 17. Each quiz was carefully vetted by ARP experts before it was released to the newspapers. In a draft for the first quiz, a correct answer stated that the "ordinary gas mask issued to civilians gives complete protection for twelve hours against any gas that can be used against us." In subsequent drafts, this draft text was crossed out and beside it was the handwritten message, "No, on no account must anything be said on this point." A note attached to the file made it clear that, as far as the administrators of civil

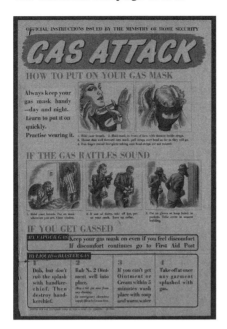

Figure 5.10a Instructions on "How to Put on Your Gas Mask" from a 1941 poster. Image and permission from The National Archives

Figure 5.10b Close-up detail from "How to Put on Your Gas Mask," a 1941 informational poster. Image and permission from The National Archives

Figure 5.11 "If the Gas Rattle Sounds," draft of a 1941 poster. Image and permission from The National Archives

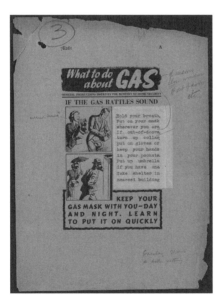

Figure 5.12 "What to Do about Gas," draft version of a 1941 poster. Image and permission from The National Archives

defense were concerned, the public must be confident that gas masks would work without needing details about the number of hours for which anti-gas protection was viable.[111]

All of the quizzes suggested that Britons must understand the reasons for gas masks rather than giving any practical information about how to use them. For example, one of the questions was whether or not a soldier or male ARP worker should give up his gas mask to a woman who lacked hers during an attack. The answer was a resounding no, for neither soldiers nor ARP workers were allowed to give up their gas masks, and thus the lesson for women was clear: They had to carry their own gas masks always. Similarly, another question asked what to do with a young child who was frightened in a gas raid and refused to put on the mask. The answer was to put the onus on the caretaker of the child to take action far in advance of a gas raid. If a terrified child struggled during an attack, "it might be too late then to calm his fears ... his struggles might make it impossible to keep gas from reaching his eyes, nose and mouth." Parents clearly needed to take time now to get children used to their gas masks: "wear your own mask and pretend to your child that it is a game ... and his fear will vanish." The clearest indication of the value of the gas mask lay in the final question, which asked what would keep Hitler from using gas, the correct response being "the knowledge that every citizen is fully protected against gas" (Fig. 5.13).[112]

Other gas raid quizzes followed this pattern. An internal government list of the main venues for all twenty of these quizzes showed the range of newspapers from national tabloids like the *Daily Express* and *Daily Mail* to more left-wing publications like the *Daily Herald*, to regional papers such as the *Yorkshire Post, Sheffield Star, Cardiff Echo*, and *Manchester Evening News*, as well as Scottish papers in Aberdeen, Dundee, Edinburgh, and Glasgow.[113] Notably, there were no quizzes in papers in Northern Ireland, although advertisements that reprinted the poster "What to Do in Case of Gas Attack" were sent to many of the same venues as the quizzes and also to the *Belfast Telegraph*.[114] The content emphasized the need for everyone to learn how to behave in a gas attack. Gas Raid Quiz No. 6, for instance, addressed the question of old and frail people, noting that they were not in greater danger from gas than others, but might become "flustered" during a sudden attack, and that they should therefore practice using the gas mask regularly. The issue of women expecting men to give up their gas masks made a reappearance here in a comment suggesting that every woman must decide for herself whether she would accept a man's offer of a gas mask and urging women to imagine their husbands in such a predicament: "wouldn't you feel ...

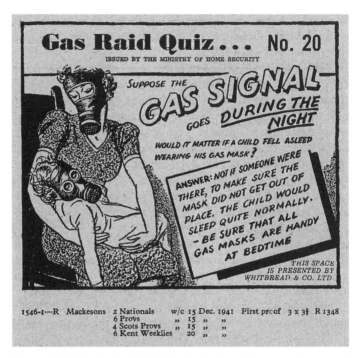

Figure 5.13 Draft of a 1941 "Gas Raid Quiz." Image and permission from The National Archives

that no woman should allow a man to risk his life for her?"[115] The solution was always the same: Women should carry their own masks.

Orchestrated efforts to persuade the public of the importance and value of the gas mask also made use of radio and film. These took the form in April of a BBC radio show in which listeners received step-by-step instructions on how to put on a gas mask with one hand.[116] In May 1941, the government started to develop two distinct films on anti-gas protection. One was a silent "training" film entitled simply *Take Care of Your Gas Mask*, while the other was a longer scripted film, with sound, entitled *The Guardian of Your Life*. The first film received approval for the script in May, with the loan of a "half dozen civilian masks, one baby's mask, two civilian duty masks" to the Marylebone Film Studio.[117] After an initial screening for representatives from Porton Down as well as the ARP Department, A. A. Sargent sent a memorandum detailing the collective critique:

It was decided that the scene dealing with the baby's helmet, in which a doll has been used, should be retaken with a live baby – this presents many difficulties, but methods of doing it were agreed upon. Apart from this, Mr. Davies, Major Martin, and I were all of the opinion that the film promised to turn out to be highly successful, Major Martin's comment being that it was much better than his best expectations.[118]

The difficulties of filming a baby in the gas helmet, and the potential solutions, were left frustratingly unspecified, but it is clear that efforts to simplify and spread knowledge about official anti-gas protection, and to use the power of mass media to distribute these ideas, formed a crucial part of the campaign of 1941.

The enthusiasm for this new media push and indications of the timeliness of *Take Care of Your Gas Mask* were partly associated with a new effort to inspect gas masks. As the war progressed, government officials grew concerned that if masks did not fit properly or were not being properly maintained, then they would be rendered useless. Thus, even if the film were not to receive widespread public distribution in cinemas, it would still prove useful to train wardens – the local and personal conduit between the officialdom of ARP and the British public. As Major Martin, one of the critics, summarized:

The film ... brings the very best demonstration directly before every individual Warden, and even directly before members of the public – in considerable numbers even with our own machinery alone, and it is hoped in still larger numbers through the co-operation of the Ministry of Information. It should represent a very big step forward in the training of both Wardens and of the public.[119]

A further memorandum on the film commented on the need to make adjustments in women's clothing in particular. Instead of showing how a shawl might aid in anti-gas protection, the officials decided to assume that "in parts of the country where shawls are used women will no doubt do it for themselves, while for other parts of the country there is little to be gained in including it in the film." Furthermore, while no hats appear in the cinematic version of the drill, the official report suggested that this might require a further note to women because their "hats cannot always be removed as quickly as men's," thus delaying their ability to put on their masks.[120] One proposed change was a new title card for the silent film: "Spectacles off – and hats, if you are wearing them." The instructional film's title cards included five basic points, starting with "Carry your gas mask everywhere" and adding notes about practicing putting it on and wearing it as well as treating the gas mask with "great care." The final point emphasized the theme of the original campaign: "Remember that ... HITLER WILL GIVE NO WARNING." These words would be the ultimate takeaway from the film.[121]

Decisions about the final script for the longer sound film prompted discussion within the ARP administration. The storyline would feature two men: Mr. Jones, representing the father of a family who did not take anti-gas protection seriously, and Mr. Wilson, a keen ARP warden determined to set Jones straight on the necessity and utility of the family's gas masks. Jones needed to be a family man, with a young child and small baby, in order to provide opportunities to illustrate the correct use of the full range of gas masks for ordinary civilians. The film makes no attempt at character development or plot or at reflecting the differing needs among various classes. Instead, it is one of many wartime artifacts that takes the white suburban middle class as its intended audience, with the assumption that others will identify with their story. This tells us something about expectations for who was willing and able to use the gas mask, thereby showing their enthusiastic participation in the national civil defense effort.

The representation of the Jones family nonchalantly indicates their middle-class accoutrements and values. In the script, young Johnny is described as "playing with a railway set," while the actual film uses a little girl playing with her doll. Disrupting an idyllic scene of a child at play, Wilson asks to see the gas mask carton and then demonstrates how to test the mask and what it would look like if incorrectly put on. Since "children grow out of their masks," adjustments must be made. The child readily follows the instructions about breathing in and out carefully. There is no indication that this child is anything but well-mannered, attentive, and obedient.

Then Mrs. Jones steps in with her further worry as a conscientious mother: "I wonder Mr. Wilson whether you would add to your kindness by telling us just how Baby's mask should be used. We're not very sure about it." Mr. Wilson obliges and carefully shows how happy the baby can be in the helmet. Given that the bellows attached to the helmet must be pumped twelve times to clear air and then steadily pumped at forty strokes per minute, the script is scrupulous about how this must be shown:

Close view of Wilson as he picks up helmet and baby. He pumps quickly and steadily.

General view of group. Wilson is holding the helmet in his arms and pumping steadily. The others are watching him closely.

The level of detail does not overwhelm the family because all participants are intent, alert, and ready to take on this task once they understand it (Fig. 5.14).

Figure 5.14 Still showing parents being shown how to use the baby's anti-gas protective helmet from the 1941 film *The Guardian of Your Life*. © Imperial War Museum

In another indication of its middle-class target audience, the film closes with an interlude involving the young female servant, Mary, who wears eyeglasses. After she "shyly" approaches him, Wilson explains that she needs special glasses to wear with a gas mask, which are available from the local council. Throughout the film, the state is shown as benevolent actor – not only bestowing the gas mask, but also ensuring that it will provide safety for all ages and despite challenges like poor eyesight. After Wilson leaves the family, having demonstrated the proper use of their gas masks and given them a leaflet explaining all that he has done, Mrs. Jones says to Mary, "Well, that has been very interesting and most useful. We shall have to try to remember all Mr. Wilson told us, because it's very important indeed. *Think Mary, our gas masks might save our lives!*"[122] The final scene begins with a workman pasting the "Hitler will send no warning" poster on a brick wall. There is a quick cutaway to a sky filled with planes and then, just as abruptly, to a hand turning a gas rattle as the bright white letters "GAS!" appear individually across a variety of scenes.

Another aspect of this new push to carry the gas mask can be observed in the forms of specific approaches to young people and children. These included the strange phenomenon advertised as the "Masked Ball [1941 Style]." Nine dance halls in London, Birmingham, Glasgow, and Brighton hosted "gas-mask dancing," offering reduced admission to anyone carrying a gas mask.[123] Newspaper columnists chimed in, one suggesting that filmmakers get leading actresses to "wear the cutest gas mask cases" in films so "that pretty soon there wouldn't be a woman in England who'd be seen without her gas mask."[124]

A government memorandum issued in April informed teachers that they should not only tell children to carry their gas masks to school but also ensure that they performed regular gas drills.[125] There is evidence that educators even in isolated areas of the nation took this seriously. In August, the principal teacher at Park Public Elementary School in County Londonderry asked the Minister of Education for Northern Ireland for assistance. Although the school had received instructions about training the eighteen children currently attending the school in the use of gas masks, "gas masks have not yet been supplied to the children of the school … and the parents … are anxious they should have them."[126] Getting children to carry gas masks, however, was not always easy. One schoolteacher reported success through telling students that only those carrying gas masks would be allowed to the victory party.[127] For those hoping to persuade children at home to use their masks, Mrs. Creswick Atkinson of the WVS, in a broadcast entitled "The Care of Children in Wartime," recommended that mothers reassure children by wearing their own masks: "make a game of it, calling it 'Mummy's Funny Face.'"[128]

The 1941 campaign insisted that gas mask carrying mattered, and that while it required some exertion, those who rejected the gas mask were questioning the value of the war effort. The new spur to carry gas masks elicited responses that did not just see the toting of the gas mask as being a matter of common sense. Popular reaction in papers such as the *Daily Mail* criticized those not carrying gas masks, with one letter to the editor urging that passengers should not be allowed to use public transport without their gas masks. Another suggested that every policeman should be allowed to collect a small fine – possibly to go to a charity – from anyone not carrying a gas mask.[129] A letter to the *Manchester Guardian* recommended the random release of tear gases to drive the message home because nothing short of a demonstration would change behavior.[130] In the *Picture Post*, a letter writer from Leicester attacked the entire campaign: "the Ministry of Home Security must have paper and money to waste. They issue posters showing hands holding a gas mask with the words, 'Hitler will send no warning.'" The public saw this as silly. If the government were serious about this, then it would have to make it a "punishable offence to leave gas masks at home." In the factory where the letter writer worked, there were notices encouraging everyone to carry gas masks but few complied, which suggested that the only solution was "to make it the law to do so. Pamphlets are no good. They are burnt. Radio is turned off when A.R.P hints are broadcast. Posters are ignored."[131] How then was the message to be delivered? The hope was to find some means of making the gas mask seamlessly a part of everyday life.

The "Hitler will send no warning" slogan became one of the iconic emblems of this campaign, but did it resonate? Having launched this effort, the government turned to Mass Observation to see whether the posters, in particular, had been effective. A report on the "Gas Mask Posters" was rapidly produced and issued on July 21, even though the cover noted that the campaign still had four weeks to run. The summation of the report compared two posters – "Warning" and "Gas Attack," representative of the admonitory and instructional efforts – of which 400,000 copies had appeared. Having investigated the campaign's effects in London and three provincial areas, it found little difference among the classes who noticed the poster. Still, of the 50 percent of the surveyed who had noticed the "Warning" poster, many liked it – something that was not true for the "Gas Attack" poster. Among the critiques of the latter poster were that it was too ordinary, that it had too many words printed in too small a font, and that several aspects were "unsuitable." For instance, green was associated with safety, and thus a poster about danger (i.e., a gas attack) should be in red. Other people found the idea of the man and woman "smiling" to be unsuitable. Mainly, the report concluded, the impact of the entire campaign had "*so far* not been considerable," but the larger problem was that the government was trying to shift people's stubborn behavior. A more emotional appeal might work, but at this stage in the war, with a lull in air raids in particular, the "strong mental resistance to the idea of poison gas" and the reluctance to carry gas masks seemed deeply rooted among citizens.[132]

Individual diarists for Mass Observation had their own personal reflections on the campaign. In Headingley, in north Leeds, a twenty-two-year-old office worker expressed her disgruntlement: The gas tests recently had been "entirely inadequate." After some substance had been scattered, anyone who wished could walk through a white cloud in their mask, but only a few hundred took advantage of this chance as it "was insufficiently publicized. ... If the Government are trying to make us gas-conscious they should do it properly or not at all."[133] A thirty-one-year-old shop assistant in Essex found out about the campaign by reading an advertisement in the *News of the World* in May 1941, and found it a good poster, "but it misses out some very important points." It should, in his opinion, have emphasized that the most important thing to do was to "take cover." In his view, "the campaign against gas, at least as conducted by the Press, has been more calculated to create a scare than to get people to do what is wanted."[134] This observer saw the campaign as orchestrated by the media, not the government, and as failing to achieve the intended purpose. The overall summary by Mass Observation on gas mask carrying and morale suggested that an uptick in aerial attacks, rather than any orchestrated campaign, prompted greater numbers to carry their gas masks.[135] The challenge was to cultivate perhaps just enough fear to alter behavior without causing undue alarm, depression, or anxiety.

Officials knew from the start that gas masks would work only if those possessing them checked them regularly, made sure they fit, cared for them, and, above all, carried them. The new posters, new leaflets, new public tests, and new films all hyped the same message: The guardian of your life worked only if you treated it properly. Thus, gas mask use became a sign that you accepted your duty to participate in the state war effort. It was designed to protect your body and help you to manage undesirable emotions such as panic or terror by making you feel safe. The knowledge contained in the Mass Observation reports – that few paid much attention to the gas masks and that the campaign did little to change their minds – must have been disappointing to these officials.

Conclusion

The Second World War was the heyday of the civilian gas mask. After its trial run in September 1938, the months leading up to Britain's official entry into the war saw scientists frantically working to perfect anti-gas protection for infants. When the war came, they were largely ready for the practical aspects of helping civilians to face the potential for chemical war with gas masks in hand. The apparatus of ARP meant that distribution of anti-gas protection would come at the level of the neighborhood, an object bestowed by the benevolent state through the local community.

Yet the state seemed unprepared for the variety of ways in which the public might respond to this gift. It had clearly made no provisions to individualize either the object or its basic case, so a new commercial field of gas mask cases for sale in a variety of styles emerged. More shocking was the outright refusal and neglect of this gift. While conscientious objectors might reject the thing itself, others were careless with this object bestowed by the government: gas masks were left in trams, trains, buses, shops, workplaces, and schools. Most frustratingly for those orchestrating civil defense, some people simply could not seem to grasp the basic message that if a poison gas could appear without warning, then the only solution was to have the mask with you always. Whenever you left the house, underneath your bed at night, taken to your shelter when the bombs began to fall – the gas mask had to be there.

The significance of this object for the state, despite there being no chemical weapons attacks in Britain, reveals the extent to which the gas mask could be seen not simply as protecting bodies or even managing emotions but as curating wartime identity. It could serve to mark out those who were willing and presumably able to help the nation cope with the potential and actual traumas of total war. As discussed here in regard to anti-gas protection for the population under five, and as will be shown more fully in the next chapter, there were limits to where the gas mask went in Britain's wartime empire. Yet within the United Kingdom, the presence of gas masks and the commitment to persuading the population of their utility reveals the ongoing militarization of individual bodies. It shows the ways in which civilians regardless of their contributions were brought ever more fully into the calculations required to wage modern war.

6   Facing Wartime
The Civilian Gas Mask's Rise and Fall, 1941–1945

Introduction

The gas awareness campaign launched in the spring of 1941 had encouraged civilians to appreciate their gas masks and to embrace the government's broader regulations for civil defense against a potential chemical attack. It is clear from personal responses, such as those recorded by Mass Observation diarists, that the campaign had limited success. In addition to the visible evidence that large numbers of people did not carry their civilian respirators, there continued to be public criticism of the gas mask. Nonetheless, the government remained committed to gas masks as the centerpiece of civil defense, continuing to inspect and replace them and to debate access to gas masks for specific populations until the end of the war.

Its insertion into the life of the nation continued as the active phase of the gas mask campaign waned. To some extent, the gas mask's firm establishment across popular culture endured, as it appeared in the official gas raid quizzes in newspapers through 1941, in humorous songs, and even in ongoing gas raid public drills, such as one in Scotland in September 1941.[1] In November 1941, in an article aimed at persuading young mothers to leave their children in the care of day nurseries so that they could take up war work, reporter Elizabeth Rowley touted not only the virtues of the light and airy babies' room in a nursery and the healthy food and the collection of toys, but also the fact that all children "get regular gas mask 'drill,'" something that they would continue to experience as schoolchildren.[2]

The rhetoric of the 1941 campaign to urge everyone to carry the gas mask everywhere suggested that this one object embodied what it meant to be prepared for total war. Yet, almost a year after the public admonishments and ubiquitous appeals to "always carry it with you," the British government had to confront some discomfiting realities about the chain of supplies that provided the resources – especially rubber – required to produce and maintain civilian anti-gas protection. The state never backed away from this object. It neither stopped giving babies' anti-gas helmets to newborns nor inspecting and repairing civilian gas masks until the bitter end. However, the government ceased to suggest that people needed to have gas masks at all times when out and about. What British subjects in the metropole and the empire made of the gas mask as the war's devastation spread sheds light on its centrality to the story of how Britain faced the horrors of modern war.

The Gas Mask and Wartime Popular Culture

Although gas mask carrying never became the law of the land, the gas mask itself became ever more deeply embedded in an array of popular culture, independent of government-sponsored efforts throughout the war. Even when it was mocked or especially when treated irreverently, it was present. The 1941 campaign aimed to get people to take it seriously, but perhaps making people aware of it was equally important. Since its introduction, elements of popular culture had used the gas mask as a source of humor, often dark-edged. In the world of popular song, the object of terror turned into an object of fun as early as 1939. The Scottish music hall performer David Willis, who had a record-setting wartime run in Glasgow, is most closely associated with a song written by John Kerr, "My Wee Gas Mask." By utilizing Scottish terms, it calls attention to Scotland specifically, but it also showcases the gas mask as a potentially unifying object:

> In ma wee gas mask,
> Im working oot a plan
> When aw the weans imagine that im just a boogey man
> The girls all smile
> And bring their friends to sae
> The nicest looking warden in the ARP[3]

The song continues to make fun of various ARP measures, but here it lays out one of the oft-repeated humorous aspects of wearing a gas mask: All the masks were identical and so everyone looked the same in them, something easily employed for sinister effect in a mystery novel and for comic relief in a song.[4] If the "weans" reacted with fear by imagining the "boogey man," one could equally claim that the mask could make the male warden mysteriously attractive. More tellingly, wearing the gas mask made it irrelevant who was the "nicest looking warden in the ARP," as it effectively camouflaged every individual facial feature. There is a whole subset of jokes that link the gas mask and the blackout, and at the end of this song, the narrating voice recounts that during a blackout, he heard a woman cry and offered, "I will save your life," but then, "Imagine the shocker I had got When I found it was me wife." In the dark as in the mask, the disappointment of not being a hero to an attractive stranger disappeared into the act of saving – as it turned out – only one's own wife.[5]

Thus, by the time George Formby was performing one of his wartime hits, "I Did What I Could with My Gas Mask," in April 1941, he was in a line of voices that had turned a potentially fearsome object designed to protect civilians against a war of aero-chemical annihilation into something humorous. As one of the biggest stars of the 1930s, the "cheeky chappie" sang silly songs accompanied often by his ukulele, and he performed regularly to boost morale during the Second World War. Some of his other wartime song releases include "Frank on His Tank," "Thirty Thirsty Sailors," "Sally the Salvage Queen," and "Guarding the Home of the Home Guard," but his ode to his gas mask released at the same time as the government campaign to encourage gas mask carrying is worth a closer look.

> Now I'm getting very fond of my gasmask I declare,
> It hardly ever leaves my side.
> I sling it on my back and I take it everywhere,
> It even comes to bed at night.
> It's been a real good pal to me I must confess
> And helped me out of many a mess.
>
> My sister had a lot of socks to mend,
> So she gave me a fat bouncing baby to tend,
> And when I felt it leaking at one end,
> Well I did what I could with my gas mask.
>
> I bought a farm because I like fresh air,
> At milking time I try to do my share.
> And when I found the bucket wasn't there
> I did what I could with my gasmask
> …
>
> For years I've courted Anabella Price
> And always found her just as cold as ice
> Until one night the lass forgot her ma's advice
> Then I did what I could with my gasmask.[6]

One could of course overanalyze these lyrics; they are certainly in keeping with a long tradition of bawdy British ballads right through to the humor found in the contemporaneous music hall. Yet the repurposing of the gas mask in these lyrics shows its thorough integration into all aspects of domestic life: it can now serve as a baby's diaper, as a milking bucket, and for some to-be-imagined sexual purpose in the final stanza. The object whose value now lies in its not being needed until a chemical weapons attack contributes to making basic aspects of domestic, bodily life easier.

By the summer of 1941, the gas mask campaign was well underway and had spread out to include informing the public about the varying kinds of poison gas as well as the inner workings of the gas mask. Yet a few voices expressed their own vision of a world that could just possibly exist beyond the mask. In the poem "Midsummer Madness," appearing in the *Manchester Guardian* on the longest day of the year, the call of spring exerts so strong a pull that the writer wants

> ... to wear no hat at all
> And just as few clothes as I dare
> And most of all, I want to sling
> That foolish gas mask far away;
> For I would bet you anything
> That Jerry will not call to-day.
>
> So if by chance I should be seen
> Blithe, unencumbered, sans a mask
> Know this ye men of graver mien –
> That none shall take me now to task

For this one day, despite the war, the poet wants to experience nature, and the most vivid emblem of the rejection of wartime reality is to do so without a gas mask.[7]

This did not stop ongoing efforts in a variety of media to continue to extol the necessity of being prepared to face chemical weapons, using humor, song, verse, images, and objects. Exhibitions to inform the public on the continuing need to always have a gas mask opened in London and thirteen other locales across the United Kingdom, including Manchester. An editorial commenting on this development in the *Manchester Guardian* reiterated the official message: Everyone needed to carry the gas mask as well as to be an informed citizen. It emphasized that while gas could be used by the enemy at any time, it was "not a killing weapon." One could escape the gas provided one had a respirator. In the event of a chemical attack, "those without masks will be the enemy's allies as well as his victims."[8] The gas mask thus remained an emblem of loyalty as well as safety.

The Limits of the Gas Mask in Wartime

While the public consumed the spectacle of gas masks throughout 1941, gas mask designers at Porton Down reported being generally pleased by the performance updates that they received. The materials were lasting as expected, and gas masks being inspected were holding up to the wear and tear of civilian life, perhaps (ironically) because many were not carrying them about. However, if millions of people carried their respirators throughout the day, as the government hoped and as many schoolchildren did, since most schools required pupils to do so in order to attend, then the likelihood of damage increased. The greatest concern at Porton Down, however, focussed on ensuring that people had masks that fit and therefore worked. This led to proposals in April 1941 to visit a selection of schools, factories, and homes to see that this crucial aspect of the gas mask was not being neglected.[9] The government's investment in the gas mask was undiminished despite the lack of chemical munitions in any of the attacks on Britain thus far, and the inspection of gas masks remained a concern throughout the remainder of the war, recounted in reports covering six-month periods until 1944.[10] Given the damage found in respirators carried by schoolchildren, the government decided to replace gas masks for those in "grant aided" (publicly funded) schools, provided the damage was due to ordinary wear and tear. When this was announced, some headmasters from private schools demanded that their pupils have their masks reserviced or replaced free of charge as well.[11]

Some remained ambivalent about having gas masks altogether. At the end of 1941, Bertram Pickard reflected in *The Friend* on how English Quakers should engage with civil defense. His essay was reprinted as a pamphlet in January 1942. Echoing earlier statements about the challenges that participating in such activities posed for pacifists, Pickard summed up the dilemma that gas mask use was not strictly about the individual: "It would be particularly unfortunate … for Friends to lay themselves open to the charge that as pacifists they were unnecessarily endangering the lives of their fellow citizens through negligence or wilful defiance of a law where no vital principle is at stake." He then explained:

I have the impression that the great majority of Friends would feel it right to carry their gas mask if only for fear (and this applies specially to women) that others, better prepared, would insist upon lending theirs in the event of danger. Some well-concerned Friends felt very strongly that this was another of those cases where pacifists should set an example in observance of law, just because they might feel obliged to break the law in other particulars, and in order not to embarrass, or even endanger, those who would be bearing the burden of responsibility in the event of the use of gas – which if it came, would almost certainly come without warning and when least expected.[12]

Pickard concluded that the issue should be left to the individual conscience to determine. In practice, some Quakers served as civil defense wardens or fire watchers and dutifully carried their gas masks.

Government officials also debated throughout the war whether to provide gas masks to individuals who were not part of the national community. Britain interned enemy aliens, including Jewish refugees, on the Isle of Man. A year into the war, the commandant of one of the internment camps wrote to the Home Office to ask about internees' access to gas masks. The problem was that few British residents who were sent to the island brought their gas masks with them, and those coming from overseas never had masks at all. As air raids intensified on the mainland, concern grew about the supply on the island, where not everyone had a respirator. ARP officials were adamant that no gas masks should go to internees until the general population of the Isle of Man possessed them and, moreover, that individual internees should pay for new masks if they had already been given them before being imprisoned.[13] In February 1941, Dame Joanna Cruickshank, the commandant of Rushen Internment Camp for Women on the Isle of Man, wrote to Sir Ernest Holderness of the Home Office stating that the local government had no interest in supplying the aliens with gas masks, so the national government needed to step in.[14] Despite other officials in the Home Office agreeing that gas masks had to be provided in part because not safeguarding this population would embarrass the government, the actual provision of gas masks took until the spring of 1942 because of disagreement over who would pay for them.[15] This example shows the ongoing challenge facing the government: It wanted to showcase its generosity and commitment to protecting the vulnerable for political as well as practical reasons, but it was reluctant in the midst of war to outlay the funds to do so if it meant including those under the control of, but not belonging to, the nation.[16]

An even greater challenge emerged relatively abruptly in the summer of 1942, when the Japanese advances in East Asia disrupted Britain's rubber supply.[17] A new policy on gas mask carrying but not on gas masks themselves emerged quickly. In July 1942, the government decided that "for the time being they would not ask citizens to carry gas masks day by day, but to care for them, to have them tested … regularly, and to have them always readily available."[18] Herbert Morrison, the Home Secretary, elaborated on the shift in policy in the Commons, suggesting that the government had been considering the recommendation "that every good citizen should carry his or her gas mask," but adding that he "was afraid that if the carrying of gas masks were conclusive proof of good citizenship … we should have come to the conclusion that there were not too many good citizens." Given the new shortages of rubber and the adequate supply of gas masks, the government had a new message: "We do not ask you to carry gas masks day by day. … But we would add this, that at home, or wherever your gas mask is, you should know where it is" and how to use it.[19]

To some extent, we can see this announcement as the government taking advantage of the genuine rubber shortage to back away from its failed campaign to persuade everyone to carry a gas mask. If this was meant to be the mark of support for the war effort – of being a good citizen – then the result would be alarming. In a face-saving gesture, the government did not back away from inspecting and repairing and giving out new masks, but indicated a desire to preserve existing supplies. Now the government promised closely to monitor the international situation, and if it felt it necessary to shift policy, then it would revise the public guidance as needed.[20] The public was told simply, "No Need to Carry a Gas Mask."[21]

Even despite the reduced and uncertain supply of rubber, which would surely impede efforts to meet the promise of providing every citizen with a gas mask, the government nonetheless continued to discuss protection for those unable to use the regular gas mask. In November 1942, Morrison wrote to Sir John Anderson, whom he had succeeded as Minister for Home Security, asking for his help with the following dilemma: Should the government use its limited rubber supply to provide special gas masks for "helpless hospital patients and those with heavily bandaged heads?" This segment of the populace could not wear the regular gas mask and needed a newly devised respirator that used bellows and was more akin to the baby's anti-gas protective helmet. Morrison continued, "I fully appreciate the possible danger of the weakening of public morale if, in the event of gas attack, there should be no provision for the helpless sick and wounded, but in view of the extreme stringency of the rubber situation, I felt very considerable hesitation in approving these proposals." Anderson soon replied that he was "definitely in favour of making the necessary provision, despite the existing acute rubber shortage." The commitment of the state to pursue protection for these special cases, and perhaps above all to be *seen* doing so as part of a commitment to protecting everyone, took precedence over concerns about limited resources.[22]

The government's reversal of its attitude toward the carrying of gas masks led to a policy of continuing "gas exercises" for civil defense personnel but halting the "gas tests" designed for civilians generally. This decision revolved around the question of "whether or not we are insisting that the public should carry their respirators continually." Once this was no longer the case, "one can scarcely risk or justify taking unawares any collection of persons ... with a gas test."[23] Adding to the growing confusion, J. B. S. Haldane, who despite his earlier role as outspoken critic of government ARP policy was now the chair of the National ARP Co-ordinating Committee, had, when addressing civil defense workers, advised everyone in Britain to keep carrying a gas mask in case of a possible attack until Hitler was defeated.[24] Despite these conflicting messages, the government tried to keep encouraging civilians to *preserve* rather than carry their gas masks, suggesting they should not become complacent. In April 1943, Morrison reiterated that the danger of gas attacks had not passed and that the population should remain vigilant about knowing where their gas mask was and how to use it.[25]

The possibility of Germany using poison gas militarily reappeared in the press in the spring and summer of 1943. Public statements about warning Russia that Germany might be planning to use gas on the Eastern Front made the issue of renewed concern that spring, especially if one read the tabloid press, in which the *Daily Mail* sensationally reported "Hitler Is About to Use Poison Gas."[26] Reports suggested that if the Axis used gas even solely on troops, the Allies had promised to retaliate and that this could escalate into an exchange of chemical arms. The *Daily Mail* quoted Labour MP Ellen Wilkson, in her capacity as Parliamentary Secretary to the Ministry of Home Security, stating, "I do not wish to raise a gas scare. It is to be hoped that Hitler will have more sense than to start a gas war. ... But. ... We can dish out much more than we may take." Consequently, in the summer of 1943, civilians were urged to have their gas masks checked in anticipation of a possible chemical attack.[27]

This headline about Hitler using poison gas obviously reads very differently to contemporary readers and begs the question of when and what the British public might have known about the actual use of poison gas during this war as a weapon of mass extermination in the Nazi death camps. The first mention of gas chambers in the *Times* appeared in December 1943 when it reported the testimony of a Dutch prisoner who had escaped from the German concentration camp at Mauthausen. During his captivity, he was subjected to poison gas when wearing a gas mask and then without one, and also witnessed gas being tested on prisoners who died as a result.[28] No other public mention of the use of poison gas in the context of the Holocaust occurred until a report in the *Times* in mid-May 1945, and its first full discussion of gas chambers at Auschwitz came at the end of the war in September.[29] A letter to the editor of the Dundee *Evening Telegraph* in 1944 makes plain that reports of the massacre of Jews "by the Hunnish favourite weapon – gas" raised questions about why the Allies threatened retribution for the use of gas bombs but not this use of poison: "Could anyone say wherein lies the difference between the gas chamber and the use of gas by bombs?" This is a powerful question, but evidence consulted shows that for the British government, the threat to its civilian population posed by gas bombs clearly demanded continued action (by the provision of gas masks) throughout the war.

Although in the end nothing came of this particular threat in 1943, the possession and maintenance of gas masks continued to be emphasized by the government throughout that year. At the end of 1943, the Ministry of Home Security announced that local authorities would repair gas masks free of charge during January and February of 1944 at local depots.[30] Prior to this point, there had been a fee to replace or fix gas masks – except for children's masks in state schools. The promotion of this mass effort to maintain gas masks at this stage of the war suggests that the commitment to the gas mask as a valuable tool for everyone was not diminishing. Public expressions linking caring for the gas mask and being a good citizen also continued into 1944.[31]

The ongoing program of gas mask maintenance despite the absence of chemical attacks on Britain can be interpreted in a few ways. In one view, the reconditioning of gas masks, including those for children, babies, and "invalids," shows the state's dedication to protecting its civilian population from the potential ravages of chemical war. The program aimed to show that a benevolent state was looking after all its inhabitants regardless of their utility for the war effort. Fixing gas masks also signaled the conservation of resources rather than wasteful production. The war had been going on for four years at this point, and the regime's access to raw materials, especially those coming from Britain's empire in Asia, was being impeded. However, officials believed that the sustaining of civilian morale could be put at risk if the population saw that the protection that they had repeatedly been told was vital was now deemed unnecessary. If this was the case in the British metropole, the issues around the provision of civilian anti-gas protection were only more complex in Britain's wartime empire.

Gas Masks in an Empire at War

As Britain moved onto a wartime footing, the policies regarding individualized anti-gas protection varied enormously between the United Kingdom and its territories. On the eve of the war, British policy was committed to providing gas masks ideally to every man, woman, and child free of charge within Britain itself, but it was not clear where and how such devices would circulate to the colonial sphere. Sending gas masks to Aden and gathering Indian women to determine what sizes of gas mask might fit them, discussed earlier, at least demonstrated some

Figure 6.1 "Indians in Civil Defence," a poster showing Indian women
with the full kit of a civil defense volunteer including the civilian duty
respirator (special ARP gas mask), c. 1942. © The Imperial War
Museum

small measure of commitment by the British government to protecting
colonial subjects from chemical attacks. Certainly, the British government went out of its way to use colonial subjects living in the British Isles
and active in ARP work as part of its propaganda, as in an image showing
Indian women holding civilian duty respirators as part of their equipment
(Fig. 6.1), but that did not mean it treated those living in its empire in
comparable terms.[32]

A full year after the worst of the German aerial attacks on the British
Isles, ARP overall was still a work in progress in India.[33] By September
1940, "as the war developed and the possibility that India might be
subjected to air raids gradually became greater," a more formal ARP
structure took shape, at least for this colonial space.[34] In 1941, the
Government of India grouped towns into categories that were to receive
differing levels of ARP. Class I locales (including most of the subcontinent's major cities such as Mumbai [Bombay in the nomenclature of the
time], Kolkata [Calcutta], Delhi, Karachi, Lahore, Chennai [Madras],
and Peshawar) as well as those labeled Class II (such as Ahmedabad,
Amritsar, Kakinada [Coconada], Gujrat, and Shimia [Simla]) could
receive the full measures available under ARP. Those with Class III

status (such as Abottabad, Coonoor, Darjeeling, and Fort Sandelman) would obtain only warning sirens and what was called "elementary training."[35] The potential weaknesses of this scheme – which stands in marked contrast to the policy of treating all locales in the United Kingdom equally – would not emerge until later.

Although the anticipated war of poison gas and flame had not arrived by this point, the government emphasized that it might yet take place, without warning, and so it continued to cultivate awareness of the risk of chemical attacks as the war progressed. In February 1942, the Colonial Office sent inquiries to all leading territorial administrators, asking them about their existing policies regarding the provision of gas masks to their general civilian population. Officials wanted to know what was being done both for the general population and for what it deemed "special categories of civilians," presumably those who were somehow assisting the wartime colonial state. They asked for the numbers of gas masks in stock (and their sizes and varieties) and whether gas masks were on order from any source.[36] Some responses came in quickly. The High Commissioner of South Africa reported that the answer was "Nil, nil, nil," that neither gas masks nor anti-gas training was available for any civilians. From Palestine, the report noted that gas masks were available free of charge in an emergency to the public in major cities such as Haifa, Ramallah, Tel Aviv, and Jerusalem; there were also close to 14,000 general service respirators available to the Palestinian Police Force, and the military authorities were seeking nearly 25,000 each of child-size gas masks and babies' gas helmets in order to be able to issue them to the public. In Transjordan, there were gas masks for police officers and ARP workers, but members of the public were encouraged to purchase their own.[37]

The Defence Department of the Colonial Office compiled a list in March 1942 that accounted for the status of anti-gas measures in the colonies. It ranked colonies according to the extent of their civilian anti-gas provision. It listed only Malta, Gibraltar, and Aden as "colonies where respirators are provided for the entire civilian population," although it noted that gas masks would not be provided "for civilians who would not remain in Aden under attack," suggesting that anyone who left the locale for fear of an attack would not receive one. The next category contained "colonies where respirators are provided for the civilian population in principal towns," which included Cyprus and Palestine. A third category comprised those colonies in which gas masks were limited to "key personnel," largely those involved in civil defense services, such as Gambia, the Gold Coast, Sierra Leone, Uganda, Zanzibar, St. Helena, Trinidad, and Transjordan (where the account also noted that "other civilians [were] encouraged to buy respirators"). The final and largest grouping listed those colonial spaces where no precautions had been taken – although in some cases, a few gas masks were on hand for training purposes. This group contained most of the West Indies (including Jamaica and Barbados); the African colonies of Northern Rhodesia, Nyasaland, Tanganyika, and Nigeria; and places as far-flung as Sri Lanka (Ceylon in the records), the Falkland Islands, and Fiji. A note next to the entry for Fiji suggests that the governor there had asked Australia and New Zealand to help supply personal anti-gas equipment.

What is striking about these calculations about the bodies and spaces to be protected is the way in which they reflect two overriding concerns. The first is a sense of needing to be alert to a potential enemy (Italy) that had used gas in the not so distant past, hence the equipping of everyone on Malta and Gibraltar. The second seems more strategic: ensuring the defense of colonial subjects and more particularly spaces in locales that would help to preserve access to India and/or other colonial sites viewed as more directly under threat. That said, there are unexplained outliers, such as the sending of gas masks of for key personnel to Trinidad, for example, but not Jamaica.[38] The wide variation in civilian anti-gas protection shows not only the absence of any sort of policy but also the failure to consider fully what protecting all civilians under British authority might require.

As a follow-up to this report, T. I. K. Lloyd of the Colonial Office wrote in late March 1942 to the Overseas Defence Committee, asking for its perspective on the overall situation regarding civilian anti-gas precautions in Britain's colonies. In Lloyd's opinion, Gambia, the Gold Coast, Sierra Leone, and Nigeria were all at similar risk, and given that it was "impractical" to supply the entire populations of these states with gas masks, especially since they deteriorated in such tropical climates, providing gas masks solely for key civilian personnel (left unspecified) was enough. According to the reports of officials in Palestine, the urban civilian population was adequately provided for, and it would be difficult to equip the remainder of the population. As far as the West Indies were concerned, the government expressed a desire to ensure that gas masks were available for "key personnel of essential civilian industries." However, Bermuda was now considering equipping all civilians, and, the report complained, "any general provision of gas masks to civilians is clearly unnecessary." The Overseas Defence Committee's reply was to suggest that every colony have a supply of gas masks sufficient for all who performed "essential civilian services," including any additional workers who might be called in to assist in case of an emergency (such as an attack); but with the exception of Sri Lanka (Ceylon), Mauritius, the Seychelles, and Britain's Indian Ocean island bases, there was no need for wider distribution of gas masks or of anti-gas training.[39] Ordinary civilians in these areas would not receive gas masks.

One colonial space of great concern given its vulnerability and value to the war effort in the Pacific was Singapore. At the end of December 1941, the British government advised Singaporean authorities "of the greater likelihood of the Japanese using gas." It therefore intended to expedite the sending of civilian gas masks to the area.[40] On February 7, 1942, the Colonial Office recorded that it had received half a million such gas masks from the Home Office but had been waiting several weeks to ship them to Singapore.[41] Singapore fell to the Japanese on February 15; some 386,000 gas masks that had been en route there were then diverted to India. There the gas masks remained held in storage rather than being distributed generally to civilians (and that number was hardly enough to have made a difference to the broader noncombatant population in that locale if they had been needed).[42]

By the spring of 1942, the British government was worried about obtaining rubber supplies for gas masks for the population in the United Kingdom, let alone how it could supply gas masks for colonial subjects. In a War Cabinet meeting, discussions noted that the reserve stocks of gas masks "were by no means lavish in relation to the demands which might be made upon them in the event of a gas attack upon this country. Any proposals therefore to supply such equipment to other countries must be carefully scrutinized."[43] Presumably "other countries" included Britain's dominions, territories, mandates, and colonies. As for whether it were even possible to provision India alone with gas masks, in a May 1942 report on India's civil defense, the government had concluded: "The subject of preparations against gas attack has been, and still remains, a very difficult one. It is impossible to put four hundred million people into gas masks, or even the 25 million to be found in the towns in which A.R.P.s are to be taken."[44] In addition, even if masks could be provided, "the illiterate portion of the population, which is very large, could not be educated to use them properly and to preserve them." Furthermore, officials expressed anxiety that too much attention to anti-gas precautions would fuel panic.[45] By August 1942, this was still the policy, although efforts had been made to "do a limited amount of unobtrusive training in more likely gas target towns," and, in connection, some equipment was stored in bulk to distribute if necessary.[46]

The supply of gas masks to Britain's empire, to the extent it existed, was calculated to aid populations in places like Aden or specific locales in

India should an enemy launch a gas attack. Perhaps in response to the targeting of civil defense establishments (ARP depots) as part of the protests against British imperial rule that constituted the Quit India movement of August 1942, the government felt reluctant to do more than keep gas masks as part of a reserve supply.[47] A gas mask census in January 1944 revealed that since respirators were not being issued to the general public but were instead kept ready to distribute to those needing to work in potentially gas-affected areas, there were nearly 71,000 civilian duty respirators, 400,000 civilian respirators, and 8,000 small children's respirators available in the subcontinent.[48] Given the ongoing famine conditions in parts of India that also faced aerial attacks, it is hard not to see the perniciousness of such a policy. Instead of supplying the basic needs of a population still under its aegis, the British government focussed on having gas masks in stock when it could.[49] It was not until April 1945 that military authorities informed the Government of India that there was no longer any gas threat and that it could dispose of all the gas masks it had in stock.

What was the purpose of sending limited supplies of gas masks to key locales in the British empire? The government had invested a great deal to try to ensure that potentially everyone in Britain received a gas mask; it never intended to offer anything comparable to its colonial subjects. Moreover, the establishment of civil defense in the empire came in part because imperial outposts had inquired about and asked for anti-gas protection since the time when, as discussed in prior chapters, poison gas was used in Ethiopia in the mid-1930s. Those planning for ARP as early as 1924 did not consider colonial subjects when thinking about the need for civilian gas masks.

However, Britain's failure to offer any anti-gas protection opened it up to criticism about being willing to sacrifice civilians, including those loyally serving its wartime regime, in these areas. Providing ARP equipment and training could also be used to justify the continuation of imperial ties if not outright colonial rule. In territories threatened externally by Japanese bombs, British could use its civil defense provisions as a reason to maintain these ties, and to some extent, this emerges in the wartime discussions. The alternative made continued justification of empire untenable, as it meant publicly acknowledging that the British government deemed the lives of its colonial subjects largely expendable. More research may well reveal how local colonial populations felt about civil defense and reflect the variety of responses seen in the metropole, yet even the limited distribution of the gas mask shows the full sweep of total war and the incorporation of civilian bodies, of persons deemed of no military value, into its waging.

The Gas Mask at the War's End

Although the Axis powers did not target British subjects at home or abroad with chemical weapons, at no point during the war did the state recall gas masks or stop defending their importance. Scientists continued to carry out tests on foreign gas masks throughout the war, and the surveys of gas mask carrying continued, as did inspections of those masks belonging to everyone from schoolchildren to old-age pensioners. Above all, the concerted volunteer labor that went into keeping gas masks in working order did not diminish.

One of the largest branches of volunteer civil defense workers was the WVS, an organization designed to enable women to participate, even on a part-time basis, in maintaining war readiness. In its monthly newsletter, a column reported on the work of regional branches. In July 1944, this featured the work of volunteers at the respirator depot in Bath, a place where "new babies are introduced to their first cradle-like container, young children come to be fitted for larger-sized respirators," and those "abnormal" or "elderly" inhabitants who needed special gas masks or special fitting received respirators. Volunteers even went to hospitals and homes for the aged to carry out their fitting and maintaining of gas masks, "so that the slogan for this branch of WVS work may well be, 'We look after them from the cradle to the grave.'"[50]

These Bath volunteers embodied the volunteer ethos of ARP and the key role that women played in the enactment of civil defense, of which anti-gas protection was an integral part. Their endeavor began in May 1938, and after being trained to fit gas masks, the women got to work with that task as soon as war was declared. Over time, the staff of volunteers learned to assemble, fit, examine, clean, and disinfect respirators, keeping up this work as the baby's helmet and modified child's ("Mickey Mouse") respirator came along in 1940. In 1941, the volunteers visited schools to examine and ensure the fit of children's gas masks and helped to repair damaged ones. The account of this work concluded as follows:

Since regular records have been kept, that is from October 1941, 21,571 respirators had been fitted by May of this year; 6,917 had been repaired during that period. In a recent quarter 194 Baby Helmets were issued and 155 "Mickey Mouse" respirators; 208 schoolchildren were fitted and 307 respirators issued to the general public. Such is the fine record of service given at the Respirator Depot at Bath.[51]

Five years into the war and still without experiencing chemical attacks, this local effort continued to occupy civilian workers. Beyond this, giving hundreds of gas masks to babies and children and ensuring that anti-gas protection was available across the spectrum of age and class signaled the ongoing symbolic value of the gas mask. Even at this late stage of the war, the government was unwilling to suggest that gas masks were no longer necessary.

Even if it was clear by the summer of 1944 that the Allies were winning the war, a new phase of terrifying aerial attacks on the British mainland was just beginning. The German V-rocket campaign, launched after a period of time when Britain had been more on the offensive than on the receiving end of air raids, renewed official anxiety about civilian morale. As the rocket campaign continued amid challenges for Allied troops in Europe, the government was again concerned that Germany might resort to deploying gas against these troops, and it was rethinking its own use of chemical arms.[52] The records do not reveal a comparable concern about poison gas attacks against civilians, but the rocket attacks coming in daylight and without warning were devastating enough. Only after the British defenses became able to destroy rockets before they reached their targets did the government feel more confident about maintaining morale, but the rockets continued to inflict damage into November and the next year.[53] The chart of wartime morale released by Mass Observation in January 1946 demonstrated a stark drop in morale around the time of the worst of the rocket attacks; according to these records, morale did not fully rebound until the spring of 1945.[54] This was not the moment to suggest withdrawing the gas mask if it had any positive, talismanic effect on the mood of civilians.

As a result, as the war was coming to an end, gas masks remained in the possession of those to whom they had been distributed, some of whom were now asking new questions suggesting that they might be ready, even eager, to give them up. D. B. Grubb of Somerset wrote to the *Times* in late August, asking, "what are we to do with our gas masks?" He had taken his to pieces and thought that the rubber might be valuable for other purposes.[55] Another letter urged that the government collect the gas masks in order to assist the Royal Society for the Prevention of Cruelty to Animals because, as its chief secretary noted, rubber from gas masks had been used by small boys to make catapults that were injuring birds, cats, and dogs.[56] In September, local authorities still awaited word about how to collect them, and as one ARP officer stated, "finding a place to put thousands of gas masks would be a real worry."[57]

Inside the government, officials had been weighing what to do with gas masks after the war since the summer of 1944. An internal government memorandum by Edward Frankland Armstrong on "Respirators after the War" evaluated the likelihood of the use of chemical arms then and now, offering the view that if "the Germans do not use gas I very much doubt whether any other nation has the mentality to do so." The effectiveness of high explosive and incendiary bombs during the war, moreover, had proved the superiority of those weapons over poison gas. At the same time, it was hard to be optimistic about the situation in Europe after the war, and therefore "it would be wrong to destroy the existing respirators." Moreover, it would be good to "get back the ordinary respirators from the public, partly from the point of view of maintaining the belief in the public mind that they are articles of value."[58] This is a revealing admission of the government's view that gas masks could be useful for maintaining civilian morale as well as for the physical protection they offered. It foreshadowed later discussions about whether or not gas masks would be of value in protecting against bacteriological as well as nuclear weapons.

Other internal government conversations show that officials pondered whether gas masks would be helpful in a future war. If the present war ended without the use of gas, they reasoned, then the nation would have available a fairly substantial reserve of unused gas masks, which were at the time being held in storage facilities. These would be in better shape than most gas masks that could be recovered from the general population.[59] Yet when the War Cabinet met in February 1945 to discuss the status of civilian respirators and whether it was advisable to ask the public either to turn them in or to preserve them, it decided that any announcement about gas masks "would have a depressing effect." Additionally, there were doubts about whether it was even worthwhile to call for the return of gas masks in order to store them after the European war ended.[60] Communicating something to the public, however, seemed vital at this juncture, so officials at the Ministry of Home Security drafted a public circular regarding gas masks that they hoped could be issued at the cessation of hostilities. In it, the government asked that local authorities stop issuing new gas masks (such as the baby's anti-gas helmet given to newborns) and repairing old gas masks. However, it also reminded them that all gas masks remained government property and requested that the public should maintain them and await further instructions.[61]

An editorial in the *Times* noted this shift in policy as the war came to an end in Europe. It reflected on the new era with the happy baby of these times who "would receive no infantile gas mask." "Good citizens," it noted, would continue to take care of their gas masks, as requested, but surely there would be some who longed for a final moment when they could play a "triumphant game of football with the family gas-masks" and give them a hearty kick. The editorial recounted the entire history of the gas mask, beginning with the times when wardens came around "like polite amateur tailors" to fit gas masks, and how "we painfully learnt the technique of putting them on ... how we laughed with perhaps a little hollow merriment at the fantastic pig-like creatures that looked back at us." Then came "days when we virtuously carried our masks on all our journeys," first in cardboard boxes and then "in neat cases of shining leather." Some of the daredevils among the population left them home, and then "we were told that we need no longer" carry them regularly. Now today, "of all the many things we have to be thankful for it is not among the least that we have never needed them, and if ever we are disposed to forget, a gas-mask makes a good memento."[62] This is a fitting summation of what the government intended for this object: gratitude for providing something to keep one safe from a potential weapon and a reminder of the benevolent state. Yet it also served as an emblem of the discomfiting incorporation of everyone into the waging (surviving) of war.

After the war ended, Stella Reading, head of the WVS, wrote to Sir William Brown in the Home Office, alerting him to the numerous inquiries that the WVS was receiving about the collection of gas masks and offering its services to retrieve them, even as the wartime civil defense services were being disbanded.[63] In a Cabinet memorandum for the Home Secretary on the preservation of civilian respirators issued in August 1945, there was some discussion of having the local authorities make use of the WVS to collect as many gas masks of all varieties as possible and to return them to the Home Office for disposal, although this could become expensive when transportation, labor, and storage costs were taken into account. However, some felt that "we cannot do otherwise than to assume in the future planning of Civil Defence that provision must be made against gas attack." And so long as the gas masks worked and were in people's homes, "the essential provision against gas attack has been made."[64]

A follow-up to this original memorandum in September was more detailed. Assuming that the babies' and children's anti-gas protection would last for twenty years and the general civilian respirator for ten, it would be possible to protect the entire population for ten years, "and we could at any time start a 'trickle' production to replace our stocks without arousing public comment." Once they were collected and scrapped, you could not replace gas masks in a hurry. Despite the fact that they had not been needed, the state was still unwilling to let go of the idea that they might someday be necessary. Acknowledging that it alarmed a population to receive gas masks, it would be better to prepare for future chemical war by just quietly maintaining the existing supply.[65]

In public, the government needed to defend its decision not to collect gas masks. The new Home Secretary, James Ede, responded to questions in the Commons by stating that the authorities had decided not to retrieve gas masks for fear of wasting manpower and storage space. He therefore repeated the request made earlier by then Home Secretary Herbert Morrison that civilians should "continue to keep their gas masks safe and free from damage." MPs laughed in response, and one asked if Ede was aware that "the continued retention of this equipment in every home indicated to most householders a considerable degree of bureaucratic inefficiency."[66] An editorial in the *Manchester Guardian* reflected on this further. Perhaps making civilians keep their gas masks was a way to keep the population in check, because someday when the exigencies of war were over and "we suddenly grow light-headed and ungrateful, the Government may sober us down by demanding, under penalty, the gas masks we never needed."[67] The future of the gas mask was undetermined; its wartime role, however, was over.

Conclusion

Multiple ironies abound when one tries to assess the wartime civilian gas mask, that vital object that ended up never being used. Perhaps one of the more tragic events happened in September 1945, after the war's end, when fourteen-year-old John Dutton, who aspired to join the RAF, put on a raincoat, a flying cap, and his gas mask and tried to parachute down the stairs. His mother found him hanging from the banister. The leather strap (presumably from the gas mask he wore) had caught on the banister and broken his neck.[68] Other deaths using gas masks were more deliberate, for accounts of suicides found wearing gas masks appeared throughout 1946.[69] The civilian gas mask during the Second World War may have saved no one's life, but it took the lives of a few both during and after the war. What are we then to make of the final, inglorious end to this object that had been designed, manufactured, and distributed by a government that then seemingly abandoned it to the cupboards and attics and dust heaps of the postwar world?

The Second World War was the heyday of the gas mask, and from 1941 onward, it entered more broadly into everyday life, faced continued (if muted) resistance, and became a central means by which the state mediated its relationship with its civilian population. Yet not everyone received a gas mask, and the issue of providing such protection was a fraught one in the British wartime empire. Throughout the war, there was tension between official statements and individual reactions. The representation of gas masks in a variety of wartime media from cartoons

Figure 6.2 Even when the government no longer asked civilians to carry their gas masks everywhere, it still emphasized the need to maintain and care for them. Here, a warden fits members of a family with their gas masks c. 1944. John Hinde/Getty Images.

to songs and the ongoing newspaper coverage of the significance of this object, despite there being no chemical weapons attacks in Britain, reveal the extent to which the gas mask could be seen not simply as managing emotions but as shaping wartime identity. It served to mark out those who were willing and presumably able to help the nation cope with the potential and actual traumas of total war. Because of its intimate connection with the body, it brought the possible horrors of war home in a way that no other artifact of this period did. As shown by a c. 1944 color photograph of a family in their home making sure their general civilian respirators work, the gas mask reveals the thorough militarization of everyday life (Fig. 6.2).

7   Conclusion

The civilian gas mask made total war normal. The processes that normalized this object contributed to making the harrowing destructive possibilities of chemical weapons targeting civilians thinkable. From the moment of its improvised introduction in 1915 to its being tossed in the dustbin after 1945, the gas mask represented a defensive object that allowed war to continue. Between the world wars, dedicated activists working to stop the spread and use of chemical arms highlighted the ugliest face of modern war, the baby in the gas mask. And while some individuals refused their gas masks, by and large the population accepted these objects, which evoked a range of emotions and attitudes, even for their babies. The state may have constructed the gas mask as something generously provided to enable its civilian population to survive total war, but in practice, the gas mask's very existence recognized the limited capacity of any government to keep out the weapons of mass destruction and make civilians safe.

The journey to integrating the gas mask into the homes and lives of Britons started in the First World War and culminated in the Second World War. Several steps along the way stand out. For instance, a year after the first set of civil defense measures – including individual anti-gas devices – had been announced, the *Daily Mirror* ran an editorial in July 1936 on "Our New Faces":

One thing is safe to assert – nobody has invented the *good-looking* gas mask. ... and really it is better that it should be so. We should be happy hypocrites if we looked well in the masks that are a feeble defence against the most ghastly form of warfare even this cruel world has ever known. Let us look ugly for ugly occasions.[1]

As the gas mask came to feature in more and more public spaces in the last few years before Britain's formal entry into war in 1939, the gas mask's ultimate purpose – to save lives – somewhat supplanted its terrifying implications. Despite its mixture of animalistic and robotic features, it became an object that, almost talisman-like, became the thing that would protect you from the ravages of industrialized warfare.

At the end of the war, the verdict on the investment of intellect and resources that had invented and widely distributed civilian gas masks was still open to debate about their utility. The gas mask makes a singular appearance in the official history of chemical defense research at Porton Down that was published to mark its seventy-fifth anniversary. Much of what happened at Porton Down was hidden (as was the case for the even less well-known facility in India), and the testing of chemical weapons on human subjects does not make for celebratory reading in the twenty-first century. That said, in this context, the gas mask receives a positive spin: it was meant to save lives, not destroy them. Rather than seeing the entire enterprise that had created the civilian gas mask as a waste of money, time, and valuable resources, the official story credits it with preventing the use of poison gas by the enemy.[2] Thus, in this official history, its deterrent effect is reason to celebrate its existence.

As deterrence came to define Cold War ideas about civil defense in the nuclear age, the British government promoted gas masks as both as defense against chemical weapons and, it hoped, a shield against atomic agents. When officials decided to let people keep their gas masks after the end of the war, they were clear that local authorities would collect the "bulky types" of gas masks such as babies' helmets, respirators for invalids, and those given to children, but that they would "continue to entrust ordinary civilian respirators to the custody of the public. ... Properly looked after, the masks will be serviceable for some years longer."[3] A government announcement about civil defense in 1949 claimed that although the atomic bomb was a "terrible weapon," there were measures that could protect against it, including "the old gas-mask," which "can keep the rays out."[4] When subsequent reports appeared in 1950 stating that a respirator would aid in giving protection against radioactive dust, a letter writer to a Dundee newspaper asked where someone could get such a respirator, hoping that the matter would be addressed by the government.[5]

In the earliest years of the Cold War, government officials thus contemplated how existing supplies could protect against future wartime methods. They also speculated about their potential utility against nuclear arms in a future war.[6] There was funding in the mid-1950s for developing a new civilian gas mask that might include the capacity to protect against nerve gas, although internal discussions expressed skepticism about the focus on this rather than other forms of civil defense for nuclear arms. A set of new designs for a civilian gas mask was also proposed in the 1970s. It is telling that nothing came of such measures in terms of production and distribution to the public, presumably because anxiety about chemical weapons lessened dramatically as concern shifted to the danger of nuclear arms and stayed there.[7] However, the ongoing if occasional interest in the gas mask long after the Second World War also tells us something about the importance of this object for a state that still needed to manage emotions and protect bodies and to do so in an era when civilians in the United Kingdom could never again be fully shielded from war. That era began with the rise of air power and chemical arms in 1915.

Of all the novel equipment carried by men in arms during the First World War that became a staple of Second World War equipment, only the gas mask fully came home to civilian populations. Developing the civilian gas mask, an apparatus of anti-chemical warfare that the state envisaged everyone could carry everywhere, meant creating an object that physically reminded Britons of the legacy of a war waged with the instruments of modern science and technology against civilians at home. Once the state started developing individual anti-gas protection for civilians, it could be seen as incorporating every man, woman, and child into the waging of modern war.

While many nations developed such safeguards in the interwar era, the British government uniquely decided to distribute gas masks free of charge within the United Kingdom, potentially to every inhabitant regardless of age, gender, or geography. As this book shows, there were limits to such protection in practice (and its boundaries are themselves revealing). This state gifted something that served as a tangible reminder that the harrowing destruction of civilian lives and of domestic life itself was no longer unimaginable or unknown. British civilians responded to their gas masks in a range of uncontrollable ways: by turning the cases used to carry them into things that were aesthetically pleasing or fashionable, by listening to songs that made fun of them, and by refusing to engage with them at all.

What should be made of an object that during the Second World War was both a marker of responsible citizenship and something mocked and disregarded, all while becoming a part of everyday life? The gas mask had a social, political, and emotional life during its heyday, and it defined an era in which the welfare and warfare state intertwined. The gas mask started as a military object. When the civil population had to be made safe in order to wage war, civilian anti-gas respirators became something that could be given to protect everyone. As the embodiment of individualized civil defense, this represented an extraordinary expansion of state power onto the bodies of ordinary civilians, all in an effort to enable them to survive. This object thus serves as a telling example of the ways in which modern wars became winnable not with a knock-out blow, but on the basis of the population's capacity to endure. The gas mask was a gift from the benevolent state, but, in return, the state expected the right sort of actions and responses; this was the social contract for the age of total war.

This history shows, however, the parameters of such an arrangement. By offering protection to only a very few colonial subjects, the provisioning of gas masks marked out the limits of the declining imperial state: not all bodies and spaces mattered equally, despite the promise of imperial civil defense as a defense of empire.

As an example of the all-encompassing modern state, the story of the age of the civilian gas mask reveals the boundaries of what a nation preparing for total war can do. The gas mask, the device created to secure human life in the face of poison gas, was fragile enough to sustain humans only in the short term. It did nothing to preserve the landscape and environment also necessary for survival. Yet, if the state had not participated actively in its development and chemical weapons had arrived, then the government would likely have been criticized for not caring about the lives of its civilian population. It had to do something about the gas menace that imaginatively lurked in the not-too-distant future.

The gas mask thus helps to demonstrate that modern war requires preparation for wars of the imagination. The long process of figuring out how to offer this particular protection was always mediated by the effort to understand not only how to protect civilians in practical terms, but also how to get them to accept the cultural transformations that such protection required. Writers of fiction as well as activists contributed to showing just what might happen to a society that faces the devastating impact of lethal chemical weapons launched en masse. Their agenda in the interwar period was to persuade readers to support disarmament by illustrating how horrific chemical attacks might be. Yet the government was also actively imagining what such a war might produce so that it could train medical personnel and the army of volunteers in civil defense to ensure that some version of civic life continued regardless of the devastation. What imagining these wars could not do was to predict how individuals would respond to an object that was provided as much to make them *feel* safe as to protect them. A government that gives out civilian gas masks is making it acceptable to factor its noncombatant population entirely into the waging of modern war.

This new relationship between the state and the individual citizen may be the most important legacy of the age of gas mask. In the civil defense state that emerged during this era, the entire population theoretically comes to have a role to play in ensuring the nation's survival. As such, civilians are given a set of practices and objects with which to carry out this task. Although active civil defense in the United Kingdom disbanded well before the end of the Cold War, the principles and means of waging war that underlined its development continue to overshadow the lives of modern citizens. In the nuclear age and in an era of violent action by non-state agents, all of us are vulnerable to attack by weapons of mass destruction for which there is no remedy, and so all of us have been enlisted in an effort to keep society safe. From the signs on the London Underground that ask us to be aware of and report suspicious parcels to the rocket launchers that fringed London during the 2012 Olympics, we live with visible reminders of the expectation that the ordinary man, woman, and child will face such risks while aiding the state. We have all become responsible for keeping calm and keeping alert and carrying on. This is not new, but it is not very old. By normalizing something for civilians that protected them from a weapon of mass destruction, the gas mask reveals a world where the only way to protect civilian life is to militarize it.

Epilogue
Five Brief Ways of Looking at a Gas Mask

The inability to breathe is a terrifying prospect. The modern era of chemical weapons that kill by asphyxiation, by deliberately poisoning the air, has provoked rightful shock and outrage since the beginning; to this day, their use is overwhelmingly condemned. When I first conceived of this book project, it was as a way of trying to figure out for myself a particular conundrum. While the First World War had in 1915 introduced almost simultaneously air raids and lethal chemical attacks, one of those weapons – aerial warfare – became acceptable whereas chemical arms resulted in unceasing, loud public outcry. To some extent, that has continued till now despite the fact that in the light of recent history, one can no longer confidently speak of chemical warfare as the one weapon of mass destruction that has been successfully eradicated via international protocols.[1] Recent events in Syria offer too stark a reminder of that. The civilian gas mask, the artifact that accompanied the arrival of lethal chemical weapons, has also undergone a strange transformation even in the years during which I have been researching as well as speaking and writing about it. While making a command appearance on countless book covers and in exhibitions associated with the hundredth anniversary of the First World War, the gas mask remains largely in the realm of the history of the world wars, soldiers' experiences in the First World War, and civilian experiences in the Second World War. Yet its powerful legacies merit some further exploration. In what follows, I want briefly to explore a few significant ways in which the state, the mask, and the individual remain entangled.

As a Vector of Popular Memory

Here is one more story told to me about a gas mask from the Second World War. A student in Ireland at the end of a seminar spoke up: "This reminds me of the first time I saw one; it was at my auntie's funeral. One

Figure E.1 Cigarette card illustrating how to use a gas mask, c. 1939.
Print Collector/Contributor/Hulton Archive/Getty Images

of the little kids must have found it in the house somewhere. Next thing you knew, they were taking turns putting it on and chasing each other round the garden." The first gas mask story that I heard and that chilled me was about a young boy being frightened by being chased by his brother who wore one; this version turns it into just another plaything, disconnected from its purpose. What happened to the gas masks at the end of the war was one of the frequent questions that I was asked. It was somehow dissatisfying to everyone to hear that they were simply abandoned. Despite widespread campaigns to make them familiar during the war, as evident in their ubiquitous appearance on posters and other printed material like cards showing individuals how to use them tucked into cigarette packs, they seemingly vanished (Fig. E.1). In official circles, there were a few years of speculation about their utility for civil defense in the nuclear age, alongside instructions to continue to keep them in good shape, given that they still belonged to the government. And then people placed their gas masks in the trash or forgot them and, thus, left them to linger in attics and cupboards. Over time, they could come to serve as decor in tea rooms, as collectables, and as objects catalogued in special collections of university libraries, where they cannot be touched because of the asbestos they contain. The device that the benevolent state bestowed upon you to protect you from inhaling hazardous air was now itself labeled a hazard.

However, as anthropologist Gabriel Moshenska recently explained, gas masks became a powerful vector of popular memory and a key piece of the material culture of wartime childhood in Britain. Moshenska makes extensive use of the BBC website "A People's History" to show this.[2] One of the photographs on that website shows three-year-old Wilma Miles (married name Gravenor) living in South Wales. Ms. Miles offers some comments on her own image:

> We must have looked like little aliens running around with our bright red rubber faces … and they were not comfortable. In the picture, I have obviously put mine on while playing in the back garden – perhaps my mother thought it was a good idea to let me familiarize myself with wearing it. I appear completely relaxed and happy … what a weird little creature I was … even dolly in the pram looks startled![3]

Gravenor's mother had, obviously, been following the instructions issued periodically by the state: The gas mask would save your children, but only if you made sure they were at ease with it; by implication, this meant that it had been domesticated into an object in which and with which one could play. The emotional toll of having such a reminder of the threat of deliberate poisoning by air as a child may be something to tease out further, but the toll on parents, especially on mothers, that constituted such a crucial concern in the 1930s and into the Second World War still has not been fully explored. Instead, the gas mask has become another thing that signals the changed circumstances of the war alongside a host of other objects and practices: blackouts, evacuations, stirrup pumps, Anderson and Morrison shelters. Yet the gas mask is unique; it alone links the military and civilian experiences of both world wars. Its tangible presence in everyone's life during the war and in many cases afterward has meant that it has resonated as a sign of the war as almost nothing else in the individual memories recounted on websites and in oral histories and memoirs.

As an Emblem of Twenty-First-Century Protest

The civilian gas mask's reappearance as the emblem of protest – be it in Istanbul or Hong Kong – directly ties into the use of tear gas to disrupt protesters. This version of the gas mask has also been turned into political art, from graffiti to the effigy of a gas-masked protester in Hong Kong to the gas masks carved in marble by Ai Weiwei. Tear gas, of course, is a chemical weapon. It is one that even those states willing to condemn the use of vesicant or asphyxiating gases wanted to retain after the First World War. This chemical agent was (and is) not allowed on battlefields but became permissible for governments, especially police forces, to use against their own populations, including strikers, protesters, and colonial subjects demanding their rights – something that should give us pause. Thus, in the twenty-first century, the gas-masked protester has become emblematic of those standing up against regimes that range from democracies like France – where tear gas permeated the air of Paris during the Gilets Jaunes protests against government measures that began in the fall of 2018 – to repressive governments like the China-backed Hong Kong government of 2019; in 2020 the United States used gas against those protesting the racist murder of George Floyd.[4]

The gas mask as a particular item of protest in modern Britain seems to coalesce around the opposition to the war in Iraq in 2003 because the false accusations of the accelerating development of weapons of mass destruction, especially chemical arms, by the Iraqi regime formed the basis of arguments that legitimized that conflict. Two prominent pieces of protest art from that year feature the gas mask. The first is a poster designed by Peter Kennard for the Stop the War Coalition, reworking an earlier design from the anti-nuclear protests of the 1980s.[5] In this Poster No. 1, a gas mask is strapped on the globe, and missiles, rather than a filter, pour out of its bottom casings. Inside the eye holes of the mask, the images of the American and British flags appear (replacing the Soviet and American ones of the initial design). The photomontage thus alludes to the claim of chemical weapons as well as the more real threat of terror being unleashed by airborne missiles.

The second piece of antiwar art with a gas mask incorporated into its design, in 2003, ended up being more controversial. British artist James Cauty created a series of prints called "Black Smoke, Stamps of Mass Destruction," for which he took the image of Queen Elizabeth II featured on postage stamps and affixed a Second World War civilian gas mask to her face. Cauty displayed this piece at the Artrepublic gallery in Brighton and quickly got into trouble with the Royal Mail for copyright infringement, because the original prints were the size of sheets of postage stamps.

Figure E.2 James Cauty, "Stamps of Mass Destruction," 2003. With kind permission of artist. The stamps have recently been repurposed as "Stamps of Mass Contamination" to commemorate the first year of Covidean Culture

At the time, Cauty responded, "I am just an artist doing my job," criticizing the Royal Mail for infringing on his artistic freedom. In the end, the unsold copies of the original prints featuring this image had to be sent to the Royal Mail, where they were destroyed, but the image reemerged in poster size (Fig. E.2).[6] Because of the alleged development of chemical weapons, the core rationale provided by Prime Minister Tony Blair to support the attack on Iraq in 2003, the depiction of the queen in the gas mask sent a pointed message about the United Kingdom's complicity in the war. The gas mask references the particular situation regarding chemical weapons inspections and weapons of mass destruction that led to the invasion; for those who had lived through the Second World War, the prints may have offered a reminder of Britain's legacy of using anti-gas protection as a way to signal loyalty to the state.

As a Piece of Popular Culture

Just as the gas mask embodied the external threats that modern war posed to civilians in interwar fiction and film, it had a long afterlife in popular culture. Arguably, the wartime civilian gas mask's most powerful modern appearance was on television in 2005 in two linked episodes of the revival of the British science fiction chronicle *Doctor Who*, "The Empty Child" and "The Doctor Dances." I was alerted to these programs, again, by questioners at public forums when I started talking about the gas mask. These episodes deserve much more attention than I can give them here, but there are a few striking features that connect this contemporary use of the gas mask with its wartime antecedent.

These two episodes were the first written by acclaimed showrunner Steven Moffat and formed part of the first season of the revived series. Whether or not the return of the gas mask as a central feature of protest a few years earlier had any impact on the development of the idea behind these episodes is unknown, but some visual moments in the episodes hearken back to photographs from the Second World War and to even earlier interwar protests against chemical arms. They may also have been influenced by the primary school exercise – so familiar to the audience for this family-oriented program – that had children dress up as Second World War evacuees, complete with cardboard gas mask boxes. Both episodes are clearly set in 1941 London, and there is even a "Hitler Will Send No Warning" poster from the gas mask campaign of that year, which helps the time-traveling Doctor determine where he is. The main challenge for the Doctor in the first episode, "The Empty Child," is figuring out why a small child in a gas mask appears asking, "Are you my mummy?" as the Doctor and his assistant Rose wander through a wartime London, bombs crashing down around them.

The boy in the children's gas mask is clearly a danger to everyone in this wartime setting, an even greater threat than the falling bombs. It becomes clear that each person who touches him eventually begins to exhibit his injuries and, most importantly, has their face replaced by a gas mask. Viewers see this take place when Doctor Who visits a local hospital and finds a ward filled with figures in gas masks who are like zombies; they are not "dead," but they are "empty." He then witnesses the local physician, Constantine, being overtaken by this "illness." When the first episode ends as the Doctor is still struggling to understand what is going on, the gas-masked figures rise up from their beds. The scene of a crowd of people walking in their gas masks bears an astonishing resemblance to the photograph of gas-masked figures in the 1935 pamphlet from the Union of Democratic Control (Fig. 3.5). They represent a terrifying future world in that era, and the gas-masked patients evoke a similar sense of a world gone terribly awry .

In the companion episode, "The Doctor Dances," the time-traveling Doctor finally uncovers what has gone wrong. Space junk that landed earlier in this wartime London contained "nanogenes," subatomic robots programmed to repair damaged humans and other species and to turn them into proto-warriors. So when they encountered a child who was killed in an air raid while wearing a gas mask, they went to work. As Doctor Who explains, having never seen a human being before,

All they've got to go on is one little body. ... They patch it up. Can't tell what's gasmask and what's skull, but they do their best ... now they think they know what people should look like, and it's time to fix all the rest. And they won't ever stop. ... The entire human race is going to be torn down and rebuilt in the form of one terrified child looking for its mother.

And it is by helping the original gas-masked child, Jamie, to find his mother that the nanogenes, recognizing the mother's superior DNA, then figure out what a real human is composed of. They then repair their earlier incarnation of Jamie to allow a normal human boy to emerge. The Doctor can thus symbolically remove the little boy's gas mask and throw the reprogrammed nanogenes at the rest of the population, who are suddenly cured (i.e., they emerge as humans who can remove their masks). The Doctor's parting words to the now restored population are, "Right you lot. Lots to do. Beat the Germans, save the world. Don't forget about the welfare state!" He himself seems rejuvenated as the episode ends with him dancing with Rose in a spaceship that is heading back to the future.[7]

The child in the gas mask in these episodes is a sign of something terribly wrong. He is at the same time horrifying and pathetic, wearing a gas mask so tightly that it completely obscures his features and crying out desperately for his mummy. The gas mask morphs here from any sort of emblem of protection, of efforts to keep women and children safe, into something that signals the most frightening consequences of modern war, a world in which the gas mask has become literally part of the body rather than a device strapped upon it. It reinvests in the horror of what the gas mask means. Of twenty-first-century British representations of the gas mask, this may be the uncanniest. And yet the Doctor's parting words, a reminder to this population that they must win a war and create a welfare state from the ruins of their country and lives, also resonate with the message of civil defence epitomized by the gas mask: that providing gas masks to all was the ultimate gesture of a state bent on the welfare of its population in order to survive a war.

As a Way to Breathe in a World on Fire

Weapons of mass destruction – biological, chemical, and nuclear – have disastrous consequences for the environment. Since I was finishing much of this book in England at the end of 2019, the protests to alert us to the

Figure E.3 Gas-masked protester in London at Global Climate Strike, November 29, 2019. Mike Kemp/Contributor/Getty Images

urgency of global climate change, especially from Extinction Rebellion, also made me think anew about how some version of the civilian gas mask might return. This time it would be to protect us not from the militarized poisoning of air by an enemy, but from the air that we have poisoned ourselves. Among the protesters at the Global Climate Strike in London in November 2019 were students in gas masks; one carried the sign "preparing for my future" (Fig. E.3).

If the images of the baby or child in the gas mask – among the most unsettling images of all the many disturbing photographs that constitute the personal archive I have assembled over the last many years – motivated action in favor of disarmament and peace, maybe it is time to resurrect them. What if we redeployed this image regularly to visualize a world in which our children cannot breathe – as, indeed, is already the case in parts of our fragile planet? During the worst episodes of air pollution in some of the world's major cities, cloth facial coverings and sometimes full-fledged gas masks have returned. For instance, people have used them during fires that have regularly devastated parts of our planet, including in the north of England in the summer of 2018, where a photograph appeared in one of the tabloid papers of a woman in a gas mask, carrying her groceries and walking along a road outside Manchester.[8] When I started this project, the idea of a gas mask being necessary for people to carry out everyday life, something that had to be made available to combatants and civilians alike, was a particular story for a very specific period of time between 1915 and 1945. While that may be the civilian gas mask's historic heyday, the gas mask may well have a renewed existence. I would like to imagine that the widespread distribution and wearing of gas masks is not our future and that of our children. The gas mask, used either to protest against climate change or to wear as a necessity in places facing it, offers a potent reminder to work toward a world where no one should ever need this device in order to carry out their daily life.

As a Way to Indicate Community

Finally, wearing masks to save lives has returned as a vital component of the response to the SARS-COVID-19 pandemic. While medical masks and the cloth masks that ordinary folks began to wear in 2020 to help prevent the spread of the virus are not gas masks, they have become objects that, like the civilian gas masks, have profound political and emotional lives. In cultures (largely but not entirely in Asia) where wearing a simple mask to cover the nose and mouth to mitigate the transmission of respiratory diseases has already been normalized, putting on such a mask has been uncontroversial.

What has been striking about the differing responses in the United Kingdom (and the United States) is how the state has responded in each case. To varying degrees, citizens have been urged to wear masks: mainly for the sake of others, to aid medical personnel heroically trying to fight an incurable, deadly ailment, and to safeguard the community. There are echoes of civilian gas mask policy in these efforts; wearing a mask in public has thus become a sign of a willingness to be a responsible citizen in the face of the pandemic. Whether or not such policy decisions are being debated in the ways in which civil defense planners talked about the gas mask, similar implications emerge. By making wearing (or in the case of the Second World War carrying) a mask voluntary rather than enforced, this simple act now signals a whole set of other attributes: community-mindedness, willingness to assist the nation in an hour of crisis, doing the right thing. It has been inspiring to watch scenes of the protests against anti-Black racism filled with people demanding justice while wearing masks that keep others safe. Almost nowhere in these states are masks being given to all who need them. Instead, individuals are being asked to make, find, or purchase such items on their own. In this sense, the mask of the pandemic clearly represents a shift in how the neoliberal state has come to see its role: it tasks the individual with actions to carry out and things to procure, without taking responsibility for providing for this new basic need for all bodies under its care. All of this serves as a reminder of the world the age of the gas mask has bequeathed us.

Notes

Chapter 1

1 Like all the memories of gas masks presented here and in the following paragraphs, this one is paraphrased from rough notes taken at the time. In hindsight, an oral history component of this project would have been fascinating to add. In its absence, I want to acknowledge the stories shared with me by those who lived during the age I am trying to understand, even when they contain errors; there were no official pink and blue gas masks, nor did those colors register as quite so gendered in 1939.

2 In addition to recounting emotions, others had stories that explained the unintended consequences of the decision to provide gas masks. The most remarkable was a story told to me in Canada at the end of this project, which stands out for its illustration of the lasting impact of the decision to issue the masks to civilians. "Listening to your talk, I was reminded of how our neighbors explained how they got to Canada. The family had a shop in London, not well off, and the father had been gassed in the first war. When the government announced they were giving gas masks to children, he decided they had to go. Sold the shop at a loss, packed everything up, and headed to Australia. Then, well, they got there, and Australia said they were going to give gas masks out. So, they packed up again and came all the way to Canada." The decision to give gas masks to everyone, in this person's experience, was not reassuring but rather an emblem of the worst that modern war could do. It offers a reminder that developing and distributing gas masks to everyone had consequences that no one – certainly no one planning how to create and use them widely – could have predicted. I am also grateful to those who shared more recent encounters with the civilian gas mask, including those living in Israel during the First Gulf War, and especially Dr. Karolina Watroba, who at the end of this project shared her experiences of twenty-first-century gas mask training as a secondary school student in Poland. They all helped me to appreciate further the human encounter with an official civilian gas mask. A focus on the gas mask and its role in shaping the childhood experiences of the Second World War is also potently explored by Gabriel Moshenska; see Gabriel Moshenska, "Gas Masks: Material Culture, Memory and the Senses," *Journal of the Royal Anthropological Institute* 16 (2010),

609–28. See also his expanded and important discussion of this in his recent book *Material Cultures of Childhood in Second World War Britain* (London and New York: Routledge, 2019), ch. 1.

3 Cicely Hamilton, *Theodore Savage: A Story of the Past or the Future* (London: Leonard Parsons, 1922); Hamilton rewrote and republished the novel at the decade's end as *Lest Ye Die: A Story from the Past or of the Future* (New York: C. Scribner's Sons, and London: J. Cape, 1928). See also Susan R. Grayzel, "Imagining War in a Post-1918 World: Cicely Hamilton's *Theodore Savage*," in "Colloquium on Key Texts for Understanding the First World War," *Contemporanea: rivista di storia dell'800 e del '900* 17:4 (2014), 660–65.

4 Put another way, the gas mask is a synecdoche for modern, total war. Air power was also a charged moment, and it provoked similar ethical debates to those that ensued when poison gas became part of war. For more on this, see Susan R. Grayzel, *At Home and under Fire: Air Raids and Culture in Britain from the Great War to the Blitz* (Cambridge: Cambridge University Press, 2012).

5 I began to explore these issues in "Protecting Which Spaces and Bodies? Civil Defence, the British Empire and the Second World War," in *An Imperial World at War*, ed. Ashley Jackson et al. (London: Ashgate, 2016), 66–83. Other related issues such as the provision of gas masks to non-citizens (e.g., internees) will be discussed in later chapters.

6 Again, for a significant anthropological study of the gas mask that situates it within the field of the archeology of modern conflict, see Moshenska, "Gas Masks" and *Material Cultures of Childhood in Second World War Britain*. Observers reacted to gas masks on children, and children reacted to having gas masks, but not always in predictable ways.

7 See J. B. S. Haldane, *Callinicus: A Defence of Chemical Warfare* (London: Routledge and Kegan Paul, 1925) and J. F. C. Fuller, *The First of the League Wars: Its Lessons and Omens* (London: Eyre and Spottiswoode, 1936), who points out on p. 85 that he had been making this argument since 1923.

8 Tim Cook, "'Against God-Inspired Conscience': The Perception of Gas Warfare as a Weapon of Mass Destruction, 1915–1939," *War & Society* 18:1 (2000), 47–69; L. F. Haber, *The Poisonous Cloud: Chemical Warfare in the First World War* (Oxford: Clarendon Press, 1986); Ulrich Trumpener, "The Road to Ypres: The Beginnings of Gas Warfare in World War I," *Journal of Modern History* 47:3 (1975), 460–80. For Britain in particular, see Marion Girard, *A Strange and Formidable Weapon: British Response to World War I Poison Gas* (Lincoln: University of Nebraska Press, 2008); Albert Palazzo, *Seeking Victory on the Western Front: The British Army and Chemical Warfare in World War I* (Lincoln: University of Nebraska Press, 2008); and Donald Richter, *Chemical Soldiers: British Gas Warfare in World War I* (Lawrence: University of Kansas Press, 1992). For works that approach this from the angle of political science, science, and international law, see Frederic J. Brown, *Chemical Warfare: A Study in Restraints* (1968; repr. New Brunswick, NJ, and London: Transaction, 2006); Richard M. Price, *The Chemical Weapons Taboo* (Ithaca, NY, and London: Cornell University Press, 1997); Edmund Russell, *War and Nature: Fighting Humans and*

Insects with Chemicals from World War I to Silent Spring (Cambridge: Cambridge University Press, 2001). See also Catherine Jefferson, "Origins of the Norm against Chemical Weapons," *International Affairs* 90:3 (2014), 647–61. For approaches that investigate the largely secret and involuntary use of chemical arms on human test subjects for the purposes of developing these weapons, see Rob Evans, *Gassed: British Chemical Warfare Experiments on Humans at Porton Down* (London: House of Stratus, 2000) and Ulf Schmidt, *Secret Science: A Century of Poison Warfare and Human Experiments* (Oxford: Oxford University Press, 2015). For important recent work on non-lethal chemical arms, see Anna Feigenbaum, *Tear Gas: From the Battlefields of WWI to the Streets of Today* (New York: Verso, 2017).

9 This project is very much part of the understudied history of civil defense before the Cold War. In Britain, its origins begin with the arrival of air power during the First World War, but the main focus of the volume covering the subject in the official history of the Second World War pays scant attention to its anti-gas elements. In the planning stages since the early 1920s and unveiled to the British public in 1935, air raid precautions (or ARP, as the British version of civil defense was known) aimed to secure the morale as well as the lives and livelihoods of the British civilian population. ARP designed preparations for the use of both conventional air attacks and chemical arms, and it was under its auspices that the civilian gas mask was developed. However, since poison gas did not, in fact, become part of the British experience of the Second World War, this aspect of civil defense tends to be relegated to the sidelines. See Terence H. O'Brien, *Civil Defence: Official History of the Second World War* (London: HMSO,1955). See also Home Office, *Air Raid Precautions* (London: HMSO, 1938). For Cold War British history, see Matthew Grant, *After the Bomb: Civil Defence and Nuclear War in Britain, 1945–68* (Basingstoke: Macmillan, 2010). For the Second World War, see Patrick Doyle, *ARP and Civil Defence in the Second World War* (Oxford: Shire, 2010); Helen Jones, *British Civilians in the Front Line: Air Raids, Productivity and Wartime Culture 1939–1945* (Manchester: Manchester University Press, 2006). Other scholars have traced the legacy of poison gas for postwar culture; see Ana Carden-Coyne, "Toxic Imaginaries and the Culture of Chemical War since 1915," manuscript essay, 2015. My thanks to Ana Carden-Coyne for sharing this with me.

10 I summarize some of the utility of this scholarship in Grayzel, "Macabre and Hilarious." The sources that I have found especially useful for this study are Arjun Appadurai, "Introduction: Commodities and the Politics of Value," in *The Social Life of Things: Commodities in Cultural Perspective*, ed. Arjun Appadurai (Cambridge: Cambridge University Press, 1986), 3–63; Bill Brown, "Thing Theory," in *Things*, ed. Bill Brown (Chicago: University of Chicago Press, 2004), 3–21; Chris Gosden, "What Do Objects Want?," *Journal of Archaeological Method and Theory* 12:3 (2005),193–211; Ian Hodder, *Entangled: An Archaeology of the Relationship between Humans and Things* (Chichester: Wiley-Blackwell, 2012); W. David Kingery, "Introduction," in *Learning from Things: Method and Theory of Material Culture Studies*, ed. W. David Kingery (Washington, DC: Smithsonian

Institution Press, 1996); Daniel Miller, *Stuff* (Malden, MA: Polity, 2010), 1–15.

11 While aware of the differences implied by using the term "things" rather than "objects" in much of this scholarship, for the purposes of this book, I am using "thing," "object," "device," and any other synonym interchangeably. In so doing, I am following the lead of Laurel Thatcher Ulrich et al., *Tangible Things: Making History through Objects* (Oxford: Oxford University Press, 2015), 2.

12 Miller, *Stuff*, 53 and ch. 2, especially 60–64.

13 Some notable examples by non-historians include studies by the anthropologist Nicholas Saunders, who points out in his *Trench Art: Materialities and Memories of War* (Oxford: Berg, 2003), 1, that the First World War demonstrates the power of industrialized modern war to transform "matter through the agency of destruction" and explores the materiality of war in two edited collections, Paul Cornish and Nicholas J. Saunders, eds., *Bodies in Conflict: Corporeality, Materiality, and Transformation* (London: Routledge, 2014) and Nicholas J. Saunders, ed., *Matters of Conflict: Material Culture, Memory, and the First World War* (London: Routledge, 2004). There is a relatively new and robust field of popular history as told by objects, usually 100 of them. This includes the most famous, Neil MacGregor, *The History of the World in 100 Objects* (New York: Viking, 2011), based on objects held by the British Museum; and the genre now ranges from histories of segments of the population (Maggie Andrews and Janis Lomas, *A History of Women in 100 Objects* (Stroud: The History Press, 2018) to epochs (Roger Moorhouse and Richard Overy, *The Third Reich in 100 Objects: A Material History of Nazi Germany* (Stroud: The History Press, 2018)). In Austin J. Ruddy, *The Home Front 1939–1945 in 100 Objects* (Barnsley: Frontline, 2019), the general civilian respirator is listed as number 6, "perhaps the most symbolic and evocative objects of the British Home Front" (12).

14 The key example remains Jared Diamond, *Guns, Germs and Steel: The Fates of Human Societies* (New York: Norton, 1997). For more recent work, see Priya Satia, *Empire of Guns: The Violent Making of the Industrial Revolution* (New York: Penguin, 2018).

15 Mats Fridlund, "Buckets, Bollards and Bombs: Towards Subject Histories of Technologies and Terrors," *History and Technology* 27:4 (2011), 397.

16 Geoffrey Parker, *The Cambridge Illustrated History of Warfare: The Triumph of the West* (revised ed., Cambridge: Cambridge University Press, 2008).

17 John Ellis, *The Social History of the Machine Gun* (1975; repr. Baltimore: Johns Hopkins University Press, 1986).

18 Joanna Bourke, *Wounding the World: How Military Violence and War-Play Invade Our Lives* (London: Virago, 2014) has a provocative related discussion about how war is made possible by both combatants and their civilian counterparts normalizing violence.

19 For an overview see Michael Howard et al., eds., *The Laws of War: Constraints on Warfare in the Western World* (New Haven, CT: Yale University Press, 1994).

20 For a helpful discussion, see Tammy M. Proctor, *Civilians in a World at War 1914–1918* (New York: New York University Press, 2010), 17–19.

21 See, for example, Isabel V. Hull, *Absolute Destruction: Military Culture and the Practice of War in Imperial Germany* (Ithaca, NY: Cornell University Press, 2005) and Michelle Moyd, *Violent Intermediaries: African Soldiers, Conquest, and Everyday Colonialism in German East Africa* (Athens: Ohio University Press, 2014) and "Color Lines, Front Lines: The First World War from the South," *Radical History Review* 131 (2018), 13–35.

22 There is room to engage with the challenges posed by modern discussions of phenomenology such as those by Sara Ahmed in *Queer Phenomenology* or Ian Bogost in *Alien Phenomenology*, both of which, in substantively different and significant ways, insist on decentering our ideas about what things do, why they matter, and how our stuff might belong at the center of the ways in which we understand the world. Sara Ahmed, *Queer Phenomenology: Orientations, Objects, Others* (Durham, NC: Duke University Press, 2006) and Ian Bogost, *Alien Phenomenology or What It's Like to Be a Thing* (Minneapolis: University of Minnesota Press, 2012).

23 Leora Auslander and Tara Zahra, "Introduction" to *Objects of War: The Material Culture of Conflict and Displacement*, ed. Leora Auslander and Tara Zahra (Ithaca, NY: Cornell University Press, 2018), 4–5.

24 Ibid., 5.

25 Jonathan Krause, "The Origins of Chemical Warfare in the French Army," *War in History* 20:4 (2013), 545–56. Krause cites a "Rapport sur l'organisation du Service du Matériel Chimique de Guerre, présenté par M. D'Aubigny, Deputé, 25 August 1915" as the source of information that the French were developing their earliest models based on respirators used in mines. See also Haber, *Poisonous Cloud*, 53.

26 "AHR Conversations: The Historical Study of Emotions: Participants: Nicole Eustace, Eugenia Lean, Julie Livingston, Jan Plamper, William A. Reddy, and Barbara H. Rosenwein," *American Historical Review* 117:5 (2012), 1487–531; discussion here drawn from Rosenwein (1515) and Lean (1519).

27 Stephanie Downes, Sally Holloway, and Sarah Randles, "A Feeling for Things, Past and Present," in *Feeling Things: Objects and Emotions through History*, ed. Stephanie Downes et al. (Oxford: Oxford University Press, 2018), 8. This is another study that excludes, largely, the objects and artifacts of war.

28 As Jean Livingston puts it: "large-scale traumatic events like ... war... can thrust familiar but latent affective possibilities into the foreground, linking recursive pasts to the present." See Livingston in "AHR Conversations: The Historical Study of Emotions," 1520.

29 There is a substantial literature on this. For a useful overview, see Tracey Loughran, "Shell Shock, Trauma and the First World War: The Making of a Diagnosis and Its Histories," *Journal of the History of Medicine and Allied Sciences* 67:1 (2012), 94–119.

30 Plamper in "AHR Conversations: The Historical Study of Emotions," 1516. See also Jan Plamper, "Soldiers and Emotion in Early Twentieth-Century Russia Military Psychology," in *Fear across the Disciplines*, ed. Jan Plamper and Benjamin Lazier (Pittsburgh, PA: University of Pittsburgh Press, 2012), 78–98.

31 Joanna Bourke captures the essence of this concept when she observes that "war domesticates terror" and that "in the face of total war, no one felt safe. Ever." See Bourke, *Fear: A Cultural History* (Emeryville, CA: Shoemaker & Hoard, 2005), 195.

32 Bourke, *Fear*: see ch. 7 for combatants and ch. 8 for civilians.

33 Fridlund, "Buckets, Bollards and Bombs," 398–402.

34 See Suzannah Biernoff, "The Rhetoric of Disfigurement in First World War Britain," *Social History of Medicine* 24:3 (2011), 666–85; Katherine Feo, "Invisibility: Memory, Masks, and Masculinities in the Great War," *Journal of Design History* 20:1 (Mar. 2007), 17–27, quote on 18.

35 Sigmund Freud, "The Uncanny" (1919), trans. Alix Strachey, in *The Standard Edition of the Complete Psychological Works of Sigmund Freud*, vol. 17: *1917–1919*, ed. James Strachey (London: Hogarth Press, 1955), 220.

36 See the discussion of letter writing in Martha Hanna, *Your Death Would Be Mine* (Cambridge, MA: Harvard University Press, 2008), and more importantly for this discussion in Michael Roper, *The Secret Battle: Emotional Survival in World War One* (Manchester: Manchester University Press, 2009). For the significance of the photograph, see Catherine Moriarty, "'Though in a Picture Only': Portrait Photography and the Commemoration of the First World War," in *Evidence, History, and the Great War: Historians and the Impact of 1914–18*, ed. Gail Braybon (New York: Berghahn, 2003), 30–47.

37 Theorists like Donna Haraway have written about the significance that the "cyborg" has for understanding new ways to configure the future of humans – complicating the "leaky distinction between animal-human (organism) and machine." (See Haraway, "A Cyborg Manifesto," in *Simians, Cyborgs and Women: The Reinvention of Nature* [New York: Routledge, 1991; repr. 2010], 150–51) Like the artificial life-extending features of technology associated with cyborgs, the gas mask as object suggests new ways to think of the body (the human and the technological); the civilian gas mask as state-sanctioned (and provided) apparatus further may open up ways in which to think about the individual body and the state.

38 One can do this without agreeing entirely with claims that one can trace the moment the twentieth century began with great precision to April 22, 1915, as it does for philosopher Peter Sloterdijk. He argues that this was the moment when military violence shifted from aiming at taking lives to destroying environments, thus begetting the age of terror and extermination: "in gas warfare, the deepest levels of people's biological condition was incorporated into the attacks on them." Peter Sloterdijk, "Airquake," in *Foams: Spheres III*, trans. Wieland Hoban (South Pasadena, CA: Semiotext(e), 2016), 97. My thanks to Charlie Huenemann for this reference.

39 I want here to acknowledge the limits of this study. Despite what I have learned from a variety of prior scholarship and different approaches, in the end, I am not a historian of science or technology, so the tale of discoveries in chemistry and weaponry will be only tangential to this study. Nor is this the study that traces – as environmental historians would do fully – all the networks of resources exploited to develop this object, from rubber to fabric to charcoal. I hope someone will write that account because it will further show how very centrally the gas mask was an imperial thing.

Chapter 2

1 Wilfred Owen, "Dulce et decorum est," composed 1917, first published posthumously in *The Poems of Wilfred Owen* (London: Chatto & Windus, 1920).

2 One attempt to address the materiality of the gas mask solely as a wartime technological object can be found in Tim Cook, "Through Clouded Eyes: Gas Masks in the First World War," *Material History Review* 47 (1998), 4–20.

3 For the more general history of chemical warfare, see Brown, *Chemical Warfare*; Price, *The Chemical Weapons Taboo*; and Russell, *War and Nature*. For more on the norm against using chemical arms, see Jefferson, "Origins of the Norm against Chemical Weapons."

4 See the extensive discussion of gas casualties in Haber, *Poisonous Cloud*, ch. 10, especially 241–44; the lower number comes from Haber's chart on 244. More recent accounts relying on official government studies account for the larger figure. See Edgar Jones, "Terror Weapons: The British Experience of Gas and Its Treatment in the First World War," *War in History* 21:3 (2014), 362.

5 For histories of chemical weapons in the First World War in addition to Jones, "Terror Weapons," see Gerald J. Fitzgerald, "Chemical Warfare and Medical Response during World War I," *American Journal of Public Health* 98:4 (2008), 611–25; Krause, "The Origins of Chemical Warfare in the French Army"; Jonathan B. Tucker, *War of Nerves: Chemical Warfare from World War I to Al-Qaeda* (New York: Anchor Books, 2007); especially for Britain, see Girard, *A Strange and Formidable Weapon*; Haber, *Poisonous Cloud*; Palazzo, *Seeking Victory on the Western Front*; and Richter, *Chemical Soldiers*. For an exploration of the cultural legacies, see Ana Carden-Coyne, "Toxic Imaginaries and the Culture of Chemical War since 1915" (unpublished essay, 2018) and Doris Kaufmann, "Gas, Gas, Gaas! The Poison Gas War in the Literature and Visual Arts of Interwar Europe," in *One Hundred Years of Chemical Warfare: Research, Deployment, Consequences*, ed. B. Friedrich et al. (Springer Nature Open, 2015), DOI: 10.1007/978-3-319-51664-6_10. My thanks to Krisztina Robert for alerting me to the Kaufmann chapter.

6 "Declaration of St. Petersburg, 19 Nov. 1868," in Avalon Project, Laws of War, http://avalon.law.yale.edu/19th_century/decpeter.asp (accessed Dec. 28, 2017); "Declaration on the Use of Projectiles the Object of Which is the Diffusion of Asphyxiating or Deleterious Gases; July 29, 1899" (accessed Dec. 28, 2017); and Article 23 of Hague Conventions 1907, http://avalon.law.yale.edu/19th_century/dec99-02.asp, http://avalon.law.yale.edu/20th_century/hague04.asp (accessed Dec. 28, 2017). The longer scope of such actions is set out in Jefferson, "Origins of the Norm against Chemical Weapons."

7 Haber, *Poisonous Cloud*.

8 Account and quote from Haber, *Poisonous Cloud*, 32. For more on Fritz Haber, see Margit Szöllösi-Janze, "The Scientist as Expert: Fritz Haber and German Chemical Warfare during the First World War and Beyond," in *One*

Hundred Years of Chemical Warfare: Research, Deployment, Consequences, ed. B. Friedrich et al. (Springer Nature Open, 2015), DOI: 10.1007/978-3-319-51664-6_10.

9 "An Account of German Cloud Gas Attacks on British Front in France," [c. 1935] The National Archives, London (TNA), WO 142/267.

10 For example, appeals appeared in such papers as *Western Times*, Apr. 29, 1915; *Hull Daily Mail*, Apr. 29, 1915; and *Manchester Evening News*, Apr. 28, 1915. The most frequently cited source for the appeal in the regional papers is "Respirators for Our Troops," *Daily Mail*, Apr. 28, 1915.

11 "Rush Job for Women," *Daily Mail*, April 29, 1915; "Will You Make a Respirator?," *Evening Despatch*, Apr. 29, 1915; "Respirators Wanted for Troops at the Front," Apr. 29, 1915; "An Opportunity for Women," *Birmingham Daily Post*, Apr. 29, 1915; "Rush to Make Respirators: Women's Response to War Office Appeal," *Daily Express*, Apr. 29, 1915.

12 "Rush to Make Respirators: Women's Response to War Office Appeal," *Daily Express*, Apr. 29, 1915.

13 "Rush to Make Respirators." See also accounts reflecting this in "An Opportunity for Women," *Birmingham Daily Post*, Apr. 29, 1915, and "Respirators Wanted," *Daily Mirror*, Apr. 29, 1915.

14 Lynn Macdonald, *1915: The Loss of Innocence* (1993; repr. Baltimore: Johns Hopkins University Press, 2000), 231–32. There were later attempts to make woolen respirators in France; see the discussion in Susan R. Grayzel, "'Needles en avant!': The Militarization of Sewing and Knitting during the First World War in France, Britain and the United States," in *French Fashion, Women, and the First World War*, ed. Maude Bass-Krueger and Sophie Kurkdjian (New Haven, CT: Yale University Press, 2019), 164–65.

15 *Manchester Evening News*, Apr. 29, 1915.

16 "Rush to Respirators: Women's Response to War Office Appeal," *Daily Express*, Apr. 29, 1915.

17 *Home Fires Burning: The Great War Diaries of Georgina Lee*, ed. Gavin Roynon (2006; Stroud: History Press, 2009), 103, entry dated Apr. 29, 1915.

18 "Deluge of Respirators," *Dundee Courier*, Apr. 30, 1915. See also "Respirators for the Troops," *Times*, Apr. 30, 1915.

19 "Respirators," *Irish Times*, Apr. 30, 1915.

20 "Women Foil the Poisoner," *Daily Mail*, Apr. 30, 1915.

21 Palazzo, *Seeking Victory*, 42–43. Like most accounts, this history pays scant attention to this call for those at home to make gas masks other than to dismiss the effort as futile. See also Haber, *Poisonous Cloud*, who records that the *Daily Mail* was the first to issue the call to women followed by the War Office on April 28 and states that "the next day women crowded the Army Clothing Depot in Pimlico" (45); and Girard, *A Strange and Formidable Weapon*, who describes "a public call to the women of England to make simple gauze masks ... an appeal that was so successful that thirty thousand masks were shipped to the War Office in thirty-six hours" (24).

22 "An Account of German Cloud Gas Attacks on British Front in France" and "Diary of Development of British Respirator" [c. 1935], TNA, WO 142/267.

23 It is unclear what happened to the useless respirators. Presumably, some of the material could be converted to bandages.

24 For biographical information about Haldane, see Martin Goodman, *Suffer and Survive: The Extreme Life of J. S. Haldane* (London: Simon and Schuster, 2007). For the development of the Black Veil respirator, see Haber, *Poisonous Cloud*, 45–46. For mourning attire, see Lucie Whitmore, "'A Matter of Individual Opinion and Feeling': The Changing Culture of Mourning Dress in the First World War," *Women's History Review* (2017), DOI: 10.1080/09612025.2017.1292631

25 Palazzo, *Seeking Victory*, 42–43. See also Haber, *Poisonous Cloud*. The main types of poison gas (excluding lachrymatory agents or gases that primarily irritated eyes or tear gases)employed during the war included chlorine (first used in Apr. 1915); phosgene (carbonyl dichloride, Oct. 1915); and disphogene (trichloromethane chloroformate, 1916) – all of which affected the lungs although in the case of the latter two in a delayed manner; and mustard gas (1, 1-thiobis 2 chloroethane, 1917), a vesicant that produced chemical burns on contact with skin or with the lungs when inhaled.

26 She later modified this device in 1917 by developing a mechanical version that was apparently never used. Ayrton herself described her early invention and its effects in "Anti-gas Fans," *Times*, May 3, 1920, from which the quote in this paragraph is taken. This provoked a series of letters to the editor from the experts H. A. Sisson (who served with the Royal Engineers), who attacked the fans as wasteful and useless, and Major H. J. Gillespie, who defended them when used properly and cited them as having a salutary effect in Armentières in the summer of 1917. See Sisson, letter to the editor, *Times*, May 6, 1920, and Gillespie, letter to the editor, *Times*, May 4, 1920. See also Haber, *Poisonous Cloud*, 104–05, who dismisses them as "big fly swats" and as "ridiculous," evidence of the last "amateur" efforts to address poison gas. Ventilation as a solution to poisoned air was out, individual protection was in.

27 Brown, *Chemical Warfare*, 10; Yigal Sheffy, "Chemical Warfare and the Palestine Campaign, 1916–1918," *Journal of Military History* 73:3 (2009), 803–44.

28 See, in addition to Brown, *Chemical Warfare*, Palazzo, *Seeking Victory*; Girard, *A Strange and Formidable Weapon*; and Olivier Lepick, *La guerre chimique: 1914–1918* (Paris: Presses Universitaires de France, 1998). For a succinct overview of the development of the gas mask within the British military, see Cook, "Through Clouded Eyes."

29 "The Man who Robbed German Gas of Its Terrors," *Birmingham Post*, Nov. 7, 1918, Imperial War Museum, London (IWM), Harrison Collection, document reference no. 15389.

30 "The Inventor of the Gas Mask," *Medical Press*, Dec. 4, 1918, IWM, Harrison Collection, document reference no 15389.

31 "Anti-gas Chief Dead," *Daily Sketch*, Nov. 7, 1918, IWM, Harrison Collection, document reference no. 15389.

32 Photograph of memorial plaque, IWM, Harrison Collection, document reference no. 15389. For accounts of the attacks on Fritz Haber, see the work of his son I. F. Haber, *Poisonous Cloud*, 1–14. John Scott Haldane would also

continue to receive praise for his work in designing earlier prototypes; other notable inventors who contributed to the invention of the gas mask included African American Garrett Morgan, who patented a safety hood and smoke protector in 1914, and Canadian Cluny Macpherson, who designed a fabric smoke helmet in 1915.

33 Lee, *Home Fires Burning*, 103–04. Lee included a newspaper clipping of the design for the respirator in the *Daily Mail*, with the handwritten notation "Respirators for the Trenches, to render German asphyxiating gas less deadly." See also "Gas Bombs on London," Daily Mail, May 24, 1915.

34 Diary of Lady Matthews [c. May 31, 1915], IWM, Department of Documents, Papers of Lady Matthews 09/36/1.

35 Advertisement for Surgical Manufacturing Company, *Times*, May 26, 1915.

36 "Gas Bombs on London," *Daily Mail*, May 24, 1915.

37 *Times*, June 2 and 10, 1915; *Daily Chronicle*, June 3, 1915.

38 Advertisement for Hospitals and General Contracts Co. Ltd., *Pall Mall Gazette*, June 9, 1915.

39 See letter dated June 16, 1915 and enclosed in diary of Lady Matthews, IWM, Department of Documents, Papers of Lady Matthews 09/36/1. Emphasis in original.

40 Other cartoons of gas masks and civilians are discussed in Girard, *A Strange and Formidable Weapon*, 150–52.

41 See a fuller discussion of this in Susan R. Grayzel, "'Macabre and Hilarious': The Emotional Life of the Civilian Gas Mask in France during and after the First World War," in *Total War: An Emotional History*, ed. Claire Langhamer, Lucy Noakes, and Claudia Siebrecht (Oxford: Oxford University Press, 2020), 40–58.

42 For more on these air raids, see Grayzel, *At Home and under Fire*, ch. 3.

43 "Air Raid Casualty Inquest," Oct. 4, 1917, TNA, HO 45/10883. Shoreditch is a neighborhood in east London.

44 New Scotland Yard Report, Nov. 3, 1917, TNA, HO 45/10883.

45 "Gas Mask Race at Army Sports" and "Gas Mask Drill at a Training Camp in England," *Daily Mirror*, Aug. 1 and Sept. 26, 1917.

46 "Football 'Frightfulness,'" *Daily Mirror*, Mar. 23, 1918. Commentary on gas masks can be found in a range of media by and for soldiers, such as this account in the *Palestine News*, May 18, 1918: "Concert parties are as essential to the well-being of the troops in this war as, say, the gas-mask. And parties as we know them are as modern in war as the gas-mask." My thanks to Mahon Murphy for this reference.

47 See Bibliothèque Nationale de France, Paris, where it is part of the collection of Agence Rol and labeled "En Pays bombardé" ("In the bombed country") with "mère et enfant" ("mother and child") in brackets; this is also available on the library's digital collection Gallica at https://gallica.bnf.fr/ark:/12148/btv1b53004018k.r=agence%20de%20pressemasque%20a%20gaz%20masque%20a%20gaz?rk=515024;0 (accessed Apr. 10, 2015); and see also IWM, Department of Photographs Q48900 – where it is labeled as a Belgian mother and child – and the learning website for the First World War hosted by the British Library, London (BL), which describes it as "Mère et enfant"

(mother and child), www.bl.uk/collection-items/mother-child-gas-masks (accessed June 1, 2016). No details about inhabitants, location, or time of the photograph are provided in any of the online or paper catalogues for these institutions.

48 See the discussion of the uncanny in Chapter 1 above.

49 For an evocative discussion of the unknown soldier, see Laura Wittman, *The Tomb of the Unknown Soldier, Modern Mourning, and the Reinvention of the Mystical Body* (Toronto: University of Toronto Press, 2011).

50 See untitled photograph, *Daily Mirror*, Jan. 15, 1918, and "Children in Gas Masks," *Daily Mirror*, Feb. 27, 1918.

51 "Scene in Village," *Daily Express*, Sept. 5, 1918.

52 For more on attitudes toward the war in Britain, see Adrian Gregory, *The Last Great War: British Society and the First World War* (Cambridge: Cambridge University Press, 2008). For cultural mobilization and remobilization, see John Horne, ed., *State, Society and Mobilization in Europe during the First World War* (Cambridge: Cambridge University Press, 1997), especially Horne's essay, "Remobilizing for 'Total War': France and Britain, 1917–1918," 195–211.

53 Boots Pure Drug Co., "Activities during Last War" and "Report Prepared for the Directorate of Industrial Planning, War Office," June 1939. My deep gratitude to Boots senior archivist Charlotte McCarthy for her assistance in tracking down this material. For the photograph, see IWM, Department of Photography, Ministry of Information First World War Official Collection, items Q28553 and Q28593. For more on the staging of such photographs, see Deborah Thom, "Making Spectaculars: Museums and How We Remember Gender in Wartime," in *Evidence, History and the Great War: Historians and the Impact of 1914–18*, ed. Gail Braybon (New York: Berghahn, 2003), 48–66.

54 John Bell, Hills & Lucas Ltd, *Lest We Forget* (London: John Bell, Hills & Lucas, Ltd, 1918) unpaginated. Similar rhetoric was used to discuss women munitions workers: see Gail Braybon, *Women Workers in the First World War* (London: Croom Helm, 1981); Laura Lee Downs, *Manufacturing Inequality: Gender Division in the French and British Metalworking Industries, 1914–1939* (Ithaca, NY: Cornell University Press, 1995); Deborah Thom, *Nice Girls and Rude Girls: Women Workers in World War I* (London: I. B. Tauris, 1997); Angela Woollacott, *On Her Their Lives Depend: Munitions Workers in the Great War* (Berkeley: University of California Press, 1994); and essays by Gail Braybon and Deborah Thom in *Evidence, History and the Great War: Historians and the Impact of 1914–18* ed. Gail Braybon (New York: Berghahn, 2003).

55 The overall efficacy of military gas masks has continued to inspire debate, and although better devices reduced mortality so too did better clinical treatment such as providing oxygen. See Haber, *Poisonous Cloud* and Jones, "Terror Weapons."

56 "Demobbed Gas Mask," *Daily Mirror*, Nov. 15, 1919.

57 "Fatal Gas Mask," *Daily Express*, June 1, 1923. The gas mask as a device was also used to commit suicide during the Second World War, a fact noted in later chapters.

58 Victor Lefebure, *The Riddle of the Rhine: Chemical Strategy in Peace and War* (1921; repr. London: Collins, 1922), 25–26, 34.

59 Lefebure,, *The Riddle of the Rhine*, 123. Lefebure went on to add: "Gas discipline thus became one of the most important features of general training, a feature which can never be abandoned by the armies of civilised nations in the future without disastrous results" (128). See also Lefebure's responses to a series of articles on the link between the chemical industry and poison gas warfare in the *Times*; Victor Lefebure, letter to the editor, *Times*, Aug. 16, 1920 and Sept. 13, 1921.

60 "Chemical Warfare," *British Medical Journal*, Dec. 1921. Among other texts published that year, see the work of American proponents of chemical weapons such as Amos Fries and Clarence West. In *Chemical Warfare* (New York: McGraw-Hill, 1921), they argued that "it is just as sportsman-like to fight with chemical weapons as it is to fight with machine guns" (437). This deliberately sought to counter one of the wartime critiques of innovations such as air raids and chemical shells: that they were atrocities used by cowards against the innocent and thus had to be stopped. In contrast, journalist Will Irwin (who covered the first gas attacks at Ypres for the *New York Tribune*), in his *"The Next War": An Appeal to Common Sense* (New York: E. P. Dutton, 1921), described the potential extension to civilian populations of all the devastating effects of modern warfare as a catastrophe that must be prevented. Tellingly, the book begins by reproducing a photo taken the U.S. Army Signal Corps and featuring "a French family equipped with gas masks" from Marbache, Meurthe-et-Moselle, September 1918, with the ominous caption "Every man, woman and child in this village was obliged, during the latter part of the war, to carry a gas mask at all times. In the next war, innumerable women and children may be obliged to wear not only gas masks, but gas-proof suits covering the entire body, as a protection against the new cell-killing gases" (ii). See also Fitzgerald, "Chemical Warfare and Medical Response during World War I."

61 Hamilton's *Theodore Savage* was republished in a revised form in 1928 as *Lest Yet Die*. Further references will appear parenthetically in the text. An even earlier portrayal of postwar environmental catastrophe, Edward Shanks's *The People of the Ruins* (London: William Collins & Sons, 1920), is less about war.

62 "Novel Notes," *Bookman*, June 1922.

63 "Fiction," *Saturday Review*, June 1922; "New Novels," *Manchester Guardian*, May 12, 1922. These times included a world in which political citizenship now applied to some women with the 1918 passage of the Representation of the People Act. The implications of the wartime passage of franchise reform that gave the vote to women over thirty or with certain qualifications have been discussed by a number of historians: see Nicoletta F. Gullace, *"The Blood of Our Sons": Men, Women, and the Renegotiation of British Citizenship during the Great War* (Basingstoke: Palgrave Macmillan, 2002); Sandra Stanley Holton, *Feminism and Democracy: Women's Suffrage and Reform Politics in Britain 1900–1918* (Cambridge: Cambridge University Press, 2003); and Martin Pugh, *Women's Suffrage in Britain, 1867–1928* (London: Historical Association, 1980). The utter inability of women to achieve equality is another key theme in the novel.

64 For more on the work of this government in inventing civil defense, see Grayzel, *At Home and under Fire*.

65 Maurice Hankey, ARP Memorandum 11, TNA, CAB 46/3. Emphasis added.

66 André Michelin, "The Danger of Aero-Chemical Attack by Germany," *English Review*, Oct. 1924, and Captain J. Brifaut, "The War of To-morrow and the Aero-chemical Menace," *English Review*, Feb. 1925.

67 Data from Circulaire d'application pour l'instruction du 9 août 1923, "La protection de la population contre les effets des bombardements aériens" ("The protection of the population from the effects of aerial bombardment"), Archives Nationales de France, Paris, F/7/13984. See also Lindsey Dodd and Marc Wiggam, "Civil Defence as a Harbinger of War in France and Britain during the Interwar Period," *Synergies* 4 (2011), 139–50, especially 145, for a good overview of differences in laws in France and Britain before and after 1935.

68 League of Nations Union, *Chemical Warfare* (London: League of Nations Union, 1924), 18. For the significance of the League of Nations Union, see Helen McCarthy, *The British People and the League of Nations: Democracy, Citizenship and Internationalism, 1918–1945* (Manchester: Manchester University Press, 2011).

69 Committee Against Scientific Warfare, newsletter, Nov. 1924, in Women's International League for Peace and Freedom Collection, IV-7-13, Archives, University of Colorado at Boulder Libraries, WILPF Papers, 1915–78 (microfilm, reel 103, frames 1801–03), cited in Alison Sobek, "How Did the Women's International League for Peace and Freedom Campaign against Chemical Warfare, 1915–1930" (State University of New York at Binghampton, 2001).

70 Annette B. Vogt, "Getrud Johanna Woker (1878–1968)," in *European Women in Chemistry*, ed. Jan Apotheker et al. (Hoboken, NJ: Wiley Blackwell, 2011), 65–69.

71 Gertrud Woker, *The Next War: A War of Poison Gas* (Washington, DC: Women's International League for Peace and Freedom, 1927); Women's International League for Peace and Freedom Collection, IV-7-14, Archives, University of Colorado at Boulder Libraries, WILPF Papers, 1915–78 (microfilm, reel 112, frames 1133–36), cited in Sobek, "How Did the Women's International League for Peace and Freedom Campaign."

72 Woker, *The Next War*

73 Britain's active interwar peace movement has received significant attention, but the key overview remains Martin Ceadel, *Pacifism in Britain, 1914–1945: The Defining of a Faith* (Oxford: Clarendon Press, 1980). For feminist anti-militarism in this era, see Jill Liddington, *The Long Road to Greenham: Feminism and Anti-militarism in Britain since 1820* (London: Virago, 1989). See also Richard Overy, *The Twilight Years: The Paradox of Britain Between the Wars* (New York: Viking, 2009) for the placement of these movements in larger cultural and political developments

74 For an overview of the work done at Porton, see the official history in G. B. Carter, *Chemical and Biological Defence at Porton Down 1916–2000* (London: HMSO, 2000), especially chs. 1 and 2.

75 See Schmidt, *Secret Science* and Evans, *Gassed* for critical perspectives on this work.
76 For a quick introduction, see V. M. Quirke, "Haldane, John Burdon Sanderson (1892–1954)," *Oxford Dictionary of National Biography* (Sept. 23, 2004), https://doi.org/10.1093/ref:odnf/33641 (accessed Jan. 20, 2017).
77 Haldane, *Callinicus*, 21, 38.
78 Ibid., 22, 35–36, 40. Pacifists and antimilitarists did indeed object to these measures when they were introduced, but Haldane suggests that preparing civilians to survive a potential gas attack should not be considered akin to preparing for war itself.
79 Haldane, *Callinicus*, 53–54. Haldane also criticized the effort by the women of England to produce the failed respirators of 1915; see 63–67.
80 For an overview of this concept, see Daniel Ussishkin, *Morale: A Modern British History* (Oxford: Oxford University Press, 2017).
81 Haldane, *Callinicus*, 81.
82 "Poisonous Gases in Future Warfare," *Times Literary Supplement*, Feb. 19, 1925.
83 "Protocol for the Prohibition of the Use in War of Asphyxiating, Poisonous or Other Gases, and of Bacteriological Methods of Warfare," June 17, 1925. See The Avalon Project: Laws of War, Yale University, http://avalon.law.yale.edu/20th_century/geneva01.asp (accessed July 1, 2016).
84 "Chemical Warfare: Prohibition Proposal Adopted," *Times*, June 6, 1925. For an assessment of the protocol in establishing anti-chemical weapons norms, see Jefferson, "Origins of the Norm against Chemical Weapons."
85 For more on tear gas, see Feigenbaum, *Tear Gas*. For British concerns about using tear gas in imperial conflict see Simeon Shoul, "British Tear Gas Doctrine between the World Wars," *War in History* 15:2 (2008), 168–90, and R. M. Douglas, "Did Britain Use Chemical Weapons in Mandatory Iraq?," *Journal of Military History* 81 (2009), 1–20, and Erik Linstrum, "Domesticating Chemical Weapons: Tear Gas and the Militarization of Policing in the British Imperial World, 1919–1981," *Journal of Modern History* 91 (2019), 557–85. The use of tear gas, as Feigenbaum notes, had often led to fatalities, and it remains prohibited in international conflict, although not when used for purposes of "policing."
86 These limits are summarized in Girard, *A Strange and Formidable Weapon*, 187 and nn. 144, 245.
87 See the list of signatories and those states that agreed to the protocol by either ratification, accession, or succession in the United Nations Office for Disarmament Affairs Treaties Database on the Geneva Gas Protocol of 1925, http://disarmament.un.org/treaties/t/1925 (accessed July 1, 2016). This treaty was succeeded by the Chemical Weapons Convention of 1993. For more on the limitations of these efforts, see E. M. Spiers, "Gas Disarmament in the 1920s: Hopes Confounded," *Journal of Strategic Studies* 29:2 (2006), 281–300.
88 Lord Halsbury [Hardinge Goulburn Giffard], *1944* (London: Thornton Butterworth, 1926), 7. Further references will appear parenthetically in the text.

89 See advertisement, "Thornton Butterworth Books Published Today," *Times Literary Supplement*, Mar. 25, 1926, noting its "2nd impression before publication" and for quote see advertisement, "Thornton Butterworth Books," *Daily Telegraph*, Apr. 16, 1926. When Giffard's death in an internment camp in German-occupied France in 1943 was reported, his role as author of the novel dominated the account: see "Forecast Poison Gas on London," *Derby Daily Telegraph*, Nov. 20, 1943.

90 Norman Anglin, *Poison Gas* (London: Jonathan Cape, 1928). Further references will appear parenthetically in the text.

91 For the full text see Yale Law School's Avalon Project: www.yale.edu/lawweb/avalon/imt/kbpact.htm (accessed Jan. 28, 2014).

92 For a summation of work done at Porton during the interwar era, see Carter, *Chemical and Biological Defence*, 29–46.

93 "Extracts from a letter dated 31/3/20 from Major Salt," TNA, WO 188/58. These are also clearly the ethnic groups identified by the British government as belonging to the "martial" races. See Heather Streets-Salter, *Martial Races: The Military, Race and Masculinity in British Imperial Culture, 1857–1914* (Manchester: Manchester University Press, 2005).

94 Salt further pointed out that "perspiration" might be a problem as well as "the oxidizing action of the sun's rays" on the masks, indicating an awareness of the environment as a variable in creating effective devices. "Extracts from a letter dated 31/3/20 from Major Salt," TNA, WO 188/58.

95 Ibid.

96 "Investigation on Possibilities of Producing a Simple Civilian Respirator," Sept. 4, 1928, TNA, WO 188/218. Emphasis added.

97 Ibid.

Chapter 3

1 ARP Circular, reproduced in its entirety in "Civilians in Air Attacks," *Times*, July 11, 1935.

2 See Norman Hammer, "The Ambulance Man Looks at Gas," *First Aid* (1935), for quotes. Subsequent installments of Hammer's piece appear under the same title in *First Aid*, Sept. 1935; Oct. 1935, Nov. 1935; Dec. 1935; and Jan. 1936.

3 See, for instance, Martin Gilbert, *The Second World War: A Complete History* (New York: Henry Holt, 1989) and Gerhard L. Weinberg, *A World at Arms: A Global History of World War II* (Cambridge: Cambridge University Press, 1994). For more context on Europe during this era, see Martin Kitchen, *Europe between the Wars* (Harlow: Pearson, 1988); and for more on Britain's domestic concerns in the 1930s, in addition to comprehensive studies of twentieth-century Britain such as Peter Clarke, *Hope and Glory: Britain 1900–2000*, 2nd ed. (London: Penguin, 2004), see Deirdre Beddoe, *Back to Home and Duty: Women between the Wars* (London: Pandora, 1989); Lucy Bland, *Modern Women on Trial: Sexual Transgression in the Age of the Flapper* (Manchester: Manchester University Press, 2013); Mo Moulton, *Ireland and the Irish in Interwar England* (Cambridge: Cambridge University Press, 2014); C. L. Mowat, *Britain between the Wars* (Chicago: University of Chicago Press, 1955); Susan Kingsley Kent, *Aftershocks: Politics and Trauma in Britain, 1918–1931* (New York: Palgrave Macmillan, 2009); Alison Light, *Forever*

England: Femininity, Literature and Conservatism between the Wars (London: Routledge, 1991); Overy, *The Twilight Years*; Susan Pennybacker, *From Scottsboro to Munich: Race and Political Culture in 1930s Britain* (Princeton, NJ: Princeton University Press, 2009); Ben Pimlott, *Labour and the Left in the 1930s* (Cambridge: Cambridge University Press, 1977).

4 See Antoinette Burton, *The Trouble with Empire: Challenges to Modern British Imperialism* (Oxford: Oxford University Press, 2017). Among other studies of unrest in the interwar British Empire that inform my perspective here, see especially Durba Ghosh, *Gentlemanly Terrorists: Political Violence and the Colonial State in India, 1919–1947* (Cambridge: Cambridge University Press, 2017), as well as Barbara Bush, *Imperialism, Race and Resistance: Africa and Britain, 1919–1945* (London: Routledge, 1999); Toyin Falola and Adam Paddock, *The Women's War of 1929: A History of Anti-colonial Resistance in Eastern Nigeria* (Durham, NC: Carolina Academic Press, 2011); Marc Matera, Misty L. Bastian, and Susan Kingsley Kent, *The Women's War of 1929: Gender and Violence in Colonial Nigeria* (New York: Palgrave Macmillan, 2012).

5 For an overview of the conflict between Italy and Ethiopia, see G. Bruce Strang, ed., *Collision of Empires: Italy's Invasion of Ethiopia and Its International Impact* (London: Routledge, 2017). The British were reluctant even to use tear gas; see Shoul, "British Tear Gas Doctrine between the World Wars," Douglas, "Did Britain Use Chemical Weapons in Mandatory Iraq?," and Erik Linstrum, "Domesticating Chemical Weapons: Tear Gas and the Militarization of Policing in the British Imperial World, 1919–1981," *Journal of Modern History* 91 (2019), 557–85. Given recent work on tear gas that persuasively suggests that this counts as a chemical arm, I want to distinguish the impact of lethal poisons during wartime. For more on this see Feigenbaum, *Tear Gas*.

6 See "Abyssinian Casualties from Poison Gas," *Times*, Oct. 16, 1935; "Bombing of the Red Cross," *Times*, Jan. 2, 1936; British Section of WILPF, minutes, 1935–36, British Library of Political and Economic Science (BLPES), London School of Economics, Papers of the British Section of WILPF, 1/11–1/12. For an overview of the use of these weapons, see Lina Grip and John Hart, "The Use of Chemical Weapons in the 1935–36 Italo-Ethiopian War," in *SIPRI Arms Control and Non-proliferation Programme* (Stockholm: Stockholm International Peace Research Institute, Oct. 2009), 1–7.

7 Carolyn J. Kitching, *Britain and the Geneva Disarmament Conference: A Study in International History* (Basingstoke: Palgrave Macmillan, 2003).

8 Statement of Organizing Committee, in *Chemical Warfare: An Abridged Report of Papers Read at an International Conference at Frankfurt am Main* (London: Williams & Norgate, 1930), 26. Emphasis in original. Interestingly enough, the French version of the proceedings appeared under the original title of the conference; see *Les méthodes modernes de guerre et la protection des populations civiles* (Paris: Marcel Rivière, 1930). Second quote from Gertrud Woker, "The Effects of Chemical Warfare," in *Chemical Warfare*, 45. According to another participant: "The new and decisive factor of the next war will be the danger to social life now that the air fleet can use its weapons for *mass attack on the civil population*. 'It is to be feared,' says the Gas Committee of the

League of Nations in its Report for 1924, 'that the less conscientious of military leaders will make no distinction between the use of poison-gas against the troops on the battlefield and the use of these gases against the centres which provide these troops with weapons.' The factory girl who makes a projectile is as important as the soldier who uses it. The transformation of warfare turns the whole of the enemy's country into a field of battle." See Captain Brunskog, "The Transformation of Warfare," in *Chemical Warfare*, 26.

9 Dr. Nestler, "Collective and Individual Protection," in *Chemical Warfare*, 77.

10 Other groups concerned with this issue include the International Red Cross; see discussion of this in Gertrud Woker, "Chemical and Bacteriological Warfare," in *What Would Be the Character of a New War?* (London: P. S. King & Son, 1931), 366–67. There were also interwar discussions about the limitations of using gas masks based on racial as well as gendered stereotypes; for more on this see Chapter 4.

11 "Geneva Gas Protocol: Ratification by Great Britain," *Times*, May 1, 1929. For additional information on Britain's interwar chemical weapons program, see Schmidt, *Secret Science*; Evans, *Gassed*; and Carter, *Chemical and Biological Defence*.

12 Victor Lefebure, *Scientific Disarmament* (London: Victor Gollancz, 1931), 101. Further references will appear parenthetically in the text.

13 As explained in the volume's preface, the Inter-Parliamentary Union was an organization that aimed to unite "in common action the Members of all Parliaments ... in order to secure the co-operation of their respective States in the firm establishment ... of the work of international peace and co-operation between nations." Its main emphasis had been on fostering international arbitration to settle disputes. After the First World War, it focussed energy on disarmament and security. See *What Would Be the Character of a New War?* (London: P. S. King & Son, 1931), preface, vii–viii. This was but one among several pro-disarmament and antimilitarist groups in the United Kingdom. For more on them, see Ceadel, *Pacifism in Britain, 1914–1945*; Overy, *The Twilight Years*.

14 Woker, "Chemical and Bacteriological Warfare," 354.

15 "Gas Masks," *Daily Telegraph*, Oct. 30, 1931.

16 See information about petitions in British Section of WILPF, minutes, July 14, 1931 and Jan. 12, 1932, BLPES, Papers of the British Section of WILPF, 1/7 and 1/8. See also discussion of the conference in Grayzel, *At Home and under Fire*, ch. 6.

17 Arthur J. Gillian, *The Menace of Chemical Warfare to Civilian Populations* (London: Chemical Worker's Union, 1932), unpaginated. Emphasis in original.

18 "Looking Forward," *Aberdeen Journal*, July 22, 1932; "Air Defence in Germany," *Nottingham Evening Post*, Aug. 4, 1932.

19 "Chemical Warfare's Prohibition," *Daily Telegraph*, Nov. 10, 1932. For more on the conference, see Kitching, *Britain and the Geneva Disarmament Conference*

20 "Peer's Gas Mask Exhibit," *Dundee Courier*, Dec. 9, 1932.

21 "Gas Mask Gifts," *Daily Mirror*, Dec. 20, 1932; "Gas Masks for Christmas," *Derby Daily Telegraph*, Dec. 19, 1932; see also an earlier photographic spread showing German anti-gas protection, "On the Continent People Are Being Taught," *London Illustrated News*, Nov. 19, 1932.

22 "Terrors of Modern War," *Times*, Jan. 2, 1933.

23 Malcolm Elwin, "Illusions of a Pacifist," *Saturday Review*, Aug. 5, 1933, 157.

24 Beverley Nichols, *Cry Havoc!* (New York: Doubley, Doran & Co., 1933), originally published in London by Jonathan Cape in 1933. Further references will appear parenthetically in the text. For more on the life and career of Nichols as the original "bright young thing," see Bryan Connon, *Beverley Nichols: A Life* (London: Constable, 1991).

25 *Cry Havoc* provoked reaction. According to one physician, it was "the usual somewhat neurotic appeals to the sensational." Furthermore, its entire discussion was emblematic of the current state of civilization. For the "more highly developed our brain becomes, ... the more easily deranged by shocks and sensitive to the horrors evoked by our imagination we of necessity become." See quotes in Frederick William Inman, "War Inescapable," in *Biological Politics: An Aid to Clear Thinking* (London: John Wright, 1935), 56, 60 – which follows this with a defense of war as a way to "weed" out the population on eugenic grounds.

26 See H. A. Gunnder, letter to the editor, *Daily Mail*, July 27, 1933, and Malcolm Elwin, "Illusions of a Pacifist," *Saturday Review*, Aug. 5, 1933, 158. The extent to which Nichols's queerness (which was well known among the intellectual elite) may have shaped his views or the responses to them is worth exploring further, but beyond the scope of this chapter.

27 Committee on Imperial Defence Sub-Committee on Air Raid Precautions, minutes of meetings, May 13, 1929, comments of Sir John Anderson and Sir Maurice Hankey, TNA, CAB 46/7. For more on the committee and these members, see Grayzel, *At Home and under Fire*.

28 Committee on Imperial Defence Sub-Committee on Air Raid Precautions, minutes of meetings, May 13, 1929, TNA, CAB 46/7.

29 "Glo'ster Red Cross Society: Course of Training in Isle of Wight," *Gloucester Citizen*, Aug. 9, 1932.

30 "Plans to Combat Gas Warfare," *Nottingham Evening Post*, Dec. 15, 1932.

31 Committee on Imperial Defence Sub-Committee on Air Raid Precautions, minutes of meetings, Feb. 23, 1931, comments of Sir John Anderson, TNA, CAB 46/8.

32 Committee on Imperial Defence Sub-Committee on Air Raid Precautions, Minutes of Meetings, Mar. 30, 1931, comments of Sir John Anderson, TNA, CAB 46/8. The committee took note, for example, of what the French were doing in terms of gas protection and training exercises, issuing a memorandum on this; see TNA, CAB 46/11.

33 See Committee on Imperial Defence Sub-Committee on Air Raid Precautions, minutes of meetings, Mar. 2, 1931, and an updated note on readiness to begin field tests made at the meeting on June 22, 1931, TNA, CAB 46/8.

34 See notes on ARP memoranda attached to Committee on Imperial Defence Sub-Committee on Air Raid Precautions, minutes of meetings, Mar. 14,

1932, referring to ARP Memorandum 118 on gas masks in Italy and ARP Memorandum 124 on France, TNA, CAB 46/8. See copies of ARP Memorandum 139 on France, ARP Memoranda 151 and 154 on Germany, and ARP Memorandum 156 on Italy, TNA, CAB 46/13.

35 Committee on Imperial Defence Sub-Committee on Air Raid Precautions, minutes of meetings, July 18, 1932, comments of Major A. T. Sumner (Chemical Research Department) and Maurice Hankey, TNA, CAB 46/9.

36 Committee on Imperial Defence Sub-Committee on Air Raid Precautions, minutes of meetings, July 18, 1932, comments of Maurice Hankey, TNA, CAB 46/9.

37 Committee on Imperial Defence Sub-Committee on Air Raid Precautions, minutes of meetings, Oct. 10, 1932 and Nov. 7, 1932, TNA, CAB 46/9.

38 Committee on Imperial Defence Air Raid Precautions (Organisation) Sub-Committee, minutes of meetings, Jan. 15, 1934, TNA, HO 45/17583.

39 Committee on Imperial Defence Sub-Committee on Air Raid Precautions, minutes of meetings, July 18, 1935, comments of Wing Commander Hodsoll and E. H. Hodgson of the Board of Trade, TNA, CAB 46/9.

40 See Committee on Imperial Defence Sub-Committee on Air Raid Precautions, minutes of meetings, Dec. 5, 1934, Feb. 25, 1935, and especially Apr. 15 and July 18, 1935, TNA, CAB 46/9. See the detailed notes from the critical Jan. 14, 1934 meeting in TNA, HO 45/17583.

41 See Committee on Imperial Defence Sub-Committee on Air Raid Precautions, minutes of meetings, Dec. 5, 1934, Jan. 14, 1935, Feb. 25, 1935, and especially Apr. 15 and July 18, 1935, TNA, CAB 46/9.

42 See Committee on Imperial Defence Sub-Committee on Air Raid Precautions, minutes of meetings, Apr. 15 and July 18, 1935, and comments of Wing Commander Hodsoll at July meeting, TNA, CAB 46/9.

43 Boyd Cable, "Poison Gas as We Knew It," *Saturday Review,* Feb. 24, 1934, emphasis in original.

44 Boyd Cable, "An Air Attack on London," *Saturday Review*, Apr. 7, 1934.

45 F. N. Pickett, *Don't Be Afraid of Poison Gas: Hints for Civilians in the Event of a Poison Gas Attack* (London: Simpkin Marshall, 1934), 1. Further references will appear parenthetically in the text.

46 See Elaine Showalter, *The Female Malady: Women, Madness, and English Culture: 1830–1980* (London: Virago, 1988); Loughran, "Shell Shock, Trauma and the First World War"; and Laurinda Stryker, "Mental Cases: British Shellshock and the Politics of Interpretation," in *Evidence, History and the Great War*, ed. Gail Braybon (New York: Berghahn, 2003), 154–71.

47 As we saw earlier, this was also something that preoccupied official civil defense planners.

48 Report on "Respirators for Civilians," May 30, 1930, TNA, WO 189/4032. There were tests of gas masks in airplanes in 1931, with a report dated July 24, 1931, TNA, WO 188/401.

49 "Memorandum on Preliminary Experiments Carried Out to Obtain Data for a Large Scale Test of the Sensitivity to Mustard Gas of British Troops in India and of Indian Troops," June 26, 1933, TNA, WO 188/493.

50 "Memorandum on the Sensitivity Test, with Particular Reference to the Sensitivity of Personnel in India," Nov. 19, 1936, TNA, WO 188/493. For

tests comparing gas masks on British and Indian troops, see "Anti-gas Respirator Efficiency Trials," Sept. 18, 1931, TNA, WO 188/401.
51 For more on British imperial civil defense, see Grayzel, "Protecting Which Spaces and Bodies?"
52 "Anti-gas Defence at Chislehurst," *Times*, Apr. 10, 1935;
53 Photograph, "Gas Drill," *Daily Express*, Apr. 10, 1935; photograph, "Anti-gas Demonstration," *Times*, Apr. 10, 1935.
54 See report in *Western Morning News*, May 27, 1935, cited in Rowan G. E. Thompson, "'Millions of Eyes Were Turned Skywards': The Air League of the British Empire, Empire Air Day, and the Promotion of Air-Mindedness, 1934–9," *Twentieth Century British History*, 30:2 (2021), 285–307, DOI: https://doi.org/10.1093/tcbh/hwaa005.
55 "Women Will Practice Gas War Drill," *Daily Express*, May 17, 1935, and see also "VADS Sign On for Gas Parade," *Daily Express*, May 18, 1935.
56 "Woman Unafraid in Gas Horror Test," *Daily Mirror*, June 20, 1935.
57 "Saturday Competition: Thanks for a Gas-Mask," *Manchester Guardian*, June 19, 1935.
58 This became known as the "ARP Circular." For more on its development and responses to its release, see Grayzel, *At Home and under Fire*, especially ch. 8.
59 Acland and Lloyd in *Parliamentary Debates – Commons*, vol. 307, cols. 1095–97 (Dec. 12, 1935).
60 "Air Raids and Poison Gas," *Lancet*, July 20, 1935.
61 Union of Democratic Control, *Poison Gas* (London: Union of Democratic Control, 1935), quotes from 13, 46, 48. There is a note on the copy in BL stating that it arrived on Aug. 10, 1935.
62 "Air Raid Precautions: Criticism of Official Circular," *British Medical Journal*, Aug. 17, 1935.
63 "Uncivilised War," *Daily Mirror*, Aug. 28, 1935.
64 "Air Raid Precautions," *Woman Teacher*, Sept. 1935.
65 Ibid. The nation that is used as a basis for comparison in highlighting the limits of British measures is France, and the article attests that the British rules are almost verbatim translations of French regulations.
66 "Air Raid Precautions: Scientists' View of the Government's Proposals," Sept. 1935, reprinted by Society of Friends Peace Committee.
67 Women's World Committee against War and Fascism – British Section, *Behind the Gas Mask: An Exposure of the Proposed Air Defence Measures* (London: WWCAWF, 1935).
68 For more on Heath's views relative to other Quaker perspectives on disarmament in the interwar period, see Maureen Waugh, "Quakers, Peace and the League of Nations: The Role of Bertram Pickard," *Quaker Studies* 6:1 (2001), 59–79.
69 Carl Heath, "Christians and Anti-gas Raid Drill," Society of Friends Peace Committee, London, July 1935. *The Friend* was (and is) a weekly journal of religious and literary content produced by the Society of Friends.
70 "400 Death-Spray 'Planes for Italy," *Daily Mirror*, Aug. 7, 1935.
71 "If War Comes: Italy's Plan of Campaign," *Manchester Guardian*, Sept. 6, 1935.

72 "Medical Help for Abyssinia," *Manchester Guardian*, Sept. 12, 1935.
73 "Abyssinians Allege Chemical War," *Daily Mail*, Oct. 10, 1935. See "Abyssinian Casualties from Poison Gas," *Times*, Oct. 16, 1935; "Bombing of the Red Cross," *Times*, Jan. 2, 1936; British Section of WILPF, minutes, 1935–36, BLPES, Papers of the British Section of WILPF, 1/11–1/12. A recent assessment of the poison gas used during the war states that the blister agent was sulphur mustard, which caused casualties directly and had a "force multiplier" effect. See Grip and Hart, "The Use of Chemical Weapons."
74 See first "Further Italian Denial of Use of Gas" and "Dum-Dums and Gas," *Manchester Guardian*, Oct. 18 and 22, 1935, respectively. For the role of the international humanitarian community in the conflict, see Rainer Baudenistei, *Between Bombs and Good Intentions: The Red Cross and the Italo-Ethiopian War, 1935–36* (New York: Berghahn Books, 2006).
75 "Fears for Britons," *Daily Mail*, Oct. 28, 1935.
76 "Peace Crusade: Mrs Zangwill's Proposals," *Scotsman*, Nov. 9, 1935. The author appears as Mrs Israel Zangwill in the press; Israel Zangwill was a writer and public intellectual.
77 For a brief discussion of the intentions behind the poster, see Laura Beers, *Your Britain: Media and the Making of the Labour Party* (Cambridge, MA: Harvard University Press, 2010), 188.
78 See in the digital collection of the Hoover Institution Library and Archives, https://digitalcollections.hoover.org/objects/28722 (accessed Dec. 1, 2020), and also collection of the People's History Museum reproduced here. See "The Campaign by Posters," *Observer*, Nov. 3, 1935.
79 See a copy of the statement cabled to Lady Gladstone in her role as chair of the Women's Advisory Council of League of Nations Union, then sent to the League of Nations general secretary in League of Nations Archives (LONA), R3648, dossier 16, ascribed to *News Chronicle* (London), Mar. 25, 1936. It is also cited in Norman Angell, *You and Mustard Gas* (London: League of Nations Union, 1936), 2. It appeared in many newspapers. The underline shows emphasis in original; the italics are my emphasis. Italy had ratified the 1925 Geneva Anti-gas Protocol in 1928. See the Disarmament Treaties Database at http://disarmament.un.org/treaties/t/1925.
80 Pamphlet, May 1943, recounting services with regard to the restoration of Ethiopia to the emperor, presentation in Westminster Abbey, May 13, 1942, but also acknowledging the death of "Princess Tsahai" (sic), as follows: "Ever since that day when she broadcast her pathetic appeal to the Allies of Ethiopia to come to the assistance of her ravaged country, we have followed her career with interest and great hope" (8). BL, Abyssinian Association Pamphlet Collection.
81 National Free Church Women's League (London), letter to Secretary General, League of Nations, undated but marked as received Apr. 23, 1936, and subsequent letter referencing the resolution of June 10, 1936, LONA, R3648, dossier 16.
82 WILPF (London), letter to Secretary General, League of Nations, c. May 12, 1936, LONA, R3648, dossier 16.

83 Women's Peace Crusade (London), letter to Prime Minister and Foreign Secretary, copied to Secretary General, League of Nations, May 8, 1936, LONA, R3648, dossier 16.

84 "Italy's Criminal Methods of Warfare: An Impressive Protest by Representative British Women," letter to the editor, *Manchester Guardian*, Apr. 7, 1936.

85 "Bombing of Swedish Hospital" and "Bombing of Red Cross," *Manchester Guardian*, Jan. 1 and 6, 1936.

86 "Red Cross Official's Protest," *Times*, Mar. 25, 1936.

87 Ibid.

88 See Hesketh Bell, "White and Black in Africa," letter to the editor, *Times*, Mar. 30, 1936.

89 The article begins on the front page with "Britain Warns Italians against Poison Gas" and continues with "Menace to Our Relations with Black Races," *Daily Express*, Mar. 31, 1936. Halifax is quoted in the article.

90 "Poison Gas in Abyssinia," *Times*, Mar. 31, 1936.

91 "The Rules of War," *Manchester Guardian*, Mar. 31, 1936.

92 David Low, "Pah! They Were Savages," *Evening Standard*, Apr. 3, 1936.

93 Mary Toulmin, "Slaughter by Bombs in Abyssinia," letter to the editor, *Manchester Guardian*, Apr. 4, 1936.

94 "Addis Expulsions," *Daily Mail*, May 18, 1936.

95 George Steer, *Caesar in Abyssinia* (1936; repr. Boston: Little, Brown & Co., 1937), 280–81. Further references will appear parenthetically.

96 "Alleged Use of Poison Gas: Gas Warfare," *Irish Examiner*, March 28, 1936.

97 See Steer, *Caesar in Abyssinia*, ch. 17 for further details.

98 See other corroborating accounts such as J. W. S. Macfie, *An Ethiopian Diary: A Record of the British Ambulance Service in Ethiopia* (Liverpool: University Press of Liverpool, 1936), 77–78. For more historical evidence accumulated by the International Committee of the Red Cross, see Baudenistei, *Between Bombs and Good Intentions*. For fuller discussions of this, see Grayzel, *At Home and under Fire* and "Protecting Which Spaces and Bodies?"

99 Fuller, *The First of the League Wars*, 80.

100 Ibid., 85.

101 For the spread of Fuller's views see J. F. C. Fuller,, "The Italo-Ethiopian War: A Military Analysis of an Eye-Witness Observer," *Army Ordnance*, May–June 1936, cited in Chemical Warfare School (US Army), *The Use of Gas in Ethiopia* (Edgewood, MD: Chemical Warfare School, 1939).

102 This is one of the most intriguing things about British policy: in contrast to both totalitarian states like Germany and democracies like France, Britain (uniquely as far as I can tell from the sources consulted) decided to provide gas masks free of charge, and to the entire population.

103 "£850,000 for Civilian Gas Masks," *Daily Mail*, July 15, 1936.

104 Hugh Cudlipp, "Don't Be Horrified, Be Thankful," *Daily Mirror*, July 22, 1936.

Chapter 4

1 For more on the interwar responses to threats of air power, see Uri Bialer, *The Shadow of the Bomber: The Fear of Air Attack and British Politics, 1932–1939* (London: Royal Historical Society, 1980); Grayzel, *At Home and under Fire*; Michele Haapamaki, *The Coming of the Aerial War: Culture and the Fear of Airborne Attack in Interwar Britain* (London: I. B. Tauris, 2014); and Brett Holman, *The Next War in the Air: Britain's Fear of the Bomber, 1908–1941* (Farnham: Ashgate, 2014). Both Haapamaki and Holman briefly discuss anti-gas preparations as merely part of these larger measures.

2 For additional critiques beyond the ones discussed in the last chapter, see Cambridge Scientists' Anti-War Group, *The Protection of the Public from Aerial Attack: Being a Critical Examination of the Recommendations Put Forward by the Air Raids Precautions Department of the Home Office* (London: Victor Gollancz, 1937).

3 "Murder in Guernica," *Daily Herald*, Apr. 28, 1937.

4 "Unmasked," *Daily Mirror*, Sept. 27, 1938.

5 "Gas Proof Kennels Ready," *Daily Mail*, Sept. 28, 1938; "Two Thirds of Britain Has Gas Masks: Babies Must Be Registered," *Daily Mail*, Sept. 28, 1938.

6 "500,000 Gas Masks Each Week," *Irish Times*, Jan. 6, 1937; "Free Gas Masks for All," *Manchester Guardian*, Jan. 13, 1937; "2,000,000 Gas Masks a Month," *Daily Mail*, Jan. 13, 1937; "First Gas-Mask Minister," *Daily Express*, Jan. 13, 1937.

7 ARP Department, Home Office, *Air Raid Precautions Handbook No. 1: Personal Protection against Gas* (London: HMSO, 1936). For the numbers in circulation see the notes in the second edition, published in March 1938 and included in TNA, HO 45/17604.

8 "Don't Be Horrified," *Daily Mirror*, July 22, 1936.

9 "Schemes for Training Medical Personnel," 1936, TNA, HO 45/17623.

10 "Miles," *The Gas War of 1940* (London: Eric Partridge, 1931). Information about the author is briefly discussed in Martin Ceadel, "Popular Fiction and the Next War, 1918–1939," in *Class, Culture and Social Change: A New View of the 1930s*, ed. Frank Gloversmith (London: Harvester Press, 1980), 171, and the novel is also addressed in I. F. Clarke, *Voices Prophesying War*, 2nd ed. (Oxford: Oxford University Press, 1992), 159. It reappeared as Neil Bell, *Valiant Clay* (London: Collins, 1934).

11 Simpson Stokes, *Air-Gods' Parade* (London: Arthur Barron, 1935).

12 I discuss all of these works and others (and some of the reactions to them) much more extensively in *At Home and under Fire*.

13 "Gas Drill Day at Westminster," *Punch*, Jan. 20, 1937.

14 Sarah Campion, *Thirty Million Gas Masks* (London: Peter Davies, 1937), 23. Further references will appear parenthetically.

15 See PPU Pamphlets, BL (received Mar. 1937).

16 "First Gas Mask Minister," *Daily Mirror*, Jan. 13, 1937.

17 "All Ready," *Daily Mirror*, Dec. 18, 1937. An account more accepting of government promises can be found in "Gas Mask Test in Every Home," *Daily Mail*, Dec. 17, 1937.

18 "Here Lies the Body," *Daily Express*, Dec. 11, 1937.

19 File on "Italy and Abyssinia: Air Raid Protection and Anti-gas Measures at Aden," Aug. 25, 1935 to Feb. 22, 1936, BL, IOR R/20/A/3760.

20 "Report on Civil Defence in India," May 30, 1942. This report begins with a detailed official chronology of the establishment of civil defense in India, from which the information in the paragraphs that follow is drawn. The 1937 executive council order responded to a suggestion made in August 1936 by the Chief of the General Staff for a "preliminary investigation" of the question. See BL, IOR L/PJ/7/4728.

21 After receiving a report from the exploratory committee in April, in June 1938, the viceroy approved a letter to be sent to all provincial governments alerting them to the main contours of what ARP must do, including establishing lighting restrictions, firefighting, warning systems, and plans to protect vital services as well as "anti-gas protection" and, significantly, "control of the civilian population." It further pointed out that "the probable vulnerable areas included all ports, the Asansol Industrial Area, the Poona-Kirkee Area, Aravankadu, certain areas of the Province of Sind and important cities in the North West of India." Those working at the local or provincial level were encouraged to send in schemes for implementing ARP, but the assistance from the central government would be "in technical matters but not with finance." On the eve of the Second World War, this meant that active preparations occurred in Bombay, Bengal, and Madras, but it was not until the outbreak of war that "paper schemes which were then in progress of preparation were converted into actual schemes" and expanded to Sind and Karachi. See discussion in BL, IOR L/PJ/7/4728. These issues will be taken up more fully in later chapters.

22 Committee of Imperial Defence Overseas Defence Committee, memorandum on "Provision of Respirators for the Families of Service Personnel Serving in the Colonies" with attached notes; Committee of Imperial Defence Overseas Defence Committee, Nov. 15, 1937, and Army Council letter, May 17, 1938, TNA, CO 323/1592/66. In addition, the CDRE continued to conduct trials for gas masks on Indian (mainly military) subjects. See "Trial of Respirators in India," 1938, BL, IOR L/MIL/7/19243.

23 For more on the production of gas masks in India c. 1930, see "Notes on a Visit to Ordnance Factories and Firms Producing Respirator Components and Material in India," May 8, 1930, TNA, WO 188/398. It is clear that experiments on types of filters and other kinds of components were being carried out to determine how to allocate the resources needed for the mask's components as well as how to reduce costs.

24 "Gas Mask Drill at the Naval Base" and "The Anti-gas Brigade of Seletar: Wives of Naval Officials Ready for Emergency," *Straits Times*, Aug. 5 and 6, 1936.

25 "Gas Mask Training: Introduction in Singapore," *Straits Times*, Apr. 26, 1937; "Gas Masks for All in Malaya," *Straits Times*, May 9, 1937.

26 "40,000,000 Pounds of Rubber: What Gas Mask Scheme Means in Sales," *Straits Times*, Sept. 18, 1936.
27 "Ceylon Selling Gas Mask Charcoal," *Morning Tribune*, Aug. 13, 1937. Perhaps anticipating challenges in obtaining commodities to produce gas masks, the use of wool filters impregnated with carbon or (according to these records, more ideally) asbestos as an alternative had already formed part of the experiments conducted on the general civilian respirator; see "Notes on an Informal Conference to Discuss the Design of Civilian Respirators," July 17, 1936, TNA, WO 33/1419. For reports on the use of carbonized coconut shells in imperial gas mask factories, see "Report on a Visit to Ordinance Factories and Firms Producing Respirator Components and Material in India," May 8, 1930, TNA, WO 188/398.
28 Telegram from Secretary of State for the Colonies to Governor of Hong Kong, Jan. 13, 1938, TNA, CO 129/565/15.
29 "Gas Mask Factory for India," *Times of India*, Feb. 7, 1938; "Gas Mask Factory for Java," *Straits Times*, Apr. 17, 1938. For a full picture of the Singapore Rubber Works, see "Singapore Makes Gas Masks," *Straits Times*, May 7, 1939. This article claims that the factory is making 200 gas masks per day.
30 They did so alongside trying out the devices of other nations. For Porton Down's test of the French civilian gas mask in 1938, see the Porton report "French Civilian Respirator," Feb. 2, 1938, TNA, WO 188/1800.
31 "First Fitting Report – General Civilian Respirator," Sept. 20, 1937, TNA, WO 189/4421.
32 "Third Fitting Report on Girls," Dec. 17, 1937, TNA, WO 189/4493; "Fifth Fitting Report on Boys," Aug. 5, 1938, TNA, WO 198/4463.
33 "Respirators for Young Children," May 1938, TNA, WO 189/4449.
34 "Physiological Trials of the General Civilian Respirator with Aged and Infirm People," Nov. 2, 1937, TNA, WO 189/4428.
35 "Trials with the General Civilian Respirator at Bristol," May 23, 1938, TNA, 189/4450.
36 "Trials of G.C.R. with Nursing Home Personnel," July 28, 1938, TNA, WO 189/4460.
37 "Chinese Respirator," May 27, 1938, TNA, WO 188/141.
38 "Fitting of Respirators to Persons of Abnormal Facial Contours," Dec. 7, 1938, TNA, WO 188/395.
39 Ninth Annual Report on Respirator Assembly Factory, 3 June 1937; quote on dermatitis from "Investigation into the Cause of Dermatitis," Nov. 20, 1937; final quote from "Tenth Annual Report on Respirator Assembly Factory," Apr. 27, 1938; all in TNA, WO 188/398.
40 "Trials of Various Protective Devices for Persons Unable to Wear the Ordinary G.C. Respirator," Nov. 20, 1939, TNA, WO 189/1227.
41 "Do Children Care?," *Daily Mirror*, Jan. 5, 1938. See accounts of youngsters testing gas masks at Empire Air Day in *The Aeroplane* in June 1938, cited in Thompson, "'Millions of Eyes Were Turned Skywards.'"
42 "Go Ahead," *Daily Mail*, Feb. 25, 1938; "Picture Gallery," *Daily Mail*, Feb. 18, 1938; "A.R.P. Activity," *Daily Mail*, Mar. 17, 1938; "Gas Masks for All," *Daily Mail*, Apr. 5, 1938; and "Gas Mask Rush Begins," *Daily Mail*, Apr. 6, 1938.

43 E. J. Hodsoll, letter to clerks of county councils, county clerks, town clerks, clerks to the district council, and chief constables, Home Office Circular, Apr. 4, 1938, TNA, HO 45/17643. That copies were circulated to some colonial outposts is evident in the appearance of these measures in Colonial Office files; see TNA, CO 323 1593/2.

44 Hodsoll, letter to clerks of county councils, etc., Home Office Circular, Apr. 4, 1938, TNA, HO 45/17643.

45 *Daily Express*, Jan. 31, 1938.

46 Charlotte Haldane, "This Shocking Photo," *Daily Mirror*, Mar. 8, 1938.

47 "Gas Masks, Hens for the Use of," *Daily Mail*, Feb. 12, 1938.

48 Photograph, *Daily Mirror*, Feb. 15, 1938. We can see this in the development of anti-gas kennels for dogs mentioned at the start of the chapter. People's deep concern for their animals, especially domestic pets, and the government's lack of planning for this meant that private enterprises as well as individuals tried to take up the slack. It also meant that almost 400,000 cats and dogs were euthanized in order to be spared the horrors of war; see Hilda Kean, *The Great Cat and Dog Massacre: The Real Story of World War Two's Unknown Tragedy* (Chicago: University of Chicago Press, 2017). For reactions to the idea of gas-proof protection for cats in 1938, for example, see ibid., 54.

49 "Thirty Million Gas Masks," *Manchester Guardian*, April 5, 1938.

50 "Gas-Masks for All within 8 Hours if Needed," *Daily Mail*, April 5, 1938.

51 "Masks Are Ready," *Daily Mail*, Apr. 5, 1938.

52 M.W., "They Think Gas Masks 'Fun,'" letter to the editor, *Daily Mail*, Apr. 23, 1938.

53 "Chapeaux," *Irish Times*, Apr. 23, 1938.

54 Charles Graves, "I See Life," *Daily Mail*, July 5, 1938.

55 "Nuns Learn All about Air Raid Precautions," *Straits Times*, July 24, 1938. It is not clear why such an article reporting on nuns in London appeared in the colonies at this particular moment.

56 "35,000,000 Gas Masks Ready," *Western Daily Press*, July 7, 1938; "35 Million Gas Masks Ready," *Dundee Courier*, July 7, 1938. The same information was also conveyed in the national press; see "35,000,000 Gas Masks for Local Storage," *Daily Telegraph*, July 7, 1938.

57 "Have You Been Fitted for Your Gas Mask?," *Derby Daily Telegraph*, Aug. 23, 1938.

58 "A.R.P.? … the Verdict Should Be RIP!," *Daily Mirror*, June 4, 1938.

59 Peace Pledge Union, *You've Got to Be Prepared* (London: Peace Pledge Union, n.d.). A note on the copy in the British Library states, "arrived 24 Jan. 1938."

60 "Unemployment and Gas-Masks: A Quaker Resolution," *Manchester Guardian*, Jan. 26, 1937.

61 "Air Raid Precautions: Statement by the Friends Peace Committee," July 1938, Library and Archive of the Society of Friends, London, Peace Committee Pamphlet 4/86.

62 Karlin Capper-Johnson, "Air Raid Precautions: An Appeal and an Alternative," Library and Archive of the Society of Friends, Peace Committee Pamphlet 4/72 [1938].

63 Summary of "Discussion at July [12, 1938] Executive Committee Meeting on Air Raid Precautions," BLPES, Papers of the British Section of WILPF, 1/14, 1938.

64 "Gas-Mask Man Will Visit You Soon," *Daily Express*, May 2, 1938.

65 "Special Pamphlet Air Raids Precautions Autumn Recruiting Campaign," c. Aug. 22, 1938, TNA, HO 45/17640. Both quotes in this paragraph are from this document.

66 The population of the United Kingdom in 1938 was determined by using figures from the *Abstract of British Historical Statistics* in mid-1938, when it was estimated at 41.2 million in England and Wales, 5 million in Scotland, and 1.2 million in Northern Ireland: a total of 47.4 million (B. R. Mitchell, *Abstract of British Historical Statistics* [Cambridge: Cambridge University Press, 1971], 10–11).

67 "Big New A.R.P. Campaign," *Daily Telegraph*, July 22, 1938.

68 "Gas Mask Drill," *Daily Telegraph*, July 15, 1938.

69 "Dogs: Too!" *Straits Times*, Aug. 28, 1938. "Even dogs wear gas masks nowadays," it proclaimed.

70 "Civilian Gas Masks Are Safe," *Daily Mail*, Aug. 18, 1938. A similar response can be found in "A.R.P. Gas Masks of Three Types," *Daily Telegraph*, Aug. 18, 1938.

71 "Gas-Mask Tests: Result of Derby Experiment," *Derby Evening Telegraph*, Aug. 19, 1938.

72 [Horace] Roye, *Nude Ego* (London: Chantry, 1958), 135.

73 "Tomorrow's Crucifixion," *North London Recorder*, as reproduced in ibid., 78.

74 There is a substantial literature on the responses to international tensions that came to be referred to as "appeasement" as well as on the Munich Crisis. For works that have most informed the discussion here, see Julie Gottlieb, *Guilty Women: Foreign Policy and Appeasement in Inter-war Britain* (London: Palgrave Macmillan, 2015); Daniel Hucker, *Public Opinion and the End of Appeasement in Britain and France* (Farnham: Ashgate, 2011); Talbot Imlay, *Facing the Second World War: Strategy, Politics, and Economics in Britain and France, 1938–1940* (Oxford: Oxford University Press, 2003); Richard Overy, *The Twilight Years: The Paradox of Britain between the Wars* (New York: Viking, 2009); and Jeffrey Record, "Appeasement: A Critical Evaluation Seventy Years On," in *The Origins of the Second World War: An International Perspective*, ed. Frank McDonough et al. (New York: Continuum, 2011), 210–23, as well as the stimulating papers presented at the conference "The Munich Crisis and the People" at the University of Sheffield, June 2018.

75 "Britain Queues Up in Millions on Gas Mask Sunday," *Daily Mirror*, Sept. 26, 1938.

76 C. Allen Newbery, "St Pancras at War, 1939–45," IWM, Department of Documents, Papers of C. A. Newberry, 97/28/1.

77 See Mitchell Library, Glasgow, UK, Glasgow City Archives (GCA), DTC 8/10/181; and for Girl Guides, see Eleanor L. Houison Craufurd, Scottish Chief Commissioner Girl Guides, letter to Glasgow Commissioner for ARP, Sept. 20, 1938. By March 1939, those in charge of civil defense were confidently asserting, "no difficulty would be experienced in supplying

respirators to others not yet in possession of a respirator"; see letter to ARP Glasgow, Mar. 29, 1939, GCA, D-CD 5.

78 Typescript journal of Denis Perkins, IWM, Department of Documents, 22/11/09/21/1.

79 "London in the Crisis," *Observer*, Oct. 2, 1938.

80 I discuss these reactions more extensively in Grayzel, *At Home and under Fire*, but see also the work of the following scholars on the Blitz and the British response: Angus Calder, *The Myth of the Blitz* (London: Pimlico, 1991); Lucy Noakes, *War and the British: Gender, Memory, and National Identity* (London: I. B. Taurus, 1998); and Sonya O. Rose, *Which People's War? National Identity and Citizenship in Wartime Britain, 1939–1945* (Oxford: Oxford University Press, 2003).

81 Sharlie Davison, letter to her family, Sept. 27, 1938, IWM, Department of Documents, Collection of Mr. and Mrs. J. G. Davison.

82 Helena Britton, Walthamstow, UK, letter to her daughter Florence Elizabeth Britton Elkus in Berkeley, CA, USA, Sept. 30, 1938, IWM, Department of Documents, Britton Collection.

83 Jan Struther, *Mrs. Miniver* (1939; repr. London: Virago, 1989), 63, 62, 157–58.

84 Margery Allingham, *The Oaken Heart: The Story of an English Village at War* (London: Michael Joseph, 1941), 28, 33–34, 36.

85 For an overview of Mass Observation and for its wartime role, see James Hinton, *The Mass Observers: A History 1937–1949* (Oxford: Oxford University Press, 2013). Daniel Todman, *Britain's War: Into Battle, 1937–1941* (Oxford: Oxford University Press, 2016), 381–84, sums up some of the conflicts that arose between Mass Observation and the government over such functions.

86 Mass Observation, Respondent 032, Day Survey, Mass Observation Online, University of Sussex, available through Adam Matthew, www.massobservation.amdigital.co.uk/Documents/Details/DaySurvey-032 (accessed Apr. 2, 2012).

87 Mass Observation, Respondent 045, Day Survey, Mass Observation Online, www.massobservation.amdigital.co.uk/Documents/Details/DaySurvey-045 (accessed Apr. 2, 2012). Final quote from Respondent 803, Day Survey, Mass Observation Online, www.massobservation.amdigital.co.uk/Documents/Details/DaySurvey-000 (accessed Apr. 2, 2012).

88 Mass Observation, Respondent 792, Day Survey, Mass Observation Online, www.massobservation.amdigital.co.uk/Documents/Details/DaySurvey-792 (accessed Apr. 2, 2012). Emphasis in original.

89 Mass Observation, Respondent 0293, Day Survey, Mass Observation Online, www.massobservation.amdigital.co.uk/Documents/Details/DaySurvey-0293 (accessed Apr. 2, 2012). For more on Haldane's increasingly critical views on ARP, see Haapamaki, *The Coming of the Aerial War*, ch. 4.

90 Mass Observation, Respondent 324, Day Survey, Mass Observation Online, www.massobservation.amdigital.co.uk/Documents/Details/DaySurvey-0324 (accessed Apr. 2, 2012). This was the view of a male insurance actuary in his early seventies.

91 "Two Thirds of Britain Has Gas Masks," *Daily Mail*, Sept. 28, 1938.

92 T.H., letter to *Daily Mail* and response, *Daily Mail*, Oct. 10, 1938.

93 "Lost Masks–Penalty?" *Daily Mirror*, Nov. 17, 1938.

94 "Huge A.R.P. Crisis Blunders," *Reynold's News*, Oct. 2, 1938.

95 "London Day by Day," *Times of India*, Sept. 28, 1938.

96 "A Letter from London: The Inquest of the Nation," *Times of India*, Nov. 12, 1938.

97 "Was under Fire, Gassed, in Her Dream!," *Daily Mirror*, Nov. 5, 1938.

98 Mass Observation, "Bad Dreams and Nightmares," reports by Mass Observers, July 1939, 14, MOA, File Report A20.

99 He further notes that this panic passed and that he and his parents began to discuss evacuation, a process that he recounts as involving watching children leaving with "our packets of sandwiches and gas masks enclosed in cardboard boxes," although he and his siblings carried theirs in cases far more "posh, for Dad had made us special holders from waste imitation leather from his works." Papers of James Angus Payne, IWM, Department of Documents, 96/32/1. This memoir reflects the retrospective accounts analyzed by Moshenska in *Material Cultures of Childhood*.

100 "A.R.P. To-Day: The Symbol of the Gas Mask," *Times*, Dec. 19, 1938.

Chapter 5

1 "To Think We've Come to This," *Manchester Guardian*, Aug. 29, 1940.

2 Ibid.

3 There is an extensive literature on the experience of civilians in Britain during the Second World War. The following works have most informed the discussion in this chapter: Maggie Andrews, *Women and Evacuation in the Second World War: Femininity, Domesticity and Motherhood* (London: Bloomsbury, 2019); Amy Bell, *London Was Ours: Diaries and Memoirs of the London Blitz* (London: I. B. Taurus, 2011); Stephen Bourne, *Mother Country: Britain's Black Community on the Home Front, 1939–45* (Stroud: History Press, 2010); Calder, *The Myth of the Blitz*; Mark Donnelly, *Britain and the Second World War* (London: Routledge, 1999); Juliet Gardiner, *Wartime Britain 1939–1945* (London: Headline, 2004); Stuart Hylton, *Their Darkest Hour: The Hidden History of the Home Front 1939–45* (Stroud: Sutton, 2001); Jones, *British Civilians in the Front Line*; Robert Mackay, *Half the Battle: Civilian Morale in Britain during the Second World War* (Manchester: Manchester University Press, 2002); Moshenska, *Material Cultures of Childhood*; Lucy Noakes, *Dying for the Nation: Death, Grief and Bereavement in Second World War Britain* (Manchester: Manchester University Press, 2020) and "'Serve to Save': Gender, Citizenship and Civil Defence in Britain 1937–1941," *Journal of Contemporary History* 47:4 (2012), 734–53; Rose, *Which People's War?*; Penny Summerfield, *Reconstructing Women's Wartime Lives: Discourse and Subjectivity in Oral Histories of the Second World War* (Manchester: Manchester University Press, 1998); Penny Summerfield and Corinna Peniston-Bird, *Contesting Home Defence: Men, Women and the Home Guard in the Second World War* (Manchester: Manchester University Press, 2007); and Philip Ziegler, *London at War* (London: Sinclair Stevenson, 1995).

4 Home Office ARP Department, Heads of Divisions Council Meeting, Feb. 24, 1939, TNA, HO 45/18198.
5 See correspondence from Home Office ARP Department to CDRD, Sept. 1938–June 1939, TNA, HO 186/2661. It concluded that some might last three years, but that there needed to be inspections and replacement parts available.
6 See "Draft Typescript of History of Civil Defence in Northern Ireland to 1939," Public Record Office of Northern Ireland, Belfast, CAB 3/A/69.
7 "The Northern Defence Bill," *Irish Times*, June 2, 1939.
8 *A.R.P. for Hampstead* (London: Hampstead Communist Party, 1938), 7. This was only part of the ongoing critiques of ARP and gas masks, mainly emanating from the left. See also *ARP: A Plan for the Safety of the People of Nottingham* (Nottingham: Nottingham Communist Party, 1938) and the magazine *Women To-Day* for views of Women's World Committee against War and Fascism on gas masks and civil defense in 1938.
9 See copies of the official pamphlet with handwritten notations in Leslie Thorne, letter, July 17, 1939, Somerset, and covering note from Home Office ARP Department, July 24, 1939, stating that county officials had decided not yet to distribute gas masks in Somerset, as well as a reply from E. T. Crutchley stating that the pamphlet was badly timed for areas that had not yet had gas masks distributed: Winifred Grace Toby, letter to Sir John Anderson, July 21, 1939; all TNA, HO 186/115.
10 For my fuller discussion of the development of the baby's anti-gas protective helmet, see Grayzel, *At Home and under Fire*, ch. 8, and see also my article "One British Thing: The Babies' Anti-gas Protective Helmet," *Journal of British Studies* 58:3 (2019), 598–601, DOI: 10.1017/jbr.2019.8.
11 The racialized as well as gendered dimensions of anti-gas protection factor into how both sides represented it, especially when it came to children, throughout the era.
12 W. H. Davies, "Armed for War," *London Mercury*, Sept. 1937, 418.
13 "A Poster Dispute Reopened: Baby in Gas Mask," *Manchester Guardian*, Mar. 4, 1938; see also coverage of the campaign in "Labour Propaganda Effort," *Times*, Mar. 5, 1938.
14 "Babies to Be Sealed in Gas-Proof Bags," *Daily Express*, Oct. 21, 1937; for a photograph of some toddlers on tricycles wearing gas masks see "Gas Masks for Babies," *Daily Telegraph*, Oct. 21, 1937.
15 "Here Is an ARP Guide," *Daily Mirror*, Sept. 28, 1938.
16 For a full discussion of this, see Grayzel, *At Home and under Fire*, ch. 9.
17 All evidence here from TNA, HO 45/17620, including letter from Mary Smith, Women's Voluntary Service for ARP, to Mr. Findlay Esq., Home Office ARP Department, Oct. 27, 1938. This organization became the Women's Voluntary Service for Civil Defence or more simply Women's Voluntary Service. For a narrative history of WVS work, see Patricia and Robert Malcolmson, *Women at the Ready: The Remarkable Story of the Women's Voluntary Services on the Home Front* (London: Abacus, 2013).
18 "Babies Safe from Gas Soon … New Device," *Daily Express*, Nov. 25, 1938; "Anti-gas 'Cages' for Babies," *Daily Telegraph*, Nov. 26, 1938.

19 See the correspondence between Alice Leigh-Smith and CDRD, c. 1938–39, TNA, WO 188/394. One of Leigh-Smith's assertions was that mothers did not like placing their babies in containers where they could not be comforted.

20 "Gas Mask for Babies Found," *Daily Express*, Feb. 3, 1939.

21 "Anderson Howled Down: Police Charge Crowds," *Daily Express*, Feb. 11, 1939.

22 See J. B. S. Haldane, *ARP* (London: Gollancz, 1938). See also Joseph S. Meisel, "Air Raid Shelter Policy and Its Critics in Britain before the Second World War," *Twentieth Century British History* 5:3 (1994). 300–19.

23 "Modern Child," *Daily Mirror*, Feb. 20, 1939.

24 "Babies in Gas Mask Show," *Daily* Mirror, Mar. 10, 1939.

25 James Agate, "Lullabye for a Baby Wearing a Gas-Mask," *Daily Express*, Mar. 18, 1939.

26 See E. J. Hodsoll, memorandum, Dec. 1938 (capitalization in the original), and G. H. Findlay, letter to CDRD, Porton Down, Jan. 6, 1939, TNA, HO 186/980.

27 *A.R.P. Newsletter* 3 (May 1, 1939), TNA, HO 186/13.

28 "Soon One Baby Gas Mask for Every 7000 People," *Daily Express*, Aug. 3, 1939.

29 Hilda Casey, memoir, 1939–43, IWM, Department of Documents, Papers of H[ilda née Woodington] Casey, 02/1/1.

30 Ireland decided to purchase gas masks from "a source outside this country," i.e., Britain, and only slowly to manufacture some its own devices; see "Ireland, Department of Defence Memo 24 August 1939," National Archives of Ireland, Dublin, TAOIS/S 1139.

31 "Attached List of Baby Helmets and Child Respirators Sent or Being Sent Abroad, and Those Left for Local Authorities," Jan. 1940, TNA, HO 186/1358.

32 "Defence of India: Report of the Expert Committee," June 16, 1939, 35, TNA, CAB 24/287.

33 William Deede, *A.R.P.: A Complete Guide to Civil Defence* (London: Daily Telegraph, 1938), 14–15. Further references will appear parenthetically.

34 S. Evelyn Thomas, *A Practical Guide to A.R.P.* (St. Albans: Rathcoole, 1939).

35 Henry F. Thuillier, *Gas in the Next War* (London: Geoffrey Bles, 1939), quotes at 91–92, 94.

36 Ibid., 174–76. Gas-mindedness, like gas discipline, was something to be cultivated.

37 Typescript diary of Miss Vera Reid, Sept. 1, 1939, IWM, Department of Documents, Micfilm 12001.

38 Diary of Nurse G. Thomas, Aug. 28 and Sept. 3, 1939, IWM, Department of Documents, 90/30/1.

39 Maggie Andrews's recent study of women and evacuation starts with the description of a small child carrying a gas mask at a train station as "one of the iconic images" of the war. See Andrews, *Women and Evacuation in the Second World War*, 1.

40 Mollie Panter-Downes, "Letter from London, 3 September," in *London War Notes 1939–1945*, ed. William Shawn (London: Longman, 1972), 4.

41 "King and Queen Visited Troops," photograph, *Daily Mirror*, Sept. 28, 1939.
42 "Masked à la Mode," *Daily Mirror*, Sept. 15, 1939. "Masking the Gas Mask," *Daily Mirror*, Oct. 6, 1939, notes a handbag designed to hold a gas mask, lipstick, and torch
43 Direct Trading Co. Leeds, advertisement, *Daily Mail*, Sept. 18 and 23, 1939.
44 Diary of Vivienne Hall, entry of Sept. 11, 1939, IWM, Department of Documents, DS/Misc/88.
45 Ibid., entry of Sept. 13, 1939.
46 See Margaret and Muriel Shean, letter to parents, Sept. 28, 1939, IWM, Department of Documents, Papers of M. J. Shean, 4734; Eileen Alexander, letter to Gershon Ellenbogen, Oct. 6, 1939, in Eileen Alexander, *Love in the Blitz: The Long-Lost Letters of a Brilliant Young Woman to Her Beloved on the Front*, ed. David McGowan and David Crane (New York: Harper Collins, 2020); Rose G. Cottrell, letter to her sister Patricia, Dec. 25, 1939, IWM, Department of Documents, Papers of R. G. Cottrell, 04/40/1. I have found many more examples than these representative few; the arrival of the gas mask and its case (cardboard box) in 1939 appears in many memoirs, oral histories, and autobiographies.
47 For more on "abnormal people and respirators," see TNA, HO 186/220 and HO 186 456.
48 Superintendent Cannon Row Station, Metropolitan Police, memorandum, Sept. 7, 1939, and statement, Sept. 12, 1939, TNA, MEPO 2 6413.
49 See files on "Respirators for British Community in France," Respirators for British Community in Paris," "Respirators for the British Community in Athens and Salonica," "Respirators for the British Community in Istanbul," and "Respirators for the British Community in Brussels," all c. Sept. 1939. See also concern from places like Cyprus and Gibraltar about the lack of gas masks during the Munich Crisis in correspondence, c. Nov. 1938, TNA, FCO 369/2528.
50 See TNA, HO 215/371.
51 See the account of Esther Bruce in Bourne, *Mother Country*, quote from 50. While there are studies that have begun to reflect on Black Britons and Britons of African, Asian, and West Indian descent and their experiences in wartime Britain, there is still a paucity of information about how such populations felt about civil defense generally and anti-gas protection in particular. All such civilians living in England, Scotland, and Wales would have received masks, but surveys of gas mask carrying did not reference race or ethnicity, and propaganda for the gas mask usually represented its users as white and middle class.
52 Excerpt from Mass Observation diary of Muriel Green, Oct. 23, 1939, in Dorothy Sheridan, ed., *Wartime Women: A Mass-Observation Anthology 1937–1945* (London: Phoenix, 1990), 57.
53 Todman, *Britain's War*, 199–222. For more on how the forgotten legacy of the war at the sea affected British armed forces early on, see Penny Summerfield, "Divisions at Sea: Class, Gender, Race and Nation in Maritime Films of the Second World War, 1939–60," *Twentieth Century British History* 22:3 (2011), 330–53.

54 Paul Addison and Jeremy A. Crang, eds., *Listening to Britain: Home Intelligence Reports on Britain's Finest Hour – May to September 1940* (London: Vintage, 2011). There are scattered notes on gas mask carrying in these snapshots of morale and public conversations across Britain; see for example reports of Aug. 29, 1940 that discuss rumors of gas attack in southeastern regions and of Aug. 30, 1940 that discuss them in the southwest regions, 376–77. For gas masks and morale more generally during the war, see Mackay, *Half the Battle*, 36–37, 56.

55 Tom Harrisson and Charles Madge, *The War Begins at Home* (London: Chatto and Windus, 1940), 166.

56 Mass Observation, Gas Mask Carrying Report, May 28, 1940, Mass Observation Archive (MOA), University of Sussex, The Keep, Brighton, TC 55, file A, box 2.

57 Mass Observation, Gas Mask Carrying Report, Sept. 17, 1940, MOA, TC 55, file A, box 2.

58 Harrisson and Madge, *The War Begins at Home*, 112–13.

59 Ibid., 72.

60 "National Day of Prayer," photograph of Churchill entering Westminster Abbey and carrying his gas mask, *Daily Mirror*, May, 25 1940; but special emphasis in "Prime Minister Carries His Gas Mask Now," *Daily Express*, Feb. 24, 1941.

61 Harrisson and Madge, *The War Begins at Home*, 111.

62 Mass Observation Diarist 5205, diary, MOA. For this diarist's response to the November directive, see Mass Observation, Respondent 1527, directive reply, Mass Observation Online, www.massobservation.amdigital.co.uk/Documents/Details/Directive-152 (accessed Feb. 19, 2020).

63 Mass Observation Diarist 5040 (male b. 1922, clerk, print costing, Margate, Kent), diary, MOA; Diarist 5040, diary, Mass Observation Online, www.massobservation.amdigital.co.uk/Documents/Details/Diarist-5040 (accessed Feb. 19, 2020).

64 W. A. Rogers, diary entry, Apr. 9, 1940, IWM, Department of Documents, Papers of W. A. Rodgers, 06/53/1.

65 Mass Observation, report, St. Peter's School, Portobello Road, London, May 24, 1940, MOA, Sussex Topic Collection, TC 55, box 1.

66 Mass Observation, report, Stratford Road, London W8, May 24, 1940, MOA, Sussex Topic Collection, TC 55, box 1.

67 "GAS!," letter to the editor, signed A.R.P., *Daily Mail*, June 7, 1940.

68 It was arguably more unpopular during the Second World War, when Britain faced greater threats. Moreover, the system for declaring one's status as a conscientious objector altered between the wars; a person seeking to obtain this designation appeared before one of nineteen regional conscientious objector tribunals run by the Minister of Labour and National Service. For conscientious objection during the Second World War, see especially Jeremy K. Kessler, "A War for Liberty: On the Law of Conscientious Objection," in *The Cambridge History of the Second World War*, vol. 3, ed. Michael Geyer and Adam Tooze (Cambridge: Cambridge University Press, 2015), 447–74. For more on wartime citizenship, see Donnelly, *Britain and the Second World War*;

Rose, *Which People's War?* For wartime pacifism in Britain, see Richard Overy, "Pacifism and the Blitz," *Past and Present* 219 (May 2013), 201–34.

69 "Pacifist with Gas Mask," *Citizen* [Gloucester], Oct. 24, 1939.

70 "Refused Gas Mask – Mother Got Him One," *Daily Mail* [Hull], Jan. 19, 1940. It had become policy rather than law to have cinemas and a few other public places deny entrance to those without a gas mask.

71 "Objector Refuses to Attend," *Manchester Guardian*, Apr. 5, 1940.

72 "Refuses Gas-Mask and Ration Book," *Courier and Advertiser* [Dundee], May 3, 1940. The view of the paper of such behavior was clear in the subheading "Mearns Conchie Is Prepared to Starve."

73 "A Roman Catholic Objector," *Manchester Guardian*, July 19, 1940.

74 "The Individual and the War," *Manchester Guardian*, Aug. 15, 1940.

75 "Eating Pastures of Religion," *Manchester Guardian*, Apr. 23, 1941.

76 Kathleen Wigham, interview (IWM Sound Archives, item 4761) as cited in Gardiner, *Wartime Britain 1939–1945*, 127. Gardiner discusses Kathleen Wigham's experiences in the context of a chapter on conscientious objection during the Second World War. She does not remark that Wigham in her oral history also reveals that she was fired for not being willing to wear a gas mask prior to her tribunal.

77 "A.R.P. Alphabet," *Daily Mirror*, July 11, 1940.

78 "Gas Mask Drill for All," *Times*, Jan. 11, 1941.

79 Mass Observation, "Morale in 1941," report, Feb. 1941, 1, 32, MOA.

80 "New Respirators," *Times*, Feb. 4, 1941.

81 "New Gas Masks for Invalids," *Times*, Feb. 4, 1941.

82 "Are YOU Still Not Carrying Your Gas Mask?," *Daily Express*, Feb. 5, 1941, and "Our Gas Masks? They're Quite Safe at Home," *Daily Express*, Feb. 13, 1941.

83 "Gas Alarm Test in Brighton," *Times*, Feb. 18, 1941.

84 "Town's Street Gas 'Attack,'" *Daily Mail*, Feb. 18, 1941. Also reported in *Daily Express*, Feb. 18, 1941.

85 "Brighton 'Masked' for a Gas 'Alert' Drill," *Illustrated London News*, Feb. 22, 1941. When Brighton held a surprise test in mid-April, the *Daily Mirror* had a photograph showing just what could happen to a child who had her gas mask with her but had not practiced putting it on. "It's a Warning to Parents," *Daily Mirror*, Apr. 16, 1941.

86 "Something Forgotten," *Manchester Guardian*, Feb. 26, 1941. Other papers began to advertise competitions to determine who could wear the gas mask the longest; see "Pasted Enemy at Home," *Daily Mirror*, Feb. 27, 1941.

87 Noel Timpson, "The Gas Weapon," letter to the editor, *Manchester Guardian*, Feb. 26, 1941.

88 "Gas Masks," *Daily Express*, Mar. 31, 1941.

89 Sir George Gater, draft letter to Monckton, undated [c. April 1941], TNA, HO 186/2247.

90 See J. R. Alderson, draft and final letter to L. N. Helsby (Treasury), Apr. 19, 1941, TNA, HO 186/2247.

91 See "Gas Publicity" memorandum, c. May 1941, and correspondence between the Ministry of Information and Treasury about paying for 15 million

copies of the leaflet as well as arranging for other materials, TNA, HO 186/2247.

92 "No Compulsion (Yet) to Carry Gas-Masks," *Daily Mail*, Mar. 28, 1941. See "Take Your Gas Mask Everywhere," IWM, Department of Art, PST 13860 (1939), and "Hitler Will Send No Warning," IWM, Department of Art, PST 13861.

93 "What to Do about Gas," *Manchester Guardian*, Apr. 7, 1941; the quotes within the article are from the pamphlet itself. See also "What to Do about Gas" (London: HMSO, 1941). See "Science and War," *Daily Telegraph*, Apr. 3, 1941.

94 "Science and War," *Daily Telegraph*, Apr. 3, 1941.

95 Quoted as appearing on the radio the previous night in "Play Teaches Gas Lessons," *Daily Mail*, Mar. 29, 1941.

96 Where is Your Gas Mask?, *Daily Mail*, April 2, 1941.

97 For more on the devastation caused by such raids and some of the reactions to them, see Amy Bell, "Landscapes of Fear: Wartime London, 1939–1945," *Journal of British Studies* 48:1 (2009), 153–75, and *London Was Ours*; Stephen Douds, *The Belfast Blitz: The People's Story* (Belfast: Blackstaff, 2011); Lara Feigel, *The Love-Charm of Bombs: Restless Lives in the Second World War* (New York: Bloomsbury, 2013); Jones, *British Civilians in the Front Line*; John MacLeod, *River of Fire: The Clydebank Blitz* (Edinburgh: Birllin, 2010); Noakes, *Dying for the Nation*; Richard Overy, *The Bombers and the Bombed: Allied Air War over Europe, 1940–45* (New York: Viking, 2013); Peter Stansky, *The First Day of the Blitz* (New Haven, CT: Yale University Press, 2008); Ziegler, *London at War*.

98 "Plea to Carry Gas Masks," *Daily Telegraph*, Mar. 29, 1941.

99 Irene Fern Smith, diary entry, Feb. 2, 1941, Bishopsgate Institute Special Collections and Archives, London, GDP/18.

100 See ibid., Feb. 11 and 13, 1941 for her daughter's gas mask; Feb. 13, 14, and 21, 1941 for rumors about gas and invasion and publicity about gas.

101 Ibid., Feb. 17 and Mar. 24, 1941.

102 Mass Observation, "Report on Gas Tests at East Molesey and Esher," Apr. 8, 1941, MOA, File Report 645.

103 Ibid.

104 Ibid. For other tests that month, see the report of one in Nottingham in "Got Your Gas Mask?," *Nottingham Evening Post*, Apr. 22, 1941.

105 For more on women and the war, see Andrews, *Women and Evacuation*; James Hinton, *Women, Social Leadership, and the Second World War: Continuities of Class* (Oxford: Oxford University Press, 2002); Noakes, *Dying for the Nation*; Summerfield, *Reconstructing Women's Wartime Lives*.

106 "Is Your Gas Mask as Efficient as His?," *Daily Mirror*, Apr. 7, 1941.

107 "What to Do about Gas," advertisement, *Manchester Guardian*, May 18, 1941. See also "What to Do about Gas," advertisement, *Observer*, May 25, 1941.

108 "What to Do about Gas: Hints to Mothers," advertisement, *Observer*, June 8, 1941.

109 See draft of "What to Do about Gas: Hints to Mothers" and correspondence between Armstrong and Williams, TNA, HO 186/2247.

110 G[ertrude] Williams, letter to J. McNulty, June 14, 1941, TNA, HO 186/2247.
111 See draft of Gas Raid Quiz No. 1, May 19, 1941, TNA, HO 186/2247.
112 "Gas Raid Quiz No. 1," *Daily Express*, June 17, 1941. The advertisement noted that this quiz came from the Ministry of Home Security, but its placement in the paper was due to the sponsorship of Whitbread & Co. Ltd. This would be the case for the series of gas raid quizzes that followed.
113 G[ertrude] Williams, letter to Dr. Armstrong, Aug. 26, 1941, TNA, HO 186/2247.
114 See list of newspapers attached to "Anti-gas Campaign: Preliminary Memorandum," Apr. 30, 1941, TNA, HO 186/2116.
115 "Gas Raid Quiz No. 6," *Daily Mail*, July 24, 1941. No one noted the contradiction that women's exclusion from combat meant that they were essentially allowing men to risk their lives for them.
116 "BBC Gives Gas-Mask Drill," *Daily Mail*, Apr. 9, 1941.
117 Memorandum to Mr. [C. D.] Soman, May 27, 1941, TNA, HO 186/752.
118 A. A. Sargent, memorandum, July 16, 1941, TNA, HO 186/752.
119 Ibid.
120 Memorandum on *Take Care of Your Gas Mask*, July 23, 1941, TNA, HO 186/752.
121 Ibid.
122 Scripts for *The Guardian of Your Life*, July 1941, TNA, HO 186/752.
123 "Masked Ball [1941 Style]," *Daily Express*, Apr. 14, 1941.
124 "Waiting for Ginger," *Daily Express*, June 14, 1941.
125 Public Record Office of Northern Ireland, Minister of Education Files, 13/1/1962.
126 Mrs. J. A. Quigley, letter to Minister of Education, Northern Ireland, Aug. 13, 1941, Public Record Office of Northern Ireland, Minister of Education Files, 13/1/1962. In theory, gas masks should have been distributed throughout Northern Ireland, but as earlier evidence showed, their initial arrival met with some concerted resistance.
127 "Peaceful Persuasion," *Manchester Guardian*, Apr. 24, 1941.
128 Mrs. Creswick Atkinson, "The Care of Children in Wartime," BBC broadcast (London: Letts Quikref Diaries, n.d.; repr. London: IWM, Department of Printed Books, 2005), 25. Publication indicates that this constitutes a transcript of the broadcast.
129 Vere Wood, "It's Your Opinion," letter to the editor; G.C.K., letter to the editor, *Daily Mail*, Apr. 1, 1941.
130 "The Gas-Mask Habit," letter to the editor, *Manchester Guardian*, Apr. 29, 1941.
131 "New Law about Gas Masks," letter to the editor, *Picture Post*, Apr. 26, 1941.
132 Mass Observation, "Report on Gas Mask Posters," July 1941, 1–3, MOA, File Report 800.
133 Mass Observation Diarist 5317, diary, Mass Observation Online, www.massobservation.amdigital.co.uk/Documents/Details/Diarist-5317 (accessed Jan. 20, 2020).

134 Mass Observation Diarist 5205, diary, Mass Observation Online, www
.massobservation.amdigital.co.uk/Documents/Details/Diarist-5205
(accessed Jan. 20, 2020).
135 See Mass Observation, "Interim Report on Gas Mask Carrying," May 16,
1941, MOA, TC 55, box 2, file L.

Chapter 6

1 See "Gas Raid Quiz," *Daily Express*, June 17, 21, 24, July 3, 10, 25, 31,
Aug. 5, 14, 27, and Sept. 9, 1941; "Mock Gas Raid on Scotland," *Daily
Telegraph*, Sept. 1, 1941.
2 Elizabeth Rowley, "This Is How a Day Nursery Is Run," *Daily Mirror*,
Nov. 6, 1941. There is evidence in the form of filmed drills and other reports
that gas drills for schoolchildren continued.
3 John Kerr, "In My Wee Gas Mask" [n.d.]. This was sung in music halls by
David Willis; see the catalog of his collection in the University of Glasgow
Library, www.gla.ac.uk/myglasgow/library/files/special/collections/STA/
Collections/willis/index.html (accessed July 31, 2019).
4 A number of works of detective fiction that appeared between 1938 and 1943
use ARP, especially the blackout and anti-gas drills, as key elements. Several
even feature a manipulated gas mask as a murder weapon. For a discussion of
these works, see Susan R. Grayzel, "Domesticating the Horrors of Modern
War: Civil Defense and the Wartime British Murder Mystery," in *British
Murder Mysteries, 1880–1960: Facts & Fictions*, eds. Laura Mayhall and
Elizabeth Prevost (Palgrave Crime Files Series in press).
5 Kerr, "In My Wee Gas Mask."
6 George Formby, "I Did What I Could with Me Gas Mask," released Apr. 8,
1941, Regal Zonophone, record no. MR3463.
7 See "Midsummer Madness," *Manchester Guardian*, June 21, 1941.
8 "Poison Gas," *Manchester Guardian*, Aug. 14, 1941. For the official statements, see TNA, HO 186/2116.
9 See memorandum "The Respirator," Apr. 29, 1941, TNA, HO 186/2661.
10 See correspondence on durability of gas masks and memorandum
"Respirators after the War," Aug. 1944, TNA, HO 186/2661. See also files
"Civilian Respirator Care after Distribution" on inspections in 1943 and
1944, TNA, HO 186/1066.
11 See Ministry of Education Circular 1551, May 10, 1942, and related correspondence, TNA, ED 136/33.
12 Bertram Pickard, "English Friends and Civil Defence" [Dec. 14, 1941],
reprinted as a pamphlet (London: The Friend, 1942), Library and Archive
of the Society of Friends, box L-15/9d. For more on Pickard's activism, see
Maureen Waugh, "Quakers, Peace and the League of Nations: The Role of
Bertram Pickard," *Quaker Studies* 6:1 (2001), 59–79.
13 See correspondence between G. D. Kirwan (ARP Department, Home Office)
and A. J. Edmunds, Sept. 30 and Oct. 1, 1940, TNA, HO 215/371.
14 Joanna Cruickshank, letter to Ernest Holderness, Feb. 27, 1941, TNA, HO
215/371.

15 See correspondence, Mar. 1941, Mar. 1942, and Oct. 1942, TNA, HO 215/
   371.
16 In addition to imprisoning resident aliens, Britain eventually took charge of
   prisoners of war. None of over thirty files in The National Archives that I was
   able to consult has anything to say about the status of gas masks for enemy
   prisoners of war in Britain, nor did I find public references to any sense that
   such masks had been distributed to them in the newspapers consulted or in
   Parliamentary Debates. Part of the reason for this may have been the timing of
   when prisoners of war (primarily first from Italy) reached the United
   Kingdom, which was not until July 1941 and in relatively small numbers.
   See Gardiner, *Wartime Britain 1939–1945*, 534–40; Dan Todman, *Britain's
   War: A New World, 1942–1947* (Oxford: Oxford University Press, 2020),
   444–46. German prisoners of war did not show up in any significant numbers
   until 1944; see Todman, *Britain's War: A New World*, 657–58.
17 For more on some of the other consequences of this shortage, see Sandra
   Trugden Dawson, "Rubber Shortages on Britain's Home Front," in *Home
   Fronts: Britain and the Empire at War, 1939–45*, ed. Mark J. Crowley and
   Sandra Trudgen Dawson (London: Boydell & Brewer, 2017), 59–75.
18 "Fire Watching and Gas Masks," *Times*, July 31, 1942.
19 See transcript of these debates in "House of Commons," *Times*, July 31,
   1942. See also Herbert Morrison in *Parliamentary Debates – Commons*,
   vol. 382, cols. 784–85 (July 30, 1942).
20 Ibid.
21 Percy Cater, "No Need to Carry a Gas Mask," *Daily Mail*, July 31, 1942.
22 Herbert Morrison, letter to John Anderson, Nov. 6, 1942, and John
   Anderson, letter to Herbert Morrison, Nov. 12, 1942, TNA, CAB 123/206.
23 See the discussion in Training Pamphlet No. 4, "Notes on Gas Tests and
   Exercises," c. Mar. 1942, TNA, HO 186/2098.
24 "Gas Mask Policy," *Daily Telegraph*, Oct. 26, 1942.
25 "Possibility of Gas Attacks," *Times*, Apr. 21, 1943. Some participants in the
   war did use gas, notably Japan. See Walter Grunden, "No Retaliation in
   Kind: Japanese Chemical Warfare Policy in World War II," in *One Hundred
   Years of Chemical Warfare: Research, Deployment, Consequences*, ed.
   B. Friedrich, D. Hoffmann, J. Renn, F. Schmaltz, and M. Wolf (Cham:
   Springer, 2017), https://link.springer.com/chapter/10.1007/978-3-319-
   51664-6_14# (accessed Oct. 21, 2018). Awareness of this usage beyond
   some sectors of the Allied military was limited.
26 "German Threat to Use Gas," *Times*, Apr. 22, 1943, and "Hitler Is About to
   Use Poison Gas," *Daily Mail*, Apr. 22, 1943. As Todman points out, the
   British government had also produced a stockpile of its own chemical agents
   but remained reluctant to start using poison gas because it felt its bases in the
   empire, especially the Middle East and India, remained especially vulnerable
   to such weapons. Todman, *Britain's War: A New World*, 267.
27 "Gas: Big Test of Masks," *Daily Mail*, June 10, 1943.
28 "Prisoners Used in Gas Tests," *Times*, Dec. 16, 1943.
29 "Murder Camps in Austria," *Times*, May 14, 1945, and "Gas Chamber at
   Auschwitz," *Times*, Sept. 22, 1945. For more on how and when the British

found out about the Holocaust, see Tony Kushner, "The Holocaust in the British Imagination: The Official Mind and Beyond, 1945 to the Present," *Holocaust Studies* 23:3 (2017), 364–84. Kushner notes the significance of the direct experience of British troops in liberating Bergen-Belsen and the subsequent publicity that this generated.

30 "Gas Mask Repairs Free for Two Months," *Times*, Dec. 29, 1943; "Free Gas Mask Repair," *Daily Mail*, Dec. 29, 1943.

31 "How to Be a Good Citizen," *Daily Express*, Jan. 31, 1944.

32 See "Indians in Civil Defence," poster, IWM, Department of Art, PST 16288. See also E. I. Ekpenyan, *Some Experiences of an African Air Raid Warden* (London: Sheldon Press, 1943). This text notes that was originally a BBC Radio Broadcast to Africa. See also Peter Fryer, *Staying Power: The History of Black People in Britain* (London: Pluto, 1984), 331 for more on Black air raid wardens in the Second World War, as well as Bourne, *Mother Country*.

33 For the definitive account of India during the Second World War, see Yasmin Khan, *The Raj at War: A People's History of India's Second World War* (London: Bodley Head, 2015). For how Churchill influenced policy toward India during the war, see Richard Toye, *Churchill's Empire: The World That Made Him and the World He Made* (New York: Henry Holt, 2010) and Madhusree Mukerjee, *Churchill's Secret War: The British Empire and the Ravaging of India during World War II* (New York: Basic Books, 2010).

34 See "Report on Civil Defence in India," 1942, which also lists the appointment in 1941 of key personnel: Raghavendra Rao as the Head of Civil Defence seated on the Executive Council (until his death and replacement by Sir J. P. Srivastava in July 1942) and A. W. Ibbotson, Director General of Civil Defence. It was also the case that the inability to decide how to finance ARP and conflicts over the extent to which the costs fell on the central government or the provinces further delayed action. This was not resolved until January 1942, when the provincial government assumed the first level of responsibility (no more than 4 percent of its budget), with expenditures split thereafter 50:50 for the next set of costs, and the central government taking on a greater percentage of the financing if and when costs increased. An advisory role, but not a financial one, was also set in place for Indian states. See BL, IOR, L/PJ/7/4728.

35 National Archives of India, New Delhi, ARP file 174/29/41. My thanks to Mahima Manchanda for her research assistance in obtaining these files. By 1942, this scheme was reflected in color coding in terms of potential exposure to air raids, as follows; red: Bengal, Assam, Bihar, and the coastal districts of Orissa together with the coastal belt twenty-five miles deep running along the coast of India from Orissa to Sind; pink: Orissa, Madras, Bombay, Central Provinces, and a portion of Uttar Pradesh southeast of the line drawn from Bombay to Cawnpore to the Nepal border together with intervening Indian states; white: the rest of India. See the summation of this and also a note in "Statement on Civil Defence for the National Defence Council," July 7, 1942, stating that that the whole of India would now be considered "the threatened area," given Japanese actions. BL, IOR L/PJ/7/4728.

36 Secretary of State for Colonies, telegram, Feb. 5, 1942, TNA, WO 193/738.
37 See High Commissioner of South Africa, telegram to Secretary of State for Colonies, Feb. 11, 1942, and Palestine, telegrams to Secretary of State for Colonies, Feb. 20 and 22, 1942 (noting policy for Transjordan), TNA, WO 193/738. For more on civilian anti-gas protection in the Middle East theater of the war, see "Anti-gas Measures in the Middle East," June 1942, TNA, CO 968/79/9.
38 "Anti-gas Civil Defence in the Colonies," Mar. 1942, TNA, WO 193/738.
39 T. I. K. Lloyd, letter to Lt. Col. C. S. Sugden, Mar. 21, 1942, and C. S. Sugden, letter to T. I. K. Lloyd, Apr. 1,1942, TNA, WO 193/738.
40 "Provision of Gas Masks for Singapore" and related correspondence, Feb. 2, 1942, TNA, CAB 120/777. See Grunden, "No Retaliation in Kind" for Japanese use of chemical arms.
41 J. N. Kennedy, "Anti-gas Protection Singapore," Feb. 7, 1942, TNA, WO 193/738. Wartime shipping was becoming an increasingly difficult issue and would only get worse through 1943; see Todman, *Britain's War: A New World*.
42 Memorandum, Sept. 21, 1943, BL, IOR L/PJ/7/4728.
43 War Cabinet, draft minutes of a meeting on "Anti-gas Precautions," Apr. 7, 1942, copy in TNA, ED 136/33.
44 "Report on Civil Defence in India," 1942, section on "Gas," BL, IOR L/PJ/7/ 4728.
45 Ibid.
46 "Memorandum on Anti-gas Measures to Be Undertaken by Provincial Governments and States," Aug. 17, 1942, BL, IOR, L/PJ/7/4728.
47 See discussion of these attacks and ARP in India in Grayzel, "Protecting Which Spaces and Bodies?," 77–78.
48 "Preparations for Chemical War," Apr. 11, 1944, BL, IOR L/PJ/7/4728.
49 See the further discussion of this in Grayzel, "Protecting Which Spaces and Bodies?"
50 "Respirator Depot at Bath," in "Work of the Regional Branches," *Women's Voluntary Service for Civil Defence Newsletter* 57 (July 1944). This article and thus the work of the Bath depot were further publicized in "Regarded as a Model," *Bath Chronicle and Weekly Gazette*, July 29, 1944. For more on this work, see Hinton, *Women, Social Leadership* and Malcolmson and Malcolmson, *Women at the Ready*. The motto may well reflect new and emerging ideas about the welfare state since it postdates the release of the Beveridge Report.
51 "Respirator Depot at Bath."
52 In late June 1944, Morrison proposed reviving prior ideas that Britain might retaliate by attacking smaller German towns with poison gas. See Todman, *Britain's War: A New World*, 583–84.
53 See the important analysis of this campaign and end of the war in Tami Davis Biddle, "On the Crest of Fear: V-Weapons, the Battle of the Bulge, and the Last Stages of World War II in Europe," *Journal of Military History* 83 (2019), 157–94; for government concern with morale, see 173 and 181, and for the threat of using gas against Allied troops, 183. For more on this, see Overy,

The Bombers and the Bombed. See also W.S.C., final memorandum, to Ministry of Home Security, Mar. 2, 1944: "Thank you for the analysis of the returns of the civilian respirator inspections which you sent to me. I see that about 9 out of every 10 people have a serviceable mask. This seems adequate insurance against the risk of the enemy's starting gas warfare at a period when we are dropping more than 30 times the tonnage of bombs on Germany that she is dropping on us." TNA, CAB 120/777.

54 Mass Observation, "War Morale Chart," Feb. 6, 1946, MOA, File Report 2332.

55 D. B. Grubb, "The Unwanted Gas Mask," letter to the editor, *Times*, Aug. 29, 1945.

56 S. G. Polhill, "The Unwanted Gas Mask," letter to the editor, *Times*, Sept. 3, 1945.

57 "End of War Surplus Counter," *Daily Mail*, Sept. 4, 1945. A follow-up statement in October noted that people were being asked to hold on to them and that no official word on whether or when to turn them in had been received: "Family Grant in August," *Daily Mail*, Oct. 12, 1945.

58 E. F. Armstrong, "Respirators after the War," Aug. 28, 1944, TNA, HO 186/2662. The memorandum went on to suggest that a new and better gas mask, as well as a sturdier design for a carrier, would be needed in the future. Edward Frankland Armstrong was a leading chemist, a Fellow of the Royal Society, and a scientific advisor to the government during the war. See C. S. Gibson and T. P. Hildreth, "Edward Frankland Armstrong," *Obituary Notices of Fellows of the Royal Society* 5 (1948), 619.

59 Draft memorandum, "Preservation of Civilian Respirators," Oct. 17, 1944, TNA, HO 186/2662.

60 "Extract from the Conclusions of the Meeting of the War Cabinet Held on Monday 26th February, 1945," TNA, HO 186/2662.

61 See drafts and the approved version of "Home Security Circular No. 36/1945: Respirators for the Public," Apr. 27, 1945. A related notice to the press, titled "Gas Masks," summarized the main aspects of the memorandum. Both in TNA, HO 186/2662.

62 "One Parting Kick," *Times*, May 7, 1945.

63 Stella Reading, letter to Sir William Brown, June 1, 1945. She notes that the WVS would be happy to do so, but "we wish to avoid putting unexpected burdens on them at the last moment when they are all tired." TNA, HO 186/2662.

64 "Cabinet Memorandum for the Home Secretary on Preservation of Civilian Respirators," Aug. 1945, TNA, PREM 8/463.

65 Ibid., additional note, Sept. 1945. There were discussions about the possible utility of gas masks against nuclear weapons and the ongoing development of civilian gas masks during the Cold War, see Special Committee of Civil Defence, City of Glasgow, minutes, May 22, 1946 for discussion of collection of babies' anti-gas helmets and children's respirators only, and especially minutes, Apr. 8, 1953, for fitting of new civilian respirators, GCA, DTC 810 348/1; see also "A Feasibility Study for a New Civilian Respirator," May 1, 1973, TNA, WO 188/2431.

66 See report of the Commons debate in "Keep Your Gas Mask Still," *Evening Telegraph* [Dundee], Oct. 11, 1945. A follow-up article quoted the statement in the "Londoner's Diary" from the *Evening Standard* that there must be 50 million gas masks now cluttering cupboards up and down the nation or rotting in warehouses while the government could not figure out what to do with them. See "Gas-Mask Mess," *Evening Telegraph* [Dundee], Nov. 27, 1945.

67 "Miscellany: How about That Gas Mask?," *Manchester Guardian*, Oct. 13, 1945.

68 "'Parachuted' Down Stairs – Broke Neck," *Daily Mirror*, Sept. 20, 1945.

69 The use of the gas mask for suicides occurred as soon as masks were distributed, as early as 1939; see "Too Old at 34, He Took His Life," *Daily Mirror*, Jan. 19, 1939. See other examples, such as "Wrote Fiancée in Own Blood," *Nottingham Evening Post*, June 29, 1945. On the immediate postwar era, see "Spinster Dead in Her Bath," *Daily Mail*, May 1, 1946; and on suspicious deaths, "Masked Chemist Found Dead," *Daily Mail*, May 2, 1946, and "Boy in Mask Suffocated," *Daily Mail*, May 11, 1946.

Chapter 7

1 "Our New Faces," *Daily Mirror*, July 20, 1936.

2 Carter, *Chemical and Biological Defence*, 59. For a history of the experiments on humans at Porton Down, see Evans, *Gassed* and Schmidt, *Secret Science*. For the use of chemical arms in the war, see Grunden, "No Retaliation in Kind" and Tucker, *War of Nerves*, especially ch. 4.

3 "Care of Gas Masks," *Times*, Dec. 7, 1945; from statement by Home Secretary James Chuter Ede in debates in the House of Commons, reprinted under the heading "Parliament."

4 "The Bomb," editorial, *Press and Journal* [Aberdeen], Oct. 19, 1949.

5 A.G., "Protection in Atomic Warfare," letter to the editor, *Dundee Courier and Advertiser*, July 28, 1950.

6 "Review of the Stocks of Civilian Respirators," Feb. 6, 1948, TNA, HO 186/2661.

7 For the 1950s, see "Production of Civilian Respirators," c. Mar. 1955, TNA, T 221/377; and for the 1970s, see "A Feasibility Study for a New Civilian Respirator," May 4, 1973, TNA, WO 188/2431. For the rise and impact of Britain's anti-nuclear movement, see Adrian Bingham, "'The Monster'? The British Popular Press and the Nuclear Culture, 1945–Early 1960s," *British Journal for the History of Science* 45:4 (2012), 609–24; Jodi Burkett, "Re-defining British Morality: 'Britishness' and the Campaign for Nuclear Disarmament 1958–68," *Twentieth Century British History* 21:2 (2010), 184–205; Liddington, *The Long Road to Greenham*; Meredith Veldman, *Fantasy, the Bomb, and the Greening of Britain: Romantic Protest, 1945–1980* (Cambridge: Cambridge University Press, 1994); Richard Taylor and Nigel Young, eds., *Campaigns for Peace: British Peace Movements in the Twentieth Century* (Manchester: Manchester University Press, 1987). For postwar civil defence, see Grant, *After the Bomb* and J. Stafford, "'Stay at Home': The Politics of Nuclear Civil Defence," *Twentieth Century British History* 23:3 (2012), 383–407.

Epilogue

1 Price, *The Chemical Weapons Taboo.*
2 Moshenska, *Material Cultures of Childhood.* For more on popular memory and the Second World War, see Lucy Noakes and Juliette Pattinson, eds., *British Cultural Memory and the Second World War* (London: Bloomsbury, 2014), especially Penny Summerfield's contribution, "The Generation of Memory: Gender and the Popular Memory of the Second World War in Britain," 25–46. See also Lucy Noakes, "Popular Memory, Popular Culture," in *The Cambridge History of the Second World War*, vol. 3, ed. Michael Geyer and Adam Tooze (Cambridge: Cambridge University Press, 2015), 675–97.
3 "WWII People's War," www.bbc.co.uk/history/ww2peopleswar/stories/04/a5960504.shtml (accessed Dec. 12, 2012). My gratitude to the family of Mrs. Gravenor, and especially to Caitlin Gravenor-Howells for sharing more of her grandmother's story.
4 For more on tear gas, see Feigenbaum, *Tear Gas.* For a representative image of a Gilets Jaunes protester in a gas mask in December 2018, see https://ici .radio-canada.ca/nouvelle/1140695/france-manifestations-des-gilets-jaunes-images (accessed Feb. 20, 2019); for a photograph of a statue of a protester in a gas mask in Hong Kong, see John Leicester and Eileen Ng, "Hong Kong's Leader Says Mask Ban Necessary to Quell Violence," *Seattle Times*, Oct. 3, 2019, www.seattletimes.com/nation-world/nation/hong-kong-protesters-rally-against-plan-for-mask-ban/ (accessed Dec. 5, 2019); and for the powerful way in which 2020 protests against anti-Black racism during the COVID-19 pandemic have incorporated gas masks, including ways to think about the meaning of "I can't breathe," see Zeynep Tufekci, "I Can't Breathe: Braving Tear Gas in a Pandemic," *Atlantic*, June 4, 2020. For how artists have powerfully responded, see "Curating the End of the World: Afrofuturism and Black Speculative Art in Times of Covid-19," https://moed.online/curat ing-the-end-of-the-world-afrofuturism-black-speculative-art-times-covid19/ (accessed July 11, 2020). My deep gratitude to Shenette Garrett-Scott for this final reference.
5 The website for the organization Stop the War explains: "In 2003 the Stop the War Coalition commissioned a series of eight anti-war posters from seven of the best graphic artists working in Britain." Peter Kennard designed the first one; see www.stopwar.org.uk/index.php/shop/612-art-against-war-1 (accessed May 20, 2020.)
6 See Sarah Left, "Royal Mail Stamps Down on Postage Art," *Guardian*, June 4, 2003, and "Row over Gas-Masked Queen," BBC News, June 4, 2003.
7 Quotations from *Doctor Who*, series 1, episode 9, "The Empty Child," and episode 10, "The Doctor Dances" (BBC, 2005).
8 See image in https://metro.co.uk/2018/06/27/woman-gas-mask-raging-wild fires-sums-true-northern-grit-7663925/ (accessed June 28, 2018). I am grateful to Jonathan Reinarz for first alerting me to this photograph.

Bibliography

Archival Sources

Archives Nationales de France, Paris
  F 7 (Series Police Générale)
Bishopsgate Institute Special Collections and Archives, London, UK
British Library (BL), London, UK
  Abyssinian Association Pamphlet Collection
  India Office Records (IOR)
  Peace Pledge Union Pamphlets
  Newspaper and Periodical Collections
In addition to a range of papers consulted about specific events, the
  following newspapers were consulted more extensively for the dur-
  ation of the period studied:
Bookman
British Medical Journal
Daily Chronicle
Daily Express
Daily Herald
Daily Mail
Daily Mirror
Daily Sketch
Daily Telegraph
English Review
Illustrated London News
Irish Times
Lancet
London Mercury
Manchester Guardian
Observer
Pall Mall Gazette
Picture Post
Punch
Saturday Review
Scotsman
Straits Times
The Times

Times Literary Supplement
Times of India
Conservative Party Archives, Bodleian Library, Oxford, UK
Imperial War Museum (IWM), London, UK
  Department of Art
  Department of Documents
  Department of Film
  Department of Photographs
Labour Party Archives, People's History Museum, Manchester, UK
League of Nations Archives (LONA), Geneva, Switzerland
Library and Archives of the Society of Friends, London, UK
  The Friend
  Pamphlet Collections
  Peace Committee Records
British Library of Political and Economic Science, London School of
  Economics, London, UK (BLPES)
  Papers of the British Section of the Women's International League
    for Peace and Freedom (WILPF)
  Women's Library Collections
Mass Observation Archive (MOA), University of Sussex, The Keep,
  Brighton, UK
Mitchell Library, Glasgow, UK
  Glasgow City Archives (GCA)
The National Archives (TNA), London, UK
  Cabinet Records (CAB)
  Colonial Office (CO)
  Foreign Office (FO)
  Home Office (HO)
  Metropolitan Police Records (MEPO)
  War Office (WO)
Public Record Office of Northern Ireland (PRONI), Belfast, UK

Printed Sources

Addison, Paul, and Jeremy A. Crang, eds. *Listening to Britain: Home Intelligence Reports on Britain's Finest Hour – May to September 1940* (London: Vintage, 2011).
Ahmed, Sara. *Queer Phenomenology: Orientations, Objects, Others* (Durham, NC: Duke University Press, 2006).
"AHR Conversations: The Historical Study of Emotions: Participants: Nicole Eustace, Eugenia Lean, Julie Livingston, Jan Plamper, William A. Reddy, and Barbara H. Rosenwein," *American Historical Review* 117:5 (2012), 1487–531.
Alexander, Eileen. *Love in the Blitz: The Long-Lost Letters of a Brilliant Young Woman to Her Beloved on the Front*, ed. David McGowan and David Crane (New York: Harper Collins, 2020).

Allingham, Margery. *The Oaken Heart: The Story of an English Village at War* (London: Michael Joseph, 1941),

Andrews, Maggie. *Women and Evacuation in the Second World War: Femininity, Domesticity and Motherhood* (London: Bloomsbury, 2019).

Angell, Norman. *You and Mustard Gas* (London: League of Nations Union, 1936).

Anglin, Norman. *Poison Gas* (London: Jonathan Cape, 1928).

Appadurai, Arjun. "Introduction: Commodities and the Politics of Value," in *The Social Life of Things: Commodities in Cultural Perspective*, ed. Arjun Appadurai (Cambridge: Cambridge University Press, 1986), 3–63.

ARP: A Plan for the Safety of the People of Nottingham (Nottingham: Nottingham Communist Party, 1938).

ARP Department, Home Office. *Air Raid Precautions Handbook No. 1: Personal Protection against Gas* (London: HMSO, 1936).

A.R.P. for Hampstead (London: Hampstead Communist Party, 1938).

Auslander, Leora, and Tara Zahra. "Introduction" to *Objects of War: The Material Culture of Conflict and Displacement* (Ithaca, NY: Cornell University Press, 2018), 1–25.

Auslander, Leora, and Tara Zahra, eds. *Objects of War: The Material Culture of Conflict and Displacement* (Ithaca, NY: Cornell University Press, 2018).

Baldoli, C., et al., eds. *Bombing, States and Peoples in Western Europe 1940–1945* (London: Continuum, 2011).

Baudenistei, Rainer. *Between Bombs and Good Intentions: The Red Cross and the Italo-Ethiopian War, 1935–36* (New York: Berghahn Books, 2006).

Beaumont, Caitríona. *Housewives and Citizens: Domesticity and the Women's Movement in England, 1928–64* (Manchester: Manchester University Press, 2013).

Beddoe, Deirdre. *Back to Home and Duty: Women between the Wars* (London: Pandora, 1989).

Beers, Laura. *Your Britain: Media and the Making of the Labour Party* (Cambridge, MA: Harvard University Press, 2010).

Bell, A. "Landscapes of Fear: Wartime London, 1939–1945," *Journal of British Studies* 48:1 (2009), 153–75.
  London Was Ours: Diaries and Memoirs of the London Blitz (London: I. B. Tauris, 2011).

Bialer, U. *The Shadow of the Bomber: The Fear of Air Attack and British Politics, 1932–1939* (London: Royal Historical Society, 1980).

Biddle, Tami Davis. "On the Crest of Fear: V-Weapons, the Battle of the Bulge, and the Last Stages of World War II in Europe," *Journal of Military History* 83 (2019), 157–94.
  Rhetoric and Reality in Air Warfare: The Evolution of British and American Ideas about Strategic Bombing, 1914–1945 (Princeton, NJ: Princeton University Press, 2002).

Biernoff, Suzannah. "The Rhetoric of Disfigurement in First World War Britain," *Social History of Medicine* 24:3 (2011), 666–85.

Bingham, Adrian. "'The Monster'? The British Popular Press and the Nuclear Culture, 1945–Early 1960s," *British Journal for the History of Science* 45:4 (2012), 609–24.

Bland, Lucy. *Modern Women on Trial: Sexual Transgression in the Age of the Flapper* (Manchester: Manchester University Press, 2013).

Bogost, Ian. *Alien Phenomenology or What It's Like to Be a Thing* (Minneapolis: University of Minnesota Press, 2012).

Bourke, Joanna. *Fear: A Cultural History* (Emeryville, CA: Shoemaker & Hoard, 2005).

Wounding the World: How Military Violence and War-Play Invade Our Lives (London: Virago, 2014).

Bourne, Stephen. *Mother Country: Britain's Black Community on the Home Front, 1939–45* (Stroud: History Press, 2010).

Braybon, Gail. *Women Workers in the First World War* (London: Croom Helm, 1981).

Braybon, Gail, ed. *Evidence, History and the Great War: Historians and the Impact of 1914–18* (New York: Berghahn, 2003).

Brown, Bill. "Thing Theory," in *Things*, ed. Bill Brown (Chicago: University of Chicago Press, 2004), 3–21.

Brown, Frederic J. *Chemical Warfare: A Study in Restraints* (1968; repr. New Brunswick, NJ, and London: Transaction, 2006).

Brunskog, Captain. "The Transformation of Warfare," in *Chemical Warfare: An Abridged Report of Papers Read at an International Conference at Frankfurt am Main* (London: Williams & Norgate, 1930).

Buckley, John J. *Air Power in the Age of Total War* (London: UCL Press, 1999).

Burkett, Jodi. "Re-defining British Morality: 'Britishness' and the Campaign for Nuclear Disarmament 1958–68," *Twentieth Century British History* 21:2 (2010), 184–205.

Burton, Antoinette. *The Trouble with Empire: Challenges to Modern British Imperialism* (Oxford: Oxford University Press, 2017).

Bush, Barbara. *Imperialism, Race and Resistance: Africa and Britain, 1919–1945* (London: Routledge, 1999).

Calder, Angus. *The Myth of the Blitz* (London: Pimlico, 1991).

Cambridge Scientists' Anti-War Group. *The Protection of the Public from Aerial Attack: Being a Critical Examination of the Recommendations Put Forward by the Air Raids Precautions Department of the Home Office* (London: Victor Gollancz, 1937).

Campion, Sarah. *Thirty Million Gas Masks* (London: Peter Davies, 1937).

Carter, G. B. *Chemical and Biological Defence at Porton Down 1916–2000* (London: HMSO, 2000).

Ceadel, Martin, *Pacifism in Britain 1914–1945: The Defining of a Faith* (Oxford: Clarendon Press, 1980).

"Popular Fiction and the Next War, 1918–1939," in *Class, Culture and Social Change: A New View of the 1930s*, ed. Frank Gloversmith (London: Harvester Press, 1980), 161–84.

Charlton, Lionel Evelyn Oswald. *War over England* (London: Longmans Greens, 1936).

Chemical Warfare: An Abridged Report of Papers Read at an International Conference at Frankfurt am Main (London: Williams & Norgate, 1930).

Chemical Warfare School (US Army). *The Use of Gas in Ethiopia* (Edgewood, MD: Chemical Warfare School, 1939).

Clarke, I. F. *Voices Prophesying War*, 2nd ed. (Oxford: Oxford University Press, 1992).

Clarke, Peter. *Hope and Glory: Britain 1900–2000*, 2nd ed. (London: Penguin, 2004).

Connelly, Mark. *We Can Take It! Britain and the Memory of the Second World War* (Harlow: Longman, 2004).

Cook, Tim. "'Against God-Inspired Conscience': The Perception of Gas Warfare as a Weapon of Mass Destruction, 1915–1939," *War & Society* 18:1(2000), 47–69.

"Through Clouded Eyes: Gas Masks in the First World War," *Material History Review* 47 (1998), 4–20.

Cornish, Paul, and Nicholas J. Saunders, eds. *Bodies in Conflict: Corporeality, Materiality, and Transformation* (London: Routledge, 2014).

Dawson, Sandra Trugden. "Rubber Shortages on Britain's Home Front," in *Home Fronts: Britain and the Empire at War, 1939–45*, ed. Mark J. Crowley and Sandra Trugden Dawson (London: Boydell & Brewer, 2017), 59–75.

Deedes, William F. *A.R.P.: A Complete Guide to Civil Defence* (London: Daily Telegraph, 1938).

Diamond, Jared. *Guns, Germs and Steel: The Fates of Human Societies* (New York: Norton, 1997).

Doan, Laura. *Disturbing Practices: History, Sexuality, and Women's Experience of Modern War* (Chicago: University of Chicago Press, 2013).

Dodd, Lindsay, and Marc Wiggam. "Civil Defence as a Harbinger of War in France and Britain during the Interwar Period." *Synergies* 4 (2011), 139–50.

Donnelly, Mark. *Britain and the Second World War* (London: Routledge, 1999).

Douds, Stephen. *The Belfast Blitz: The People's Story* (Belfast: Blackstaff, 2011).

Douglas, R. M. "Did Britain Use Chemical Weapons in Mandatory Iraq?," *The Journal of Military History* 81 (2009), 1–29.

Downes, Alexander B. *Targeting Civilians in War* (Ithaca, NY: Cornell University Press, 2008).

Downes, Stephanie, Sally Holloway, and Sarah Randles. "A Feeling for Things, Past and Present," in *Feeling Things: Objects and Emotions through History*, ed. Stephanie Downes et al. (Oxford: Oxford University Press, 2018), 8–26.

Downs, Laura Lee. *Manufacturing Inequality: Gender Division in the French and British Metalworking Industries, 1914–1939* (Ithaca, NY: Cornell University Press, 1995).

Doyle, Patrick. *ARP and Civil Defence in the Second World War* (Oxford: Shire, 2010).

Edgerton, David. *Warfare State: Britain, 1920–1970* (Cambridge: Cambridge University Press, 2006).

Ekpenyan, E. I. *Some Experiences of an African Air Raid Warden* (London: Sheldon Press, 1943).

Ellis, John. *The Social History of the Machine Gun* (1975; repr. Baltimore: Johns Hopkins University Press, 1986).

Evans, Rob. *Gassed: British Chemical Warfare Experiments on Humans at Porton Down* (London: House of Stratus, 2000).

Falola, Toyin, and Adam Paddock. *The Women's War of 1929: A History of Anti-Colonial Resistance in Eastern Nigeria* (Durham, NC: Carolina Academic Press, 2011).

Feigel, Lara. *The Love-Charm of Bombs: Restless Lives in the Second World War* (London: Bloomsbury, 2013).

Feigenbaum, Anna. *Tear Gas: From the Battlefields of WWI to the Streets of Today* (New York: Verso, 2017).

Fell, Alison S., and Susan R. Grayzel. "Women's Movements, War and the Body," in *Women Activists between War and Peace: Europe, 1918–1923*, ed. I. Sharp and M. Stibbe (London: Bloomsbury, 2017), 221–50.

Feo, Katherine. "Invisibility: Memory, Masks, and Masculinities in the Great War," *Journal of Design History* 20:1 (Mar. 2007), 17–27.

Fitzgerald, Gerald J. "Chemical Warfare and Medical Response during World War I," *American Journal of Public Health* 98:4 (2008), 611–25.

Foote, Nicola, and Nadya Williams, eds. *Civilians and Warfare in World History* (Abingdon: Routledge, 2018).

Freemantle, Michael. *Gas! Gas! Gas! Quick, Boys! How Chemistry Changed the First World War* (Stroud: The History Press, 2013).

Freud, Sigmund. "The Uncanny" (1919), trans. Alix Strachey, in *The Standard Edition of the Complete Psychological Works of Sigmund Freud*, vol. 17: *1917–1919*, ed. James Strachey (London: Hogarth Press, 1955).

Fridlund, Mats. "Buckets, Bollards and Bombs: Towards Subject Histories of Technologies and Terrors," *History and Technology* 27:4 (2011), 391–416.

Fries, Amos A., and Clarence J. West. *Chemical Warfare* (New York: McGraw-Hill, 1921).

Fryer, Peter. *Staying Power: The History of Black People in Britain* (London: Pluto, 1984).

Fuller, J. F. C. *The First of the League Wars: Its Lessons and Omens* (London: Eyre and Spottiswoode, 1936).

Gardiner, Juliet. *Wartime Britain 1939–1945* (London: Headline, 2004).

Ghosh, Durba. *Gentlemanly Terrorists: Political Violence and the Colonial State in India, 1919–1947* (Cambridge: Cambridge University Press, 2017).

Gibson, C. S., and T. P. Hildreth. "Edward Frankland Armstrong," in *Obituary Notices of Fellows of the Royal Society* 5 (1948), 619.

Gilbert, Martin. *The Second World War: A Complete History* (New York: Henry Holt, 1989).

Gillian, Arthur J. *The Menace of Chemical Warfare to Civilian Populations* (London: Chemical Worker's Union, 1932).

Girard, Marion. *A Strange and Formidable Weapon: British Responses to World War I Poison Gas* (Lincoln: University of Nebraska Press, 2008).

Goodman, Martin, *Suffer and Survive: The Extreme Life of J. S. Haldane* (London: Simon and Schuster, 2007).

Gosden, Chris. "What Do Objects Want?," *Journal of Archaeological Method and Theory* 12:3 (2005), 193–211.

Gottlieb, Julie. *Guilty Women: Foreign Policy and Appeasement in Inter-war Britain* (London: Palgrave Macmillan, 2015).

Grant, Matthew. *After the Bomb: Civil Defence and Nuclear War in Britain 1945–1968* (Basingstoke: Palgrave Macmillan, 2010).

Grayling, A. C. *Among the Dead Cities* (London: Bloomsbury, 2006).

Grayzel, Susan R. *At Home and under Fire: Air Raids and Culture in Britain from the Great War to the Blitz* (Cambridge: Cambridge University Press, 2012).

"The Baby in the Gas Mask: Motherhood, Wartime Technology, and the Gendered Division between the Fronts during and after the First World War," in *Gender and the First World War*, ed. C. Hämmerle et al. (Basingstoke: Palgrave Macmillan, 2014), 127–43.

"Defence against the Indefensible: The Gas Mask, the State, and British Culture during and after the First World War," *Twentieth Century British History* 25:3 (2014), 418–34.

"Imagining War in a Post-1918 World: Cicely Hamilton's Theodore Savage," *Contemporanea: rivista di storia dell'800 e dell'900* 17:4 (2014), 660–65.

"'Macabre and Hilarious': The Emotional Life of the Civilian Gas Mask in France during and after the First World War," in *Total War: An Emotional History*, ed. Claire Langhamer, Lucy Noakes, and Claudia Siebrecht (Oxford: Oxford University Press, 2020), 40–58.

"'Needles en Avant!': The Militarization of Sewing and Knitting during the First World War in France, Britain and the United States," in *French Fashion, Women, and the First World War*, ed. Maude Bass-Krueger and Sophie Kurkdjian (New Haven, CT: Yale University Press, 2019), 133–67.

"One British Thing: The Babies' Anti-gas Protective Helmet," *Journal of British Studies* 58:3 (2019), 598–601, DOI: 10.1017/jbr.2019.8.

"Protecting Which Spaces and Bodies? Civil Defence, the British Empire and the Second World War," in *An Imperial World at War*, ed. Ashley Jackson et al. (London: Ashgate, 2016), 66–83.

Grayzel, Susan R., and Lucy Noakes. "Defending the Home(land): Gendering Civil Defence from the First World War to the War on Terror," in *Gender and Conflict since 1914*, ed. Ana Carden-Coyne (Basingstoke: Palgrave Macmillan, 2012), 29–40.

Gregory, Adrian. *The Last Great War: British Society and the First World War* (Cambridge: Cambridge University Press, 2008).

Grip, Lina, and John Hart. "The Use of Chemical Weapons in the 1935–36 Italo-Ethiopian War," *SIPRI Arms Control and Non-proliferation Programme* (Stockholm: Stockholm International Peace Research Institute, Oct. 2009), 1–7.

Grunden, Walter. "No Retaliation in Kind: Japanese Chemical Warfare Policy in World War II," in *One Hundred Years of Chemical Warfare: Research, Deployment, Consequences*, ed. B. Friedrich, D. Hoffmann, J. Renn, F. Schmaltz, and M. Wolf (Cham: Springer, 2017), https://link.springer.com/chapter/10.1007/978-3-319-51664-6_14# (accessed Oct. 21, 2018).

Gullace, Nicoletta F. *"The Blood of Our Sons": Men, Women, and the Renegotiation of British Citizenship during the Great War* (New York: Palgrave Macmillan, 2002).

Haapamaki, Michele. *The Coming of the Aerial War: Culture and the Fear of Airborne Attack in Interwar Britain* (London: I. B. Tauris, 2014).

Haber, L. F. *The Poisonous Cloud: Chemical Warfare in the First World War* (Oxford: Clarendon Press, 1986).

Haden-Guest, Leslie. *If Air War Comes: A Guide to Air Raid Precautions and Anti-gas Treatment* (London, 1937).

Haldane, John Burdon Sanderson. *A.R.P.* (London: Victor Gollancz, 1938).

Callinicus: A Defence of Chemical Warfare (London: Kegan Paul, 1925).

Halsbury, Lord [Hardinge Goulburn Giffard]. *1944* (London: Thornton Butterworth, 1926).

Hamilton, Cicely. *Lest Ye Die: A Story from the Past or of the Future* (New York: C. Scribner's Sons, and London: J. Cape, 1928).

Theodore Savage: A Story of the Past or the Future (London: Leonard Parsons, 1922).

Hanna, Martha. *Your Death Would Be Mine* (Cambridge, MA: Harvard University Press, 2008).

Haraway, Donna J. "A Cyborg Manifesto," in *Simians, Cyborgs and Women: The Reinvention of Nature* (New York: Routledge, 1991; repr. 2010), 150–51.

Harrisson, Tom, and Charles Madge. *The War Begins at Home* (London: Chatto and Windus, 1940).

Hinton, James. *The Mass Observers: A History 1937–1949* (Oxford: Oxford University Press, 2013).

Women, Social Leadership, and the Second World War: Continuities of Class (Oxford: Oxford University Press, 2002).

Hipper, Thomas. *Governing from the Skies: A Global History of Aerial Bombing*, trans. D. Ferbach (London: Verso, 2017).

Hodder, Ian. *Entangled: An Archaeology of the Relationships between Humans and Things* (Chichester: Wiley-Blackwell, 2012).

Hogg, Jonathan G. "The Family That Feared Tomorrow: British Nuclear Culture and Individual Experience in the Late 1950s," *British Journal for the History of Science* 45:4 (2012), 535–49.

Holman, Brett. *The Next War in the Air: Britain's Fear of the Bomber, 1908–1941* (Farnham: Ashgate, 2014).

Holton, Sandra Stanley. *Feminism and Democracy: Women's Suffrage and Reform Politics in Britain 1900–1918* (Cambridge: Cambridge University Press, 2003).

Home Office, *Air Raid Precautions* (London: HMSO, 1938).

Horne, John. "Remobilizing for 'Total War': France and Britain, 1917–1918," in *State, Society and Mobilization in Europe during the First World War*, ed. John Horne (Cambridge: Cambridge University Press, 1997), 195–211.

Horne, John, ed. *State, Society and Mobilization in Europe during the First World War* (Cambridge: Cambridge University Press, 1997).

Howard, Michael, et al., eds. *The Laws of War: Constraints on Warfare in the Western World* (New Haven, CT: Yale University Press, 1994).

Hucker, Daniel. *Public Opinion and the End of Appeasement in Britain and France* (Farnham: Ashgate, 2011).

Hull, Isabel V. *Absolute Destruction: Military Culture and the Practices of War in Imperial Germany* (Ithaca, NY: Cornell University Press, 2005).

A Scrap of Paper: Breaking and Making International Law during the Great War (Ithaca, NY: Cornell University Press, 2014).

Hunt, Krista, and Kim Rygiel, eds. *(En)gendering the War on Terror: War Stories and Camouflaged Politics* (Aldershot: Ashgate, 2006).

Hyde, H. M., and G. R. Falkiner Nuttall. *Air Defence and the Civil Population* (London: Cresset, 1937).

Hylton, Stuart. *Their Darkest Hour: The Hidden History of the Home Front 1939–45* (Stroud: Sutton, 2001).

Imlay, Talbot. *Facing the Second World War: Strategy, Politics, and Economics in Britain and France, 1938–1940* (Oxford: Oxford University Press, 2003).

Inman, Frederick William. *Biological Politics: An Aid to Clear Thinking* (London: John Wright, 1935).

Inter-Parliamentary Union. *What Would Be the Character of a New War?* (London: P. S. King & Son, 1931).

Irwin, Will. *"The Next War": An Appeal to Common Sense* (New York: E. P. Dutton, 1921).

Jefferson, Catherine. "Origins of the Norm against Chemical Weapons," *International Affairs* 90:3 (2014), 647–61.

John Bell, Hills & Lucas Ltd. *Lest We Forget* (London: John Bell, Hills & Lucas Ltd, 1918).

Jones, Edgar. "Terror Weapons: The British Experience of Gas and Its Treatment in the First World War," *War in History* 21:3 (2014), 355–75.

Jones, Helen. *British Civilians in the Front Line: Air Raids, Productivity and Wartime Culture 1939–1945* (Manchester: Manchester University Press, 2006).

Kaufmann, Doris. "Gas, Gas, Gaas! The Poison Gas War in the Literature and Visual Arts of Interwar Europe," in *One Hundred Years of Chemical Warfare: Research, Deployment, Consequences*, ed. B. Friedrich et al. (Springer Nature Open, 2015), DOI: 10.1007/978-3-319-51664-6_10.

Kean, Hilda. *The Great Cat and Dog Massacre: The Real Story of World War Two's Unknown Tragedy* (Chicago: University of Chicago Press, 2017).

Kendall, James. *Breathe Freely: The Truth about Poison Gas* (London: G. Bell & Sons, 1938).

Kennett, Lee. *A History of Strategic Bombing* (New York: Scribner, 1982).

Kent, Susan Kingsley. *Aftershocks: Politics and Trauma in Britain, 1918–1931* (New York : Palgrave Macmillan, 2009).

Kessler, Jeremy K. "A War for Liberty: On the Law of Conscientious Objection," in *The Cambridge History of the Second World War*, vol. 3, ed. Michael Geyer and Adam Tooze (Cambridge: Cambridge University Press, 2015), 447–74.

Khan, Yasmin. *The Raj at War: A People's History of India's Second World War* (London: Bodley Head, 2015).

Kingery, W. David. "Introduction," in *Learning from Things: Method and Theory of Material Culture Studies*, ed. W. David Kingery (Washington, DC: Smithsonian Institution, 1996), 1–15.

Kingery, W. David, ed. *Learning from Things: Method and Theory of Material Culture Studies* (Washington, DC: Smithsonian Institution, 1996).

Kitchen, Martin. *Europe between the Wars* (Harlow: Pearson, 1988).

Kitching, Carolyn J. *Britain and the Geneva Disarmament Conference: A Study in International History* (Basingstoke: Palgrave Macmillan, 2003).

Kramer, Alan. *Dynamic of Destruction: Culture and Mass Killing in the First World War* (Oxford: Oxford University Press, 2007).

Krause, Jonathan. "The Origins of Chemical Warfare in the French Army," *War in History* 20:4 (2013), 545–56.

Kushner, Tony. "The Holocaust in the British Imagination: The Official Mind and Beyond, 1945 to the Present," *Holocaust Studies* 23:3 (2017), 364–84.

Langdon-Davies, J. *Air Raid: The Technique of Silent Approach High Explosive Panic* (London: George Routledge & Sons, 1938).

Langhamer, Claire, Lucy Noakes, and Claudia Siebrecht, eds. *Total War: An Emotional History* (Oxford: Oxford University Press, 2020).

League of Nations Union. *Chemical Warfare* (London: League of Nations Union, 1924).

Lee, Georgina. *Home Fire Burning: The Great War Diaries of Georgina Lee* (2006; Stroud: History Press, 2009).

LeFebure, Victor. *The Riddle of the Rhine: Chemical Strategy in Peace and War* (London: W. Collins & Sons, 1921).

Scientific Disarmament (London: Victor Gollancz, 1931).

Lepick, Olivier. *La guerre chimique: 1914–1918* (Paris: Presses Universitaires de France, 1998).

Liddington, Jill. *The Long Road to Greenham: Feminism and Anti-militarism in Britain since 1820* (London: Virago, 1989).

Light, Alison. *Forever England: Femininity, Literature and Conservatism between the Wars* (London: Routledge, 1991).

Lindqvist, Sven. *A History of Bombing*, trans. Linda Haverty Rugg (New York: New Press, 2001).

Linstrum, Erik. "Domesticating Chemical Weapons: Tear Gas and the Militarization of Policing in the British Imperial World, 1919–1981," *Journal of Modern History* 91 (2019), 557–85.

Loughran, Tracey. "Shell Shock, Trauma and the First World War: The Making of a Diagnosis and Its Histories," *Journal of the History of Medicine and Allied Sciences* 67:1 (2012), 94–119.

Macdonald, Lynn. *1915: The Death of Innocence* (1993; repr. Baltimore: Johns Hopkins University Press, 2000).

MacFie, John William Scott. *An Ethiopian Diary: A Record of the British Ambulance Service in Ethiopia* (Liverpool: University Press of Liverpool, 1936).

Mackay, Robert. *Half the Battle: Civilian Morale in Britain during the Second World War* (Manchester: Manchester University Press 2002).

MacLeod, John. *River of Fire: The Clydebank Blitz* (Edinburgh: Birllin, 2010).

McCarthy, Helen. *The British People and the League of Nations: Democracy, Citizenship and Internationalism, 1918–1945* (Manchester: Manchester University Press, 2011).

Malcolmson, Patricia and Robert. *Women at the Ready: The Remarkable Story of the Women's Voluntary Service on the Home Front* (London: Abacus, 2013).

Matera, Marc, Misty L. Bastian, and Susan Kingsley Kent. *The Women's War of 1929: Gender and Violence in Colonial Nigeria* (London: Palgrave Macmillan, 2012).

Meilinger, P. S. "Clipping the Bomber's Wings: The Geneva Disarmament Conference and the Royal Air Force, 1932–1934," *War in History* 6:3 (1999), 306–30.

Meisel, Joseph S. "Air Raid Shelter Policy and Its Critics in Britain before the Second World War," *Twentieth Century British History* 5:3 (1994), 300–19.

"Miles." *The Gas War of 1940* (London: Eric Partridge, 1931).

Miller, Daniel. *Stuff* (Malden, MA: Polity, 2010).

Mitchell, B. R. *Abstract of British Historical Statistics* (Cambridge: Cambridge University Press, 1976).

Moriarty, Catherine. "'Though in a Picture Only': Portrait Photography and the Commemoration of the First World War," in *Evidence, History, and the Great War: Historians and the Impact of 1914–18*, ed. Gail Braybon (New York: Berghahn, 2003), 30–47.

Moshenska, Gabriel. "Gas Masks: Material Culture, Memory and the Senses," *Journal of the Royal Anthropological Institute* 16 (2010), 609–28.

Material Cultures of Childhood in Second World War Britain (London: Routledge, 2019).

Moulton, Mo. *Ireland and the Irish in Interwar England* (Cambridge: Cambridge University Press, 2014).

Mowat, Charles Loch. *Britain between the Wars* (Chicago: University of Chicago Press, 1955).

Moyd, Michelle. "Color Lines, Front Lines: The First World War from the South," *Radical History Review* 131 (2018), 13–35.

Violent Intermediaries: African Soldiers, Conquest, and Everyday Colonialism in German East Africa (Athens: Ohio University Press, 2014).

Mukerjee, Madhusree. *Churchill's Secret War: The British Empire and the Ravaging of India during World War II* (New York: Basic Books, 2010).

Mumford, Philip S. *Humanity, Air Power and War* (London: Jarrolds, 1936).

Munch, P. Preface to *What Would Be the Character of a New War? Enquiry Organised by the Inter-Parliamentary Union* (London: P. S. King & Sons, 1931).

Nestler, Dr. "Collective and Individual Protection," in *Chemical Warfare: An Abridged Report of Papers Read at an International Conference at Frankfurt am Main* (London: Williams & Norgate, 1930).

Nichols, Beverley. *Cry Havoc!* (New York: Doubley, Doran & Co., 1933).

Noakes, Lucy. *Dying for the Nation: Death, Grief and Bereavement in Second World War Britain* (Manchester: Manchester University Press, 2020).

"Popular Memory, Popular Culture," in *The Cambridge History of the Second World War*, vol. 3, ed. Michael Geyer and Adam Tooze (Cambridge: Cambridge University Press, 2015), 675–97.

"'Serve to Save': Gender, Citizenship and Civil Defence in Britain 1937–1941," *Journal of Contemporary History* 47:4 (2012), 734–53.

War and the British: Gender, Memory, and National Identity (London: I. B. Taurus, 1998).

Noakes, Lucy, and Juliette Pattinson, eds. *British Cultural Memory and the Second World War* (London: Bloomsbury, 2014).

O'Brien, Terence H. *Civil Defence: Official History of the Second World War* (London: HMSO, 1955).

Omissi, David E. *Air Power and Colonial Control: The Royal Air Force, 1919–1939* (Manchester: Manchester University Press, 1990).

Overy, Richard, *The Bombers and the Bombed: Allied Air War over Europe, 1940–1945* (New York: Viking, 2013).

"Pacifism and the Blitz," *Past and Present* 219 (May 2013), 201–34.

The Twilight Years: The Paradox of Britain between the Wars (New York: Viking, 2009).

Owen, Wilfred. "Dulce et decorum est," in *The Poems of Wilfred Owen* (London: Chatto & Windus, 1920).

Palazzo, Albert. *Seeking Victory on the Western Front: The British Army and Chemical Warfare in World War I* (Lincoln: University of Nebraska Press, 2008).

Panchasi, Roxanne. *Future Tense: The Culture of Anticipation in France between the Wars* (Ithaca, NY: Cornell University Press, 2009).

Pankhurst, E. Sylvia. *The Home Front* (London, 1932; repr. London: Cresset, 1987).

Panter-Downes, Mollie. "Letter from London, 3 September," in *London War Notes 1939–1945*, ed. William Shawn (London: Longman, 1972), 4.

Pape, Robert A. *Bombing to Win: Air Power and Coercion in War* (Ithaca, NY: Cornell University Press, 1996).

Parker, Geoffrey, ed. *The Cambridge Illustrated History of Warfare: The Triumph of the West* (revised ed., Cambridge: Cambridge University Press, 2008).

Peace Pledge Union. *You've Got to Be Prepared* (London: Peace Pledge Union, n. d.).

Pedersen, Susan. "Gender, Welfare and Citizenship in Britain during the Great War," *American Historical Review* 95:4 (1990), 983–1006.

The Guardians: The League of Nations and the Crisis of Empire (Oxford: Oxford University Press, 2015).

Pennybacker, Susan. *From Scottsboro to Munich: Race and Political Culture in 1930s Britain* (Princeton, NJ: Princeton University Press, 2009).

Pickett, Francis Norman. *Don't Be Afraid of Poison Gas: Hints for Civilians in the Event of a Poison Gas Attack* (London: Simpkin Marshall, 1934).

Pimlott, Ben. *Labour and the Left in the 1930s* (Cambridge: Cambridge University Press, 1977).

Plamper, Jan. "Soldiers and Emotion in Early Twentieth-Century Russia Military Psychology," in *Fear across the Disciplines,* ed. Jan Plamper and Benjamin Lazier (Pittsburgh, PA: University of Pittsburgh Press, 2012), 78–98.

Price, Richard M. *The Chemical Weapons Taboo* (Ithaca, NY, and London: Cornell University Press, 1997).

Proctor, Tammy M. *Civilians in a World at War 1914–1918* (New York: New York University Press, 2010).

Pugh, Martin. *Women's Suffrage in Britain, 1867–1928* (London: Historical Association, 1980).

Quirke, V. M. "Haldane, John Burdon Sanderson (1892–1954)," *Oxford Dictionary of National Biography* (Sept. 23, 2004), https://doi.org/10.1093/ref:odnf/33641 (accessed Jan. 20, 2017).

Record, Jeffrey. "Appeasement: A Critical Evaluation Seventy Years On," in *The Origins of the Second World War: An International Perspective*, ed. Frank McDonough et al. (New York: Continuum, 2011), 210–23.

Records of the Conference for the Reduction and Limitation of Armaments, series D, vol. 3 (Geneva: League of Nations, 1936).

"Respirator Depot at Bath," in "Work of the Regional Branches," *Women's Voluntary Service for Civil Defence Newsletter* 57 (July 1944).

Richter, Donald. *Chemical Soldiers: British Gas Warfare in World War I* (Lawrence: University of Kansas Press, 1992).

Roper, Michael. *The Secret Battle: Emotional Survival in World War One* (Manchester: Manchester University Press, 2009).

Rose, Sonya. O. *Which People's War? National Identity and Citizenship in Wartime Britain, 1939–1945* (Oxford: Oxford University Press, 2003).

Roye, [Horace]. *Nude Ego* (London: Chantry, 1958).

Ruddy, Austin J. *The Home Front 1939–1945 in 100 Objects* (Barnsley: Frontline, 2019).

Russell, Edmund. *War and Nature: Fighting Humans and Insects with Chemicals from World War I to Silent Spring* (Cambridge: Cambridge University Press, 2001).

Saint-Amour, Paul K. *Tense Future: Modernism, Total War, Encyclopedic Form* (Oxford: Oxford University Press, 2015).

Saler, Michael. *As If: Modern Enchantment and the Literary Prehistory of Virtual Reality* (Oxford: Oxford University Press, 2012).

Satia, Priya. "The Defense of Inhumanity: Air Control and the British Idea of Arabia," *American Historical Review* 111:1 (2003), 16–51.

   Empire of Guns: The Violent Making of the Industrial Revolution (New York: Penguin, 2018).

   Spies in Arabia: The Great War and the Cultural Foundations of Britain's Covert Empire in the Middle East (Oxford: Oxford University Press, 2008).

Saunders, Nicholas J. *Trench Art: Materialities and Memories of War* (Oxford: Berg, 2003).

Saunders, Nicholas J., ed. *Matters of Conflict: Material Culture, Memory, and the First World War* (London: Routledge, 2004).

Scarry, Elaine. *The Body in Pain: The Making and Unmaking of the World* (Oxford: Oxford University Press, 1985).

Schmidt, Ulf. *Secret Science: A Century of Poison Warfare and Human Experiments* (Oxford: Oxford University Press, 2015).

Sebald, W. G. *On the Natural History of Destruction*, trans. Anthea Bell (1999; repr. New York: Modern Library, 2004).

Shanks, Edward. *The People of the Ruins* (London: William Collins & Sons, 1920).

Shapira, Michal. *The War Inside: Psychoanalysis, Total War, and the Making of the Democratic Self in Postwar Britain* (Cambridge: Cambridge University Press, 2013).

Sheffy, Yigal. "Chemical Warfare and the Palestine Campaign, 1916–1918," *Journal of Military History* 73:3 (2009), 803–44.

Sheridan, Dorothy, ed. *Wartime Women: A Mass-Observation Anthology 1937–1945* (London: Phoenix, 1990).

Shoul, Simeon. "British Tear Gas Doctrine between the World Wars," *War in History* 15:2 (2008), 168–90.

Showalter, Elaine. *The Female Malady: Women, Madness, and English Culture: 1830–1980* (London: Virago, 1988).

Slim, Hugo. *Killing Civilians: Method, Madness and Morality in War* (New York: Columbia University Press, 2008).

Sloterdijk, Peter. "Airquake," in *Foams: Spheres III*, trans. Wieland Hoban (South Pasadena, CA: Semiotext(e), 2016).
Sobek, Allison. "How Did the Women's International League for Peace and Freedom Campaign against Chemical Warfare, 1915–1930?" (State University of New York at Binghampton, 2001).
Sontag, Susan. *Regarding the Pain of Others* (New York: Picador, 2003).
Spiers, E. M. "Gas Disarmament in the 1920s: Hopes Confounded," *Journal of Strategic Studies* 29:2 (2006), 281–300.
Stafford, James "'Stay at Home': The Politics of Nuclear Civil Defence," *Twentieth Century British History* 23:3 (2012), 383–407.
Stansky, Peter. *The First Day of the Blitz* (New Haven, CT: Yale University Press, 2008).
Steer, George. *Caesar in Abyssinia* (1936; repr. Boston: Little, Brown & Co., 1937).
Stokes, Simpson. *Air-Gods' Parade* (London: Arthur Barron, 1935).
Strang, G. Bruce, ed. *Collision of Empires: Italy's Invasion of Ethiopia and Its International Impact* (London: Routledge, 2017).
Streets-Salter, Heather. *Martial Races: The Military, Race and Masculinity in British Imperial Culture, 1857–1914* (Manchester: Manchester University Press, 2005).
Struther, Jan. *Mrs Miniver* (1939; repr. London: Virago, 1989).
Stryker, Laurinda. "Mental Cases: British Shellshock and the Politics of Interpretation," in *Evidence, History and the Great War*, ed. Gail Braybon (New York: Berghahn, 2003), 154–71.
Summerfield, Penny. "Divisions at Sea: Class, Gender, Race and Nation in Maritime Films of the Second World War, 1939–60," *Twentieth Century British History* 22:3 (2011), 330–53.
"The Generation of Memory: Gender and the Popular Memory of the Second World War in Britain," in *British Cultural Memory and the Second World War*, ed. Lucy Noakes and Juliette Pattinson (London: Bloomsbury, 2014), 25–46.
Reconstructing Women's Wartime Lives: Discourse and Subjectivity in Oral Histories of the Second World War (Manchester: Manchester University Press, 1998).
Summerfield, Penny, and Corinna Peniston-Bird. *Constructing Home Defence: Men, Women and the Home Guard on the Second World War* (Manchester: Manchester University Press, 2007).
Swanwick, Helena. *Frankenstein and His Monster: Aviation for World Service* (London: Women's International League, 1934).
Szöllösi-Janze, Margit. "The Scientist as Expert: Fritz Haber and German Chemical Warfare during the First World War and Beyond," in *One Hundred Years of Chemical Warfare: Research, Deployment, Consequences*, ed. B. Friedrich et al. (Springer Nature Open, 2015), DOI: 10.1007/978-3-319-51664-6_10.
Tanaka, Toshiyuki Y., and Marilyn B. Young, eds. *Bombing Civilians: A Twentieth-Century History* (New York: New Press 2009).
Taylor, Richard, and Nigel Young, eds. *Campaigns for Peace: British Peace Movements in the Twentieth Century* (Manchester: Manchester University Press, 1987).

Thom, Deborah. "Making Spectaculars: Museums and How We Remember Gender in Wartime," in *Evidence, History and the Great War: Historians and the Impact of 1914–18*, ed. Gail Braybon (New York: Berghahn, 2003), 48–66.

Nice Girls and Rude Girls: Women Workers in World War I (London: I. B. Tauris, 1997).

Thomas, S. Evelyn. *A Practical Guide to A.R.P.* (St. Albans: Rathcoole, 1939).

Thompson, Rowan G. E. "'Millions of Eyes Were Turned Skywards': The Air League of the British Empire, Empire Air Day, and the Promotion of Air-Mindedness, 1934–9," *Twentieth Century British History* 30:2 (2021), 285–307, DOI: https://doi.org/10.1093/tcbh/hwaa005.

Thuillier, Henry F. *Gas in the Next War* (London: Geoffrey Bles, 1939).

Todman, Dan. *Britain's War: A New World, 1942–1947* (Oxford: Oxford University Pres, 2020).

Britain's War: Into Battle, 1937–1941 (Oxford: Oxford University Press, 2016).

Toye, Richard. *Churchill's Empire: The World That Made Him and the World He Made* (New York: Henry Holt, 2010).

Trumpener, Ulrich. "The Road to Ypres: The Beginnings of Gas Warfare in World War I," *Journal of Modern History* 47:3 (1975), 460–80.

Tucker, Jonathan B. *War of Nerves: Chemical Warfare from World War I to Al-Qaeda* (New York: Anchor Books, 2007).

Ulrich, Laurel Thatcher, et al. *Tangible Things: Making History through Objects* (Oxford: Oxford University Press, 2015).

Union of Democratic Control. *Poison Gas* (London: Union of Democratic Control, 1935).

Ussishkin, Daniel. *Morale: A Modern British History* (Oxford: Oxford University Press, 2017).

Veldman, Meredith. *Fantasy, the Bomb, and the Greening of Britain: Romantic Protest, 1945–1980* (Cambridge: Cambridge University Press, 1994).

Vogt, Annette B. "Gertrud Johanna Woker (1878–1968)," in *European Women in Chemistry* (Hoboken, NJ: Wiley Blackwell, 2011), 65–69.

Waugh, Maureen. "Quakers, Peace and the League of Nations: The Role of Bertram Pickard," *Quaker Studies* 6:1 (2001), 59–79.

Weinberg, Gerhard L. *A World at Arms: A Global History of World War II* (Cambridge: Cambridge University Press, 1994).

"What to Do about Gas" (London: HMSO, 1941).

What Would Be the Character of a New War? (London: P. S. King & Son, 1931).

Whiting, Charles. *Britain under Fire: The Bombing of Britain's Cities, 1940–45* (London: Leo Cooper, 1999).

Whitmore, Lucie. "'A Matter of Individual Opinion and Feeling': The Changing Culture of Mourning Dress in the First World War," *Women's History Review* (2017), DOI: 10.1080/09612025.2017.1292631.

Willis, Kirk. "The Origins of British Nuclear Culture 1895–1939," *Journal of British Studies* 34:1 (1995), 59–89.

Winner, Langdon. *The Whale and the Reactor: A Search for Limits in an Age of High Technology* (Chicago: University of Chicago Press, 1989).

Wittman, Laura. *The Tomb of the Unknown Soldier, Modern Mourning, and the Reinvention of the Mystical Body* (Toronto: University of Toronto Press, 2011).

Woker, Gertrud. "Chemical and Bacteriological Warfare," in *What Would Be the Character of a New War?* (London: P. S. King & Son, 1931).

"The Effects of Chemical Warfare," in *Chemical Warfare: An Abridged Report of Papers Read at an International Conference at Frankfurt am Main* (London: Williams & Norgate, 1930).

Der kommende Giftgaskrieg (Leipzig, 1925).

The Next War: A War of Poison Gas (Washington, DC: Women's International League for Peace and Freedom, 1927).

Women's World Committee Against War and Fascism – British Section. *Behind the Gas Mask: An Exposure of the Proposed Air Defence Measures* (London: WWCAWF, 1935).

Woollacott, Angela. *On Her Their Lives Depend: Munitions Workers in the Great War* (Berkeley: University of California Press, 1994).

Woolf, Virginia. Thoughts on Peace in an Air Raid," *The New Republic*, Oct. 20, 1940; repr. in *Thoughts on Peace in an Air Raid* (London: Penguin, 2009).

Three Guineas (1938; repr. Harmondsworth: Penguin, 1982).

Ziegler, Philip. *London at War* (London: Sinclair Stevenson, 1995).

Films and Television Shows

British Pathé. "Mock Gas Attack – Esher 1941," news reel film ID 1657.02, www .britishpathe.com/video/mock-gas-attack-esher (accessed Apr. 10, 2020).

Doctor Who, series 1, episode 9, "The Empty Child," and episode 10, "The Doctor Dances" (BBC, 2005).

Ministry of Information. *The Guardian of Your Life* (1941).

Things to Come, dir. William Cameron Menzies (London Films Production, 1936).

Index